# Network Administrator Street Smarts

## A Real World Guide to CompTIA Network+® Skills

Toby Skandier

Wiley Publishing, Inc.

Acquisitions and Development Editor: Jeff Kellum
Technical Editor: Kevin Lundy
Production Editor: Sarah Groff-Palermo
Copy Editor: Judy Flynn
Production Manager: Tim Tate
Vice President and Executive Group Publisher: Richard Swadley
Vice President and Executive Publisher: Joseph B. Wikert
Vice President and Publisher: Neil Edde
Book Designers: Judy Fung, Bill Gibson
Compositor: Chris Gillespie, Happenstance Type-O-Rama
Proofreader: Ian Golder
Indexer: Ted Laux
Cover Designer: Ryan Sneed

ISBN-13: 9-780-470-04724-8
ISBN-10: 0-470-04724-0

For general information on our other products and services or to obtain technical support, please contact our Customer Care Department within the U.S. at (800) 762-2974, outside the U.S. at (317) 572-3993 or fax (317) 572-4002.

Wiley also publishes its books in a variety of electronic formats. Some content that appears in print may not be available in electronic books.

Library of Congress Cataloging-in-Publication Data is available from the publisher.

10 9 8 7 6 5 4 3

*For my loving and supportive wife, Karen. As the wife of an author, you make it without me and still manage to stand by me. 143*

# Acknowledgments

Not that a simple acknowledgment is sufficient, but I want to recognize the father of the Street Smarts series, Jeff Kellum. Jeff came to me in the fall of 2005 with his idea. Less than a year later, multiple titles were in the works. I'm sincerely grateful that Jeff considered me for the networking installment in the series. Networking has always been my greatest passion in the computing world. Thanks, Jeff.

I'm indebted to Kevin Lundy for keeping me honest in my discussions. A better technical editor I could not have asked for. I'm simply in awe of Sarah Groff-Palermo and Judy Flynn. Their mastery of the English language is a beautiful thing.

Of course, all those who work long hours supporting an author and his book I cannot thank enough. My crude drawings come to life in exacting detail. My manuscript is typeset in a professional and alluring style. My work is bound and marketed to the masses. Your expertise is necessary, and I appreciate it more than you can know.

My gratitude goes out to my Embarq Corporation management team, Rich Hake, Jackie Stecher, and Al Smith, as well as to my colleagues in the Talent Management organization. You constantly challenge me and provide me opportunities for growth.

Finally, thank you to my incredible kids, Toby, Tiffani, Trey, and Taylor. You guys support and encourage your dad through your own hard work and determination. You make quite a family.

# About the Author

Toby Skandier has been in the networking field since the early 1990s and general computing since the mid-1980s. He is a Technical Trainer for Embarq™ Corporation tasked with developing and delivering technical courses for Embarq associates and affiliates. Toby is also the author of the Sybex titles *Network+ Study Guide* and *CCNP: Complete Study Guide*, as well as technical editor for many others. Toby holds the following industry and vendor certifications: Network+, A+, i-Net+, Server+, CTT+, CCNP, CCIP, CCDP, and MCSE.

# Contents at a Glance

# Contents

# Introduction

The Network+ certification was developed by the Computer Technology Industry Association (CompTIA) to provide an industry-wide means of certifying the competency of computer service technicians in the basics of computer networking. The Network+ certification is granted to those who have attained a level of knowledge and networking skills that show a basic competency with the networking needs of both personal and corporate computing environments.

While most books targeted toward certification candidates present material for you to memorize before the exam, this book is different. It guides you through procedures and tasks that solidify related concepts, allowing you to devote your memorization efforts to more abstract theories because you've mastered the more practical topics through doing. Even if you do not aspire to become Network+ certified, this book might still be a valuable primer for your networking career.

## What Is Network+ Certification?

The Network+ certification was created to offer an introductory step into the complex world of IT networking. You only need to pass a single exam to become Network+ certified. But obtaining this certification does not mean you can provide sufficient networking services to a company. In fact, this is just the first step toward true networking knowledge and experience. Hopefully, by obtaining Network+ certification, you will be able to obtain more networking experience and gain an interest in networks in order to pursue more complex and in-depth network knowledge and certifications.

For the latest pricing on the exam and updates to the registration procedures, call Prometric at (866) 776-6387 or (800) 776-4276. You can also go to either www.2test.com or www.prometric.com for additional information or to register online. If you have further questions about the scope of the exams or related CompTIA programs, refer to the CompTIA website at www.comptia.org.

## Is This Book for You?

*Network Administrator Street Smarts* is designed to give the insight into the world of a typical network administrator by walking you through some of the daily tasks you can expect on the job. Some investment in equipment is advised to get the full effect from this book. However, much value can be derived from simply reading through the tasks without performing the steps on live equipment. Organized classes and study groups are the ideal structures for obtaining and practicing with the recommended equipment.

The *Network+ Study Guide, Fourth Edition* or *Deluxe Edition* (Sybex 2005) is a recommended companion to this book in your studies for the CompTIA Network+ certification.

# How This Book Is Organized

This book is organized into four phases of network administration.

Each phase is separated into individual tasks. The phases represent broad categories under which related responsibilities are grouped. The tasks within each phase lead you step-by-step through the processes required for successful completion. When performed in order, the tasks in this book approximate those required by a network administrator over an extended period of time. The four phases and their descriptions follow.

- *Phase 1—Designing an Internetwork* presents common tasks recommended for most projects in order to make sure your internetwork is planned properly to minimize surprises down the road.

- *Phase 2—Implementing and Configuring the Design* puts your design into action, taking into account the practical tasks necessary to implement a networking plan.

- *Phase 3—Maintaining and Securing the Network* gives you tools to enhance your network and keep it safe.

- *Phase 4—Troubleshooting the Network* provides a reference and guide for using various tools and utilities to minimize the amount of downtime your network must endure.

Each task in this book is organized into sections aimed at giving you what you need when you need it. The first section introduces you to the task and any key concepts that can assist you in understanding the underlying technology and the overall procedure. Descriptions of the remaining sections follow.

- *Scenario*—This section places you in the shoes of the network administrator, describing a situation in which you will likely find yourself. The scenario is closely related to and often solved by the task at hand.

- *Scope of Task*—This section is all about preparing for the task. It gives you an idea of how much time is required to complete the task, what setup procedure is needed before beginning, and any concerns or issues to look out for.

- *Procedure*—This is the actual meat of the task itself. This section informs you of the equipment required to perform the task in a lab environment. It also gives you the ordered steps to complete the task.

- *Criteria for Completion*—This final section briefly explains the outcome you should expect after completing the task. Any deviation from the result described is an excellent reason to perform the task again and watch for sources of the variation.

## How to Contact the Publisher

Sybex, an imprint of John Wiley & Sons Inc., welcomes feedback on all of its titles. Visit the Sybex website at www.sybex.com for book updates and additional certification information. You'll also find forms you can use to submit comments or suggestions regarding this or any other Sybex title.

## How to Contact the Author

Toby Skandier welcomes your questions and comments. You can reach him by email at tskandier@hotmail.com.

# The Network+ Exam Objectives

The following are the areas (referred to as domains by CompTIA) in which you must be proficient in order to pass the Network+ exam.

**Domain 1: Media and Topologies**    This content area deals with basics of the logical and physical shape of various networks and how the topology of the network affects the technologies used in the network. You should also know common network devices and the connectors that you can use to form various types of networks.

**Domain 2: Protocols and Standards**    This content area deals with the OSI model of communication and how all of the network devices and network protocols are organized based on the model. The focus is on the TCP/IP suite of protocols and how it differentiates between all of the protocols in the suite.

**Domain 3: Network Implementation**    This content area deals with connecting the various components of a network to create a functioning network. It also covers firewalls, VLANs, fault tolerance, and disaster recovery.

**Domain 4: Network Support**    This content area deals with troubleshooting a network. You should know about the tools and utilities that you can use to troubleshoot a network as well as a troubleshooting methodology that has been proven effective.

 At the beginning of each of the four phases of this book, we include the supported domains of the Network+ exam objectives. Exam objectives are subject to change at any time without prior notice and at CompTIA's sole discretion. Please visit the Network+ Certification page of CompTIA's website (www.comptia.org/certification/network) for the most current listing of exam objectives.

Following are the specific objectives grouped by domain.

## Domain 1.0 Media and Topologies

1.1 Recognize the following logical or physical network topologies given a diagram, schematic, or description:

- Star
- Bus
- Mesh
- Ring

1.2 Specify the main features of 802.2 (Logical Link Control), 802.3 (Ethernet), 802.5 (Token Ring), 802.11(wireless), and FDDI (Fiber Distributed Data Interface) networking technologies, including:

- Speed
- Access method (CSMA/CA [Carrier Sense Multiple Access/Collision Avoidance] and CSMA/CD [Carrier Sense Multiple Access/Collision Detection])
- Topology
- Media

1.3 Specify the characteristics (for example, speed, length, topology, and cable type) of the following cable standards:

- 10BaseT and 10BaseFL
- 100BaseTX and 100BaseFX
- 1000BaseTX, 1000BaseCX, 1000BaseSX, and 1000BaseLX
- 10GBaseSR, 10GbaseLR, and 10GBaseER

1.4 Recognize the following media connectors and describe their uses:

- RJ-11 (Registered Jack)
- RJ-45 (Registered Jack)
- F-Type
- ST (Straight Tip)
- SC (Standard Connector)
- IEEE1394 (FireWire)
- LC (Local Connector)
- MTRJ (Mechanical Transfer Registered Jack)

1.5 Recognize the following media types and describe their uses:

- Category 3, 5, 5e, and 6
- UTP (Unshielded Twisted Pair)
- STP (Shielded Twisted Pair)
- Coaxial cable
- SMF (Single Mode Fiber) optic cable
- MMF (Multimode Fiber) optic cable

1.6 Identify the purposes, features, and functions of the following network components:

- Hubs
- Switches
- Bridges

- Routers
- Gateways
- CSU/DSU (channel service unit/data service unit)
- NICs (network interface card)
- ISDN (Integrated Services Digital Network) adapters
- WAPs (wireless access point)
- Modems
- Transceivers (media converters)
- Firewalls

1.7 Specify the general characteristics (for example, carrier speed, frequency, transmission type and topology) of the following wireless technologies:

- 802.11 (frequency hopping spread spectrum) 802.11x (direct sequence spread spectrum)
- Infrared
- Bluetooth

1.8 Identify factors which affect the range and speed of wireless service (for example, interference, antenna type, and environmental factors).

## Domain 2.0 Protocols and Standards

2.1 Identify a MAC (Media Access Control) address and its parts.

2.2 Identify the seven layers of the OSI (Open Systems Interconnection) model and their functions.

2.3 Identify the OSI (Open Systems Interconnection) layers at which the following network components operate:

- Hubs
- Switches
- Bridges
- Routers
- NICs (network interface card)
- WAPs (wireless access points)

2.4 Differentiate between the following network protocols in terms of routing, addressing schemes, interoperability, and naming conventions:

- IPX / SPX (Internetwork Packet Exchange/Sequence Packet Exchange)
- NetBEUI (Network Basic Input/Output System Extended User Interface)
- AppleTalk/AppleTalk over IP (Internet Protocol)
- TCP/IP (Transmission Control Protocol/Internet Protocol)

2.5 Identify the components and structure of IP (Internet Protocol) addresses (IPv4, IPv6) and the required setting for connections across the Internet.

2.6 Identify classful IP (Internet Protocol) ranges and their subnet masks (for example, Class A, B, and C).

2.7 Identify the purpose of subnetting.

2.8 Identify the differences between private and public network addressing schemes.

2.9 Identify and differentiate between the following IP (Internet Protocol) addressing methods:

- Static

- Dynamic

- Self-assigned (APIPA [Automatic Private Internet Protocol Addressing])

2.10 Define the purpose, function, and use of the following protocols used in the TCP / IP (Transmission Control Protocol/Internet Protocol) suite:

- TCP (Transmission Control Protocol)

- UDP (User Datagram Protocol)

- FTP (File Transfer Protocol)

- SFTP (Secure File Transfer Protocol)

- TFTP (Trivial File Transfer Protocol)

- SMTP (Simple Mail Transfer Protocol) HTTP (Hypertext Transfer Protocol)

- HTTPS (Hypertext Transfer Protocol Secure)

- POP3/IMAP4 (Post Office Protocol version 3/Internet Message Access Protocol version 4)

- Telnet

- SSH (Secure Shell)

- ICMP (Internet Control Message Protocol)

- ARP / RARP (Address Resolution Protocol/Reverse Address Resolution Protocol)

- NTP (Network Time Protocol)

- NNTP (Network News Transport Protocol)

- SCP (Secure Copy Protocol)

- LDAP (Lightweight Directory Access Protocol)

- IGMP (Internet Group Multicast Protocol)

- LPR (Line Printer Remote)

2.11 Define the function of TCP/UDP (Transmission Control Protocol/User Datagram Protocol) ports.

2.12 Identify the well-known ports associated with the following commonly used services and protocols:

- 20 FTP (File Transfer Protocol)
- 21 FTP (File Transfer Protocol)
- 22 SSH (Secure Shell)
- 23 Telnet
- 25 SMTP (Simple Mail Transfer Protocol)
- 53 DNS (Domain Name Server)
- 69 TFTP (Trivial File Transfer Protocol)
- 80 HTTP (Hypertext Transfer Protocol)
- 110 POP3 (Post Office Protocol version 3)
- 119 NNTP (Network News Transport Protocol)
- 123 NTP (Network Time Protocol)
- 143 IMAP4 (Internet Message Access Protocol version 4)
- 443 HTTPS (Hypertext Transfer Protocol Secure)

2.13 Identify the purpose of network services and protocols (for example, DNS [Domain Name Service], NAT [Network Address Translation], ICS [Internet Connection Sharing], WINS [Windows Internet Name Service], SNMP [Simple Network Management Protocol], NFS [Network File System], Zeroconf [Zero configuration], SMB [Server Message Block], AFP [Apple File Protocol], and LPD [Line Printer Daemon]).

2.14 Identify the basic characteristics (for example, speed, capacity, and media) of the following WAN (Wide Area Network) technologies:

- Packet switching
- Circuit switching
- ISDN (Integrated Services Digital Network)
- FDDI (Fiber Distributed Data Interface)
- T1 (T Carrier level 1)/E1/J1
- T3 (T Carrier level 3)/E3/J3
- OCx (Optical Carrier)
- X.25

2.15 Identify the basic characteristics of the following Internet access technologies:

- xDSL (Digital Subscriber Line)
- Broadband Cable (Cable modem)
- POTS/PSTN (Plain Old Telephone Service/Public Switched Telephone Network) Satellite Wireless

2.16 Define the function of the following remote access protocols and services:

- RAS (Remote Access Service)
- PPP (Point-to-Point Protocol)
- SLIP (Serial Line Internet Protocol)
- PPPoE (Point-to-Point Protocol over Ethernet)
- PPTP (Point-to-Point Tunneling Protocol)
- VPN (Virtual Private Network)
- RDP (Remote Desktop Protocol)

2.17 Identify the following security protocols and describe their purpose and function:

- IPSec (Internet Protocol Security)
- L2TP (Layer 2 Tunneling Protocol)
- SSL (Secure Sockets Layer)
- WEP (Wired Equivalent Privacy)
- WPA (Wi-Fi Protected Access)
- 802.1x

2.18 Identify authentication protocols (for example, CHAP [Challenge Handshake Authentication Protocol], MS-CHAP [Microsoft Challenge Handshake Authentication Protocol], PAP [Password Authentication Protocol], RADIUS [Remote Authentication Dial-In User Service], Kerberos, and EAP [Extensible Authentication Protocol]).

## Domain 3.0 Network Implementation

3.1 Identify the basic capabilities (for example, client support, interoperability, authentication, file and print services, application support and security) of the following server operating systems to access network resources:

- UNIX/Linux/Mac OS X Server
- NetWare
- Windows
- Appleshare IP (Internet Protocol)

3.2 Identify the basic capabilities needed for client workstations to connect to and use network resources (for example, media, network protocols, and peer and server services).

3.3 Identify the appropriate tool for a given wiring task (for example, wire crimper, media tester/certifier, punch down tool, or tone generator).

3.4 Given a remote connectivity scenario comprised of a protocol, an authentication scheme, and physical connectivity, configure the connection. Includes connection to the following servers:

- Unix/Linux/MAC OS X Server
- NetWare
- Windows
- Appleshare IP (Internet Protocol)

3.5 Identify the purpose, benefits, and characteristics of using a firewall.

3.6 Identify the purpose, benefits, and characteristics of using a proxy service.

3.7 Given a connectivity scenario, determine the impact on network functionality of a particular security implementation (for example, port blocking/filtering, authentication, and encryption).

3.8 Identify the main characteristics of VLANs (virtual local area networks).

3.9 Identify the main characteristics and purpose of extranets and intranets.

3.10 Identify the purpose, benefits, and characteristics of using antivirus software.

3.11 Identify the purpose and characteristics of fault tolerance:

- Power
- Link redundancy
- Storage
- Services

3.12 Identify the purpose and characteristics of disaster recovery:

- Backup / restore
- Offsite storage
- Hot and cold spares
- Hot, warm, and cold sites

## Domain 4.0 Network Support

4.1 Given a troubleshooting scenario, select the appropriate network utility from the following:

- Tracert/traceroute
- ping
- arp
- netstat
- nbtstat
- ipconfig/ifconfig
- winipcfg
- nslookup/dig

4.2 Given output from a network diagnostic utility (for example, those utilities listed in objective 4.1), identify the utility and interpret the output.

4.3 Given a network scenario, interpret visual indicators (for example, link LEDs [Light Emitting Diode] and collision LEDs [Light Emitting Diode]) to determine the nature of a stated problem.

4.4 Given a troubleshooting scenario involving a client accessing remote network services, identify the cause of the problem (for example, file services, print services, authentication failure, protocol configuration, physical connectivity, and SOHO [small office/home office] router).

4.5 Given a troubleshooting scenario between a client and the following server environments, identify the cause of a stated problem:

- Unix/Linux/Mac OS X Server
- NetWare
- Windows
- Appleshare IP (Internet Protocol)

4.6 Given a scenario, determine the impact of modifying, adding, or removing network services (for example, DHCP [Dynamic Host Configuration Protocol], DNS [Domain Name Service], and WINS [Windows Internet Name Server]) for network resources and users.

4.7 Given a troubleshooting scenario involving a network with a particular physical topology (for example, bus, star, mesh, or ring) and including a network diagram, identify the network area affected and the cause of the stated failure.

4.8 Given a network troubleshooting scenario involving an infrastructure (for example, wired or wireless) problem, identify the cause of a stated problem (for example, bad media, interference, network hardware, or environment).

4.9 Given a network problem scenario, select an appropriate course of action based on a logical troubleshooting strategy. This strategy can include the following steps:

1. Identify the symptoms and potential causes.
2. Identify the affected area.
3. Establish what has changed.
4. Select the most probable cause.
5. Implement an action plan and solution including potential effects.
6. Test the result.
7. Identify the results and effects of the solution.
8. Document the solution and process.

# Phase

# 1

# Designing an Internetwork

Although this phase is often skipped, the proper design of an internetwork can guarantee great efficiency during the life of simple networks and complex internetworks alike. Conversely, omitting this phase can guarantee a never-ending struggle to optimize the performance of even the smallest networks. As you'll find, developing the habit of advance planning is more straightforward and painless than you might expect. The tasks in this phase indoctrinate you in the art of network design as well as prepare you for various aspects of the CompTIA Network+ exam.

Phase 1 consists of a set of tasks that lead you through the primary responsibilities of the network administrator in the design and development on a complex internetwork. Topics include designing the internetwork and identifying the actual devices and how they are to be deployed. Identifying your components is not a final process. Once you know what a device is, you can begin to categorize it in a number of ways. Aligning components with their corresponding layer in the OSI reference model is one of the most beneficial forms of categorization you can perform.

Another important piece of the design phase is addressing, both physical and logical. This phase familiarizes you with Ethernet and IP addresses alike. Finally, while discharging their regular duties, most administrators find a need to group end devices in a non-geographical way. This is where virtual LANs come in. You will develop a keen understanding of each topic through detailed tasks designed to help you develop skills through doing, which is the point of this entire book.

Let's start by drawing out your internetwork, based on detailed facts of how it is laid out.

The tasks in this phase map to domains 1, 2, and 3 in the objectives for the CompTIA Network+ exam.

# Task 1.1: Drawing an Internetwork

In this task, you will practice laying out a complete complex internetwork based only on information you might receive as a managerial directive. Sketching out your physical network, even when you are in possession of an existing drawing, helps to solidify even the smallest details of the infrastructure for which you are responsible.

There is much publicized advice circulating out there for the practical portion of advanced certifications such as the Cisco Certified Internetwork Expert (CCIE) and the Juniper Networks Certified Internet Expert (JNCIE). The advice is that even though you have a diagram of the internetwork you are expected to configure, you should draw your own copy. This is true mainly for the kinesthetic learning benefit, but it's also useful in that you can mark up your copy of the internetwork drawing as you make your way through the exam and use the originals only for reference. Such rationale will also serve you well in your administration of a real-world network.

## Scenario

You are the network administrator of a regional site that is part of a larger internetwork implemented by a multinational organization. Your company has offices in five continents. Your CIO has outlined a list of requirements for the internetwork and asked you to head the initiative. You've organized these requirements by site, as listed later in the procedure section.

As a good administrator, you recognize the importance of proper documentation before, during, and after implementation. Therefore, your plan is to illustrate the components of the proposed internetwork, including any nonstandard cables that will be required, such as cross-over cables between similar devices.

## Scope of Task

### Duration

This task should take 1 to 2 hours.

### Setup

For this task, you'll practice making quick yet meaningful sketches of networking infrastructure. Instead of using professional sketching materials or putting effort into making a final electronic drawing using software such as Microsoft's Visio, simply arm yourself with a good-sized sheet of sketch paper to hold your entire drawing or a basic notepad that you can use to continue your drawing over multiple pages. You should use a pencil so that major and minor changes do not require starting your sketch over again. A dedicated eraser of some sort comes in handy as well.

This task has a basic setup in that all you need is some space to spread out and draw as you follow the subsequent procedure. Be prepared for a bit of erasure fleck buildup, which may require attention when you're cleaning up. Such a byproduct additionally may influence your workspace selection.

### Caveat

Don't overdraw the diagram. Be efficient where possible, but be as detailed as necessary. Look for central structures in your diagram and extend the drawing from there. Compartmentalize major pieces of your illustration and then interconnect the components into the complete diagram.

# Procedure

The following list of items for you to complete in this lab is very loosely structured. You may find that it works best for you to complete some items out of order.

## Geographical Aspects

Your internetwork spans the entire globe. You have equipment in the following sites:

- New York
- Los Angeles
- London
- Tokyo
- Sydney
- Cairo

## Equipment Used

You will use a variety of devices, LAN topologies, and WAN circuits. These include the following:

- Hubs
- Multistation access units (MAUs)
- Switches
- Servers
- Workstations
- Modems
- Channel service unit/data service units (CSU/DSUs)
- Routers
- T1s
- E1s
- 56Kbps digital data service (DDS)
- DSL
- Cable modem
- Plain old telephone service (POTS)

## Details

### New York

- New York connects to Los Angeles and London using two WAN routers—A and B—and four T1 circuits to each remote location. The CSU/DSUs are all external.

- The two WAN routers attach directly to one another with a Gigabit Ethernet (GE) connection.

- An additional router—router C—connects directly to the two WAN routers. Router C also connects to the LAN, through switch 1, using Fast Ethernet (FE).

- Sixty workstations interconnect using FE.

  - Twenty workstations connect to a hub that then connects to Ethernet switch 1.

  - Forty workstations connect to a large Ethernet switch, switch 2, which is also connected to switch 1.

- Fifteen older workstations tie together with 10Base2 coaxial cable, which also connects to a BNC connector in switch 2.

- The DNS server for the entire internetwork connects to switch 1.

- A server running DHCP and WINS for the New York LAN connects to switch 1.

- A remote access server (RAS) named NY1 connects to switch 1 as well as to a bank of modems connected to the public switched telephone network (PSTN) with POTS lines.

- Five telecommuters connect from home to the RAS using modems.

### Los Angeles

- The central Los Angeles site connects to New York and Tokyo with a single WAN router, router D (which contains internal CSU/DSUs), using four T1 circuits to New York and two T1 circuits to Tokyo.

- Router D attaches directly to another router, router E, with a GE connection.

- Router E connects through switch 3 to the LAN using FE.

- One hundred five workstations interconnect using FE through switch 3.

- A second LA site has two routers—F and G—that connect to the central LA site, router F with a T1 and router G with a 56Kbps DDS circuit.

- Router F attaches to a GE switch, switch 4, which also connects to RAS server LA1. Twenty DSL subscribers attach through LA1 over the Internet to the corporate LAN.

- To connect to the Internet, LA1 attaches through a GE connection directly to an Internet-attached router, router H.

- Router G attaches to an FE switch, switch 5, which also connects to remote access services (RAS) server LA2, through which three cable modem subscribers attach over the Internet to the corporate LAN.

- LA2 attaches to the Internet through a FE connection directly to an Internet-attached router, router I.
- A server running DHCP and WINS for the LA LANs has a GE connection to switch 4.

## Tokyo

- Tokyo connects to Los Angeles and Sydney with a single WAN router, router J, using two T1 circuits to each remote destination. Router J contains internal CSU/DSUs.
- Additionally, router J has the following direct connections:
    - FE connection to switch 6, which also attaches to 35 workstations.
    - GE connection to a server running DHCP and WINS.
    - GE connection to router K, which uses FE to connect through switch 7 to 10 workstations.

## Sydney

- Sydney connects to Tokyo through router L using two T1 circuits. Router L contains internal CSU/DSUs.
- Router L is dual-attached to an FE interface on an FE blade in a large concentrator, switch 8, and to a 16Mbps Token Ring (TR) interface on a TR MAU blade in the same concentrator.
    - The FE blade also connects to switch 9, which attaches to 25 workstations and a server running DHCP and WINS.
    - The ring-out (RO) port of the MAU blade connects to the ring-in (RI) port on a stand-alone MAU, which attaches to 22 workstations and RAS server SY1.
- SY1 also attaches by FE to router M, which connects directly to the Internet.
- Ten remote employees use cable modems to attach over the Internet through SY1 to the LAN.

## London

- London connects to New York and Cairo with a single router, router N, which uses internal CSU/DSUs for four T1 circuits to New York and external CSU/DSUs for two E1 circuits to Cairo.
- Router N connects directly to a MAU, to which a server running DHCP and WINS and five workstations are attached.
- Router N also connects to a large modular GE switch, switch 10, which networks 52 workstations and RAS server LN1, which connects to the Internet through router O using GE.
- Twenty employees use DSL to attach to the LAN over the Internet through LN1.
- Fifteen employees use cable modems to attach to the LAN over the Internet through LN1.

### Cairo

- Cairo connects to London through router P, using external CSU/DSUs and two E1 circuits.

- Router P attaches to FE switch 11, which connects to a server running DHCP and WINS, a database server, and 20 workstations.

- Router P attaches to RAS server CA1 using GE.

- CA1 gains Internet access through router Q.

- Twelve employees use DSL to connect to the LAN over the Internet through CA1.

## Criteria for Completion

You have completed this lab when you have produced a diagram that illustrates all stated components and circuits and shows proper interconnectivity. It is acceptable for your drawing to consolidate where raw detail does not add to the solution.

For example, it is not necessary to draw out all 40 workstations in New York that connect to switch 2, assuming they are interchangeable devices. Instead, you can draw the device once and use a multiplier to explain the quantity, as shown in the following diagram.

x 40

Additionally, when you need to represent a network, like the Internet or the PSTN, it's best to use a generic cloud to avoid the quagmire of detailing those components that may be considered irrelevant to the task at hand, such as Internet core routers and telephone-network central office switches. For example, the following diagram depicts a possible solution for the Internet cloud in London, through which the 20 DSL and 15 cable modem subscribers connect to the London LAN by way of the LN1 RAS server.

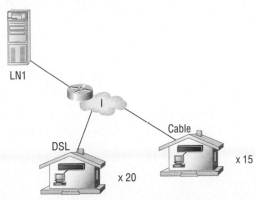

Figure 1.1 depicts one possible solution to the portion of the task involving Tokyo and Sydney. Note the detail of the type of Ethernet cable needed in nonstandard situations, such as a crossover cable between two DTE devices (routers and computers) or two DCE devices (switches) and thicker lines to represent cables of network segments of higher bandwidth. For example, a GE cable's line is bolder than that of a 16Mbps Token Ring.

Note that including the entire solution would be impossible due to this book's trim size.

**FIGURE 1.1**    Sample solution for the Tokyo and Sydney portion of the intranet

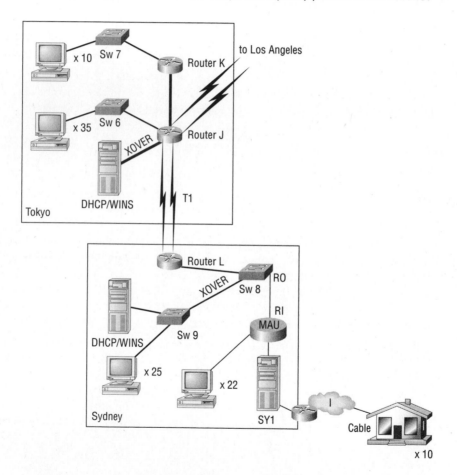

# Task 1.2: Identifying Network Components

One of the biggest mistakes a network administrator can make is to attempt to incorporate devices into their network without first understanding their function, let alone their identity. This task encourages you to collect and identify the components of your internetwork before attaching them and configuring them.

## Scenario

Your supervisor has ordered a series of devices and had them delivered to your site. In the process of unpacking each component, you take the time to read the documentation and perform a physical examination. Your visual inspection includes the identification of each and every external interface for interconnectivity and function.

## Scope of Task

### Duration

This task should take about 1 hour.

### Setup

For this task, you need to surround yourself with only the devices you expect to implement in your own internetwork and their documentation. Be sure to have enough space to spread out to make sure you don't mix up the components and their documentation and packaging. Alternatively, you can deal with a single item at a time.

### Caveat

If you decide to identify your equipment one device at a time, be sure to make a drawing of the components and how they connect with one another. It's a good idea to do this anytime you're working with network components. It is simply easier to envision the interconnectivity of the devices when they are all in front of you at the same time.

An interface that will not connect to any other device for the time being is not necessarily an interface you want to ignore. Interfaces that currently are not connected merely offer opportunities for future expansion. You should be familiar with all the capabilities of your equipment.

# Procedure

There is really only a simple series of steps in this lab, but it needs to be repeated for each device you have.

## Equipment Used

The equipment you use will depend on the equipment you have available to you. It could include, but is not limited to, any of the following:

- Hubs
- MAUs
- Switches
- NIC cards, installed or not
- Modems (analog, DSL, cable)
- CSU/DSUs
- ISDN devices (terminal adapters, NT1s, etc.)
- Routers
- Wireless access points and other components
- Cables related to any of these components

## Details

1. Choose a device.
2. Unpack it, if necessary.
3. Visually inspect the external interfaces of the device.
4. Through a combination of observing the interface labels and looking them up in the accompanying documentation, if available, familiarize yourself with all external interfaces of the device.
5. Optionally, draw a block diagram of the device showing its interfaces. If this is not the first component you selected, also show how it connects to any other devices you have drawn already.

# Criteria for Completion

You have completed this task when you can readily identify each interface of each device, including wireless antennas, without hesitation. Being quizzed by an assistant or mentor can prove helpful in confirming your competency in this lab.

The following figures are examples of devices and their interfaces. These images are meant as a reference, not a solution.

Figures 1.2 through 1.5 illustrate the commonality of the eight-pin modular connector. Be sure you know the function of connectors that are easily confused with one another.

**FIGURE 1.2**    Three modular interfaces on a Cisco router

**FIGURE 1.3**    ISDN BRI interface on a Cisco router

**FIGURE 1.4**    Fast Ethernet trunk ports on a Cisco switch

**FIGURE 1.5**     Fast Ethernet interface On a 3Com NIC card

Figures 1.6 and 1.7 show two types of DB-15 female connector. The DB-15 female joy-stick and AUI ports—Figure 1.6 shows the AUI—are also identical connectors with vastly different functions. One is a game port and the other is the classic 10Mbps Ethernet interface. Figure 1.7 is the high-density 15-pin female connector found on graphics cards. This is where your monitor's data cables plugs in.

**FIGURE 1.6**     Ethernet AUI interface on a Cisco switch

**FIGURE 1.7**    DB-15HD interface on a VGA video adapter

The next two graphics show serial interfaces on a Cisco router. Figure 1.8 is the modern version, while Figure 1.9 can be seen on older systems. Cisco and other manufacturers use the V.35 connector shown in Figure 1.10.

**FIGURE 1.8**    Smart-Serial V.35 interfaces on a Cisco router

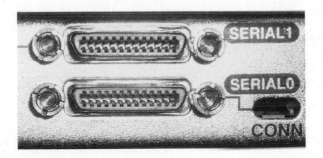

**FIGURE 1.9**    DB-60HD serial interface on a Cisco router

**FIGURE 1.10** Winchester V.35 connector on a cable

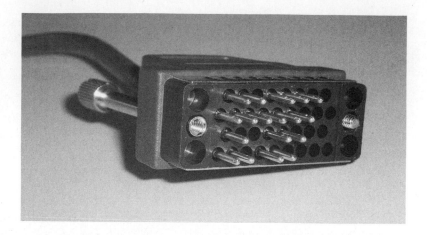

Figure 1.11 might look quite familiar to you. It's a common USB connector, the type that most often interfaces with the ports on the computer side of the cable.

**FIGURE 1.11** Type A USB interface on a cable

# Task 1.3: Differentiating Ethernet Devices

If you are able to readily identify the wired or wireless orientation of the components of your network, you will be more likely to deploy them properly when it is time. Many surprises are in store for the network administrator who waits until the last minute to identify the applicability of network devices. One of the biggest differences between Ethernet devices depends on whether they are for wired networks or wireless networks.

Wired devices follow one of the many Institute of Electrical and Electronics Engineers (IEEE) 802.3 Physical layer specifications, such as 802.3ab for Gigabit Ethernet over unshielded twisted pair (UTP) copper. Wireless devices adhere to one of fewer IEEE standards, such as 802.11g for 54Mbps wireless LANs at a frequency of 2.4GHz.

## Scenario

Having sketched out the layout of your internetwork and having identified its components, it is time to familiarize yourself with how everything interconnects. Therefore, before mounting any devices or otherwise committing to the placement of any component, you decide to make sure you are familiar with the physical attachment requirements of each item in your collection.

## Scope of Task

### Duration

This task should take about 30 minutes.

### Setup

For this task, gather the Ethernet devices you expect to implement in your own internetwork and their documentation. Be sure to have enough space to spread out comfortably.

### Caveat

Some devices, such as routers, may have many interfaces in addition to Ethernet interfaces. Be sure you don't discount these devices but instead consider them as part of this procedure. Also try not to confuse similar eight-pin modular connectors with Ethernet interfaces, possibly leading to misidentification and setbacks.

## Procedure

Demarcate three areas in your workspace. You will use each area to place similar devices: one area for devices based on 802.3 characteristics only, one for devices based on 802.11 characteristics only, and one area for both.

## Equipment Used

The equipment you use will depend on the equipment you have available to you. It could include, but is not limited to, any of the following:

- Hubs
- Switches
- NIC cards, installed or not
- Modems (DSL, cable)
- ISDN terminal adapters with Ethernet attachment
- Routers
- Wireless access points
- Wireless adapters of various system connectivity (expansion slot, USB, etc.)

## Details

1. Make sure you have three distinct areas in your workspace identified for placement of network devices.

2. Choose a device.

3. Unpack it, if necessary.

4. Visually inspect the method of attachment for the device.

5. If the component exhibits a physically attached Ethernet interface, such as the one in the following photo, place it in the first of the three areas you formed.

6.  If the component appears to have an antenna for wireless access, such as the device in the following illustration, place it in the second area, among the three that you demarcated earlier.

7.  If the device conforms to both an 802.3 wired and an 802.11 wireless specification, as depicted in the following illustration, place it in the third area that you prepared for this task.

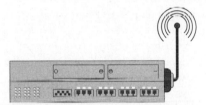

8.  Optionally, draw a block diagram of the device, showing its interfaces. If this is not the first component you selected, also show how it connects to any other devices you have drawn already. Use waveforms, as shown in the following illustration to simulate wireless communication.

## Criteria for Completion

You have completed this task when you have separated your Ethernet devices into three distinct categories of connectivity. The first category consists entirely of those devices that must be attached to the network using some form of cabling, the second category, of those that attach without cables of any kind, and the third category, of those that use either method of attachment or both.

# Task 1.4: Discovering and Filtering MAC Addresses

There are various methods of filtering traffic in an internetwork. While this lab may seem to fit better in Phase 3, "Maintaining and Securing the Network," it is presented here because of its value in discovering and cataloging the Media Access Control (MAC) addresses of the devices in your network. Such a task should always be performed as early as possible in the deployment of an internetwork, preferably not later than the time of official deployment.

Recall that the MAC address is a 48-bit numerical value, most often expressed as a 12-digit hexadecimal number. These addresses are somewhat permanently stored in read-only memory (ROM) on those devices with a LAN interface meant for network attachment. There are nearly as many ways to ascertain the MAC address of a network interface as there are network interfaces. This lab will present a variety of utilities for discovering your MAC addresses. Anything from a spreadsheet to a database to a specially written application can be used to catalog your results.

The first six hexadecimal digits of a MAC address are referred to as the organizationally unique identifier (OUI) and can be matched to a manufacturer using various utilities, both online and offline.

## Scenario

You have been tasked with putting together a list of MAC addresses for the Ethernet devices to be deployed in your internetwork. You expect to restrict access to only certain devices in one or more areas of your network. You also realize you will need to be able to reverse-lookup the identities of devices that show up in error messages and reports by their MAC addresses alone.

## Scope of Task

### Duration

This task should take about 2 hours.

## Setup

For this task, you need all LAN devices in your installation. You also need a computer with a serial port and the appropriate adapters for any devices you have that require serial attachment for configuration but no external MAC address labeling.

## Caveat

Ethernet switches and hubs have multiple eight-pin modular interfaces but generally only one MAC address. The MAC address for these devices is used for management, not normal user traffic. For management functions, such as pinging, telneting, and SNMP control, only one MAC address to bind a single IP address to is sufficient. Therefore, do not expect to find more than one or a very few MAC addresses assigned to such devices.

# Procedure

It may help to organize your components by the method you expect to use to ascertain the MAC address. For example, place all the uninstalled and labeled NICs and other devices with readily visible address labels together, separate from those devices that require electronic access for MAC determination.

## Equipment Used

The equipment you use will depend on the equipment you have available to you. It could include, but is not limited to, any of the following:

- Hubs
- Switches
- NIC cards installed or not
- Computers with built-in wireless NICs
- Modems (DSL, cable)
- ISDN terminal adapters with Ethernet attachment
- Routers
- Wireless access points
- Wireless adapters of various system connectivity (expansion slot, USB, etc.)

## Details

The procedure for discovering the MAC address for certain interfaces requires electronic craft interface (like a console port on a Cisco router) access to the device. Although you may feel it is a bit early to obtain such access to certain devices, it is not necessary to deploy the components in order to obtain the addresses of their interfaces. Sometimes, just the device in question and a handy PC or laptop with appropriate cabling and adapters are enough to get the job done.

### Using a Third-Party Utility

Figure 1.12 shows a screen shot from an application known as A-Mac Address 5.0, which can be used to scan a range of IP addresses for corresponding MAC addresses and hostnames. This feature allows you to catalog existing addresses and keep an eye out for unauthorized infiltration. For Unix, you can download arpwatch from `www-nrg.ee.lbl.gov/nrg.html` to help keep track of IP-MAC pairings.

With such software, you can also alter the MAC address that corresponds to one or more of the NICs in the machine on which the software is installed. A similar capability is helpful when, for example, an ISP tracks the MAC address it sees coming from the device you attach to its WAN circuit. If you replace your equipment, you will have to notify the ISP of the new MAC address. Many more sophisticated components have a utility built in that can spoof your MAC address back to the old one the ISP is suspecting.

### Visual Inspection

1. Choose a NIC or other device that has an exposed label with a hexadecimal code on it, as shown in the following picture.

2. Look for a 12-digit hexadecimal value, which will be made up of some combination of the numbers 0 through 9 and the letters *A* through *F*.

3. Because you may not see evidence that the code you are looking at is the MAC address, such as the letters *EA* for Ethernet address, it may help to use a lookup utility, such as the IEEE's online utility, to confirm that the first six digits actually correspond to the company that appears to have manufactured the device. Otherwise, you may be looking at the wrong number. It may be possible that there is no MAC address actually listed on the device and an electronic discovery will have to be made.

**FIGURE 1.12** A-MAC address utility

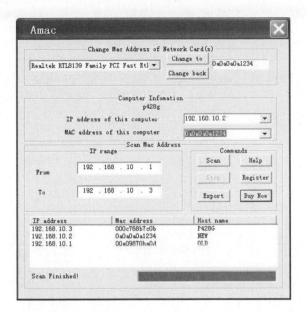

## Decoding OUIs

OUIs are assigned by the IEEE, so the online utility provided by the IEEE at http://standards
.ieee.org/regauth/oui/index.shtml is likely to be the most accurate and up-to-date. The following screen shot shows the result of a search for the OUI of a Linksys Wireless-G Broadband Router with SpeedBooster, perhaps as found in the ARP cache of a PC attached to the
router. You'll see how to produce such output later in this task.

Here are the results of your search through the public section of the IEEE Standards OUI database report for **001217**:

```
00-12-17   (hex)          Cisco-Linksys, LLC
001217     (base 16)      Cisco-Linksys, LLC
                          121 Theory Dr.
                          Irvine CA 92612
                          UNITED STATES
```

Your attention is called to the fact that the firms and numbers listed may not always be obvious in product implementation. Some
manufacturers subcontract component manufacture and others include registered firms' OUIs in their products.

[IEEE Standards Home Page] -- [Search] -- [E-mail to Staff]
Copyright © 2006 IEEE

## Use of *winipcfg*

If you have one of the earlier Windows operating systems, such as 9x or Me, you might have access to a handy graphical user interface (GUI) called winipcfg. If not, you might have a similar utility installed. Check in your system tray. Figure 1.13 shows a sample output from winipcfg.

1.  If you have winipcfg, the first step to running it is to click the Start button.

2.  Click Run.

3.  Enter **winipcfg** on the Open line.

4.  Click OK.

5.  You may need to click the down arrow to the right of the initial adapter name that appears in order to be able to select the adapter you wish to identify.

**FIGURE 1.13**     MAC address by winipcfg

## Use of *ipconfig*

The ipconfig utility has been available from Microsoft since the days of Windows 98. A similar command-line utility, known as ifconfig, can be found in the Macintosh and Unix/Linux operating systems. The ipconfig utility is available in those operating systems that do not offer winipcfg or its equivalent.

1.  Open a command prompt. For Windows 98 SE, and Me, click Start ➤ Run.

    For later versions of Windows, click Start ➤ Run ➤ cmd.

    Alternatively, you can click Programs ➤ Accessories ➤ Command Prompt in most Windows operating systems.

2.  Enter the command **ipconfig/all**. This will display the MAC address of the installed network interfaces.

With earlier operating systems on machines that contain two or more NICs, it may be necessary to have the Ctrl+Break key sequence ready as soon as you press Enter to execute the command form the previous step. This is because the scroll-back feature was not introduced until Windows 2000. It may take a few executions of the command to get your timing right.

Look through the output of the command for each NIC you wish to catalog and pay attention to the Physical Address field. This is the MAC address of the NIC, so called because it is said to be burned into the NIC permanently in ROM and therefore physically associated with the NIC.

Figure 1.14 shows the `ipconfig` output for the same adapter from the `winipcfg` output of Figure 1.13. Note the same MAC address.

**FIGURE 1.14**   MAC address by ipconfig

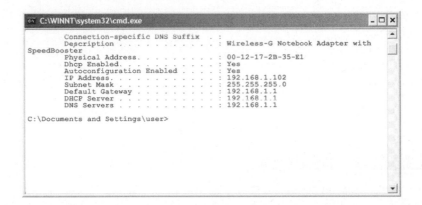

## Use of *net config*

If the output of the `ipconfig` prompt is a bit too busy for you, and if you are currently active on a network with the interface of which you wish to identify the MAC address, you can use the `net config workstation` command to display pertinent information for your active interfaces. It's a little tougher to spot the MAC address in the output of the `net config` command, but it is there, nonetheless.

1. Open a command prompt.

2. Enter the command **net config workstation**.

3. In the output, locate the MAC address for the NIC. In Figure 1.15, the MAC address for the same interface shown in Figures 1.13 and 1.14 is displayed as (0012172B35E1).

**FIGURE 1.15**   MAC address by net config

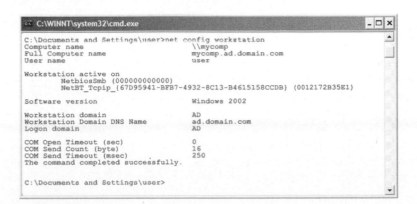

### Use of *arp*

If you are interested in identifying the MAC address of a remote device on your own IP subnet but do not have access to a third-party utility capable of scanning for MAC addresses, you can use the built-in utility arp with either the -a or -g switch. It bears repeating that the ARP cache contains only IP-to-MAC associations within the IP subnet of the workstation issuing the command. For addresses of devices outside of a given IP subnet, you need to issue the arp command on a workstation that shares the subnet with the target device.

1.  Open a command prompt.

2.  Because a workstation caches only addresses it has used, and because they age out of the cache every couple of minutes, it is most often necessary to generate traffic to the device in question before issuing the arp command. This is done easily by pinging the IP address of the target device. Generally, a workstation is in frequent contact with its default gateway, so pinging the default gateway's IP address may not be necessary as often as pinging other devices. Ping the IP address of the device that you wish to discover the MAC address for.

3.  Enter the command **arp -a** or **arp -g**.

In the following output, the MAC address you need to record is in the Physical Address column on the line corresponding to the Internet address of the device in question.

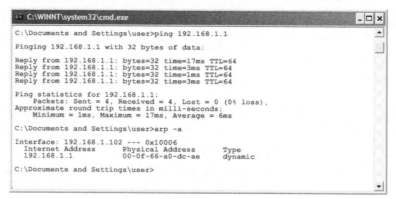

The Type column in the arp output shows the fact that the address was learned dynamically through the ARP broadcast process. Using the arp -s command, you can create an association permanently, which shows as static in the Type column.

### MAC Address Filtering on a Linksys Wireless Router

The following procedure guides you through enabling and configuring the Linksys Wireless-G Broadband Router to filter out unwanted connections by devices identified by unauthorized MAC addresses. The procedure for other brands of similar devices differs slightly, but you get the general idea of the broad tasks that you must perform to filter on MAC addresses from the following steps:

1. If you do not know the IP address for your Linksys router, one way to determine it, provided your workstation receives its IP address assignment directly from the Linksys, is to open the command prompt and issue the `ipconfig` command. The Linksys's IP address, given the aforementioned conditions, is specified on the Default Gateway line.

2. Open a web browser and specify **http://*ip_address***, where *ip_address* is the IP address of the Linksys wireless router identified in the previous step.

3. As shown in the following screen shot, you will be asked for a username and password to access the configuration pages of your Linksys. Depending on the model of router, the default username could be blank, meaning do not put anything in that field, or admin. The default password is likely admin. Obviously, the defaults are subject to change, and you will enter whatever username and password are currently set on your Linksys.

4. Figure 1.16 shows the Wireless MAC Filter page of the Wireless tab, selected by clicking the corresponding link near the top of the screen. On this page, you must click the Enable radio button to activate the Prevent and Permit choices on the page, if they're not already selected.

5. Select the Prevent radio button if you would like to prohibit MAC addresses from accessing the wireless network. Otherwise, if the list of allowed addresses is shorter than the list of the unauthorized addresses, select the Permit Only radio button to specify only those MAC addresses that will be allowed access to the wireless network, prohibiting all others from connecting.

6. To build the list of MAC addresses allowed or prohibited access to the wireless network, click the Edit MAC Filter List button at the bottom of the page. This produces the screen in Figure 1.17.

7. Notice that Linksys wants MAC addresses entered in hexadecimal with no punctuation, but the system will convert them to colon-separated bytes. You can enter the addresses in the colon-separated format as well. Start with MAC 01 and enter the MAC addresses in consecutive fields, with a maximum of 40.

**FIGURE 1.16**     Linksys router Wireless tab

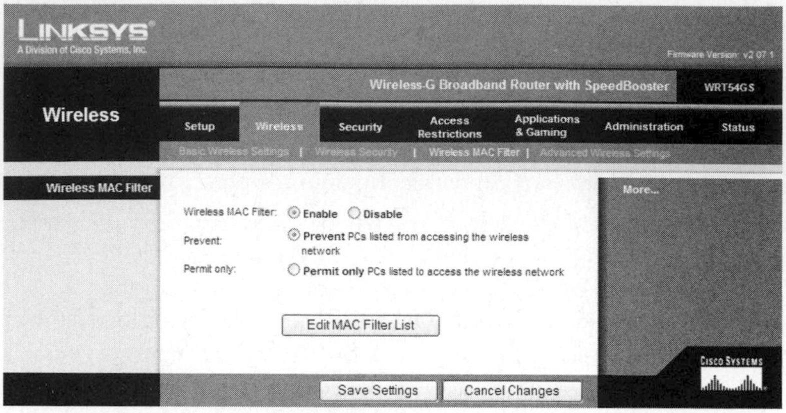

**FIGURE 1.17**     Linksys router MAC Address Filter List screen

8.  Alternatively, or in addition to manually entering addresses, you can choose to click the Wireless Client MAC List button, producing the following screen, populated by devices that are or have been connected recently to the Linksys.

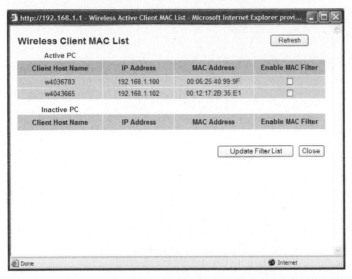

9.  Putting a check mark in the Enable MAC Filter box to the right of the desired entries and clicking the Update Filter list button automatically adds the corresponding MAC addresses to the MAC Address Filter List screen, as shown in the following screen shot.

10. Click the Save Settings button at the bottom of the screen when you are finished entering MAC addresses.

11. If the settings are saved successfully, click the Continue button to return to the MAC Address Filter List screen, where you can click the X in the upper-right corner of the screen to close the filter list. If you know you have no more MAC addresses to enter, you may click the X in the upper-right corner of the screen with the Continue button without compromising your settings, which have been saved already.

12. Back in the Wireless MAC Filter page (Figure 1.16), be sure to click the Save Settings button at the bottom of the page to keep from losing your settings on this particular page.

13. Finally, you can opt to click the Continue button on the resulting screen if you have more changes to make, or, because there is no official method to log out of the router, you can simply click the X in the upper-right corner of the Continue screen or any screen thereafter to exit your configuration session.

## Filtering MAC Addresses on a Cisco Catalyst 2950 Switch

Consider the sample network segment between two routers in Figure 1.18. The switch called 2950A ties the two routers together on the segment. A malfunctioning Ethernet interface on the HR router is creating unwanted jabber on the segment, so you need to temporarily prohibit the HR router from accessing the network.

**FIGURE 1.18**   The HR-IT LAN segment

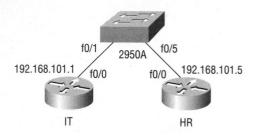

The following procedure shows how to configure switch 2950A to prohibit the HR router from accessing the network, limiting the jabber to the physical link between router HR and switch 2950A. Note that it is not necessary to filter MAC addresses on other interfaces of the HR router or on interfaces of devices on the other side of the HR router because at Layer 2, the HR router will be the source of all traffic that it places on the segment shown in the diagram.

1.   The HR router's Ethernet interface still has reliable functionality beyond its jabber (that is, its continuous corrupted and useless transmission), allowing you to confirm the HR router's current connectivity by pinging the IT router, as shown in the following output.

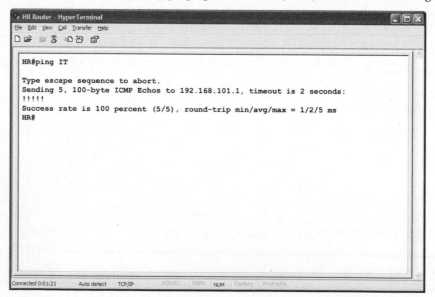

2. The same connectivity can be confirmed from the perspective of the IT router, as shown in the following output.

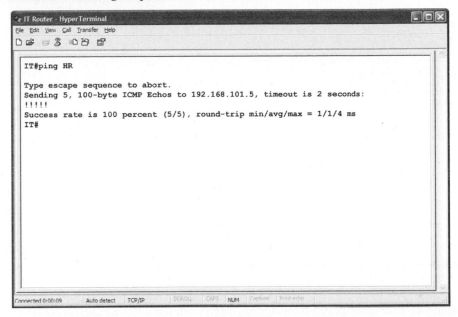

```
IT#ping HR

Type escape sequence to abort.
Sending 5, 100-byte ICMP Echos to 192.168.101.5, timeout is 2 seconds:
!!!!!
Success rate is 100 percent (5/5), round-trip min/avg/max = 1/1/4 ms
IT#
```

3. By using the show interface f0/0 command on the HR router, you can ascertain the MAC address for the HR router's interface on this segment, as can be seen in the following screen shot.

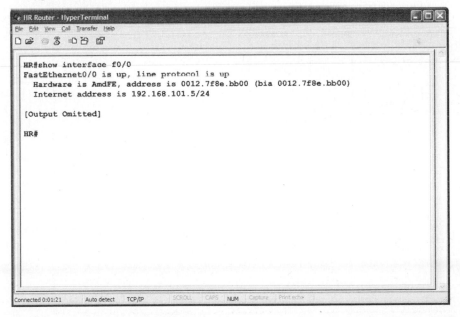

```
HR#show interface f0/0
FastEthernet0/0 is up, line protocol is up
   Hardware is AmdFE, address is 0012.7f8e.bb00 (bia 0012.7f8e.bb00)
   Internet address is 192.168.101.5/24

[Output Omitted]

HR#
```

4. Using this information, you can enter the commands in the following output to prohibit access by the HR router's f0/0 interface.

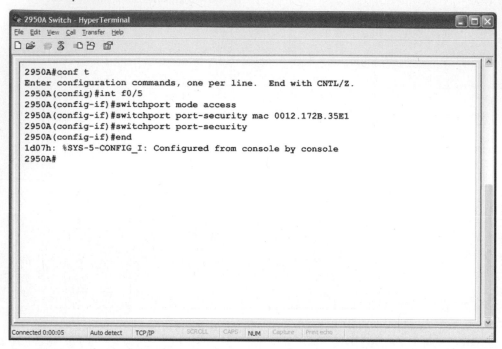

```
2950A#conf t
Enter configuration commands, one per line.  End with CNTL/Z.
2950A(config)#int f0/5
2950A(config-if)#switchport mode access
2950A(config-if)#switchport port-security mac 0012.172B.35E1
2950A(config-if)#switchport port-security
2950A(config-if)#end
1d07h: %SYS-5-CONFIG_I: Configured from console by console
2950A#
```

Note that this technique plays on the fact that by default, port security on the Catalyst switch allows a maximum of 1 MAC address per secured interface, configurable up to 132. By keeping the default of 1, any MAC address other than the one you wish to prohibit will result in the desired effect.

The switchport commands shown are entered on the 2950 interface to which the HR router is directly connected, interface f0/5. The first switchport command sets the allowed MAC address on the interface. The second switchport command begins enforcing the port security on interface f0/5.

The reason the MAC address is entered before security is enforced is because the jabber from the HR router will steal the one MAC address allowed for a dynamic entry of its own MAC address, defeating the purpose of the task at hand.

The following output shows how to confirm your settings.

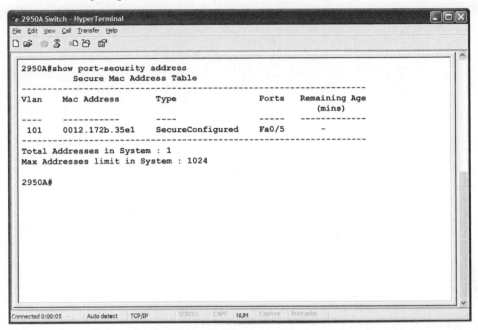

```
2950A#show port-security address
            Secure Mac Address Table
-------------------------------------------------------------
Vlan    Mac Address      Type            Ports    Remaining Age
                                                     (mins)

----    -----------      ----            -----    --------------
 101    0012.172b.35e1   SecureConfigured  Fa0/5     -
-------------------------------------------------------------
Total Addresses in System : 1
Max Addresses limit in System : 1024

2950A#
```

You'll find that now, access to and from the HR router across the LAN segment is not possible. Trying to ping from either router to the other produces the following results.

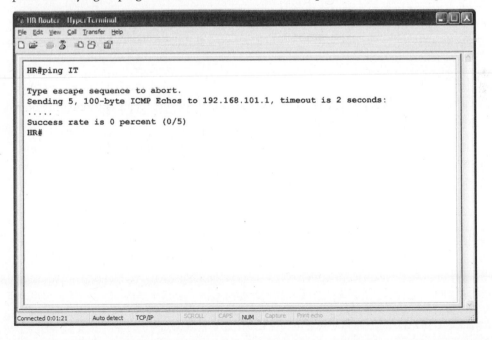

```
HR#ping IT

Type escape sequence to abort.
Sending 5, 100-byte ICMP Echos to 192.168.101.1, timeout is 2 seconds:
.....
Success rate is 0 percent (0/5)
HR#
```

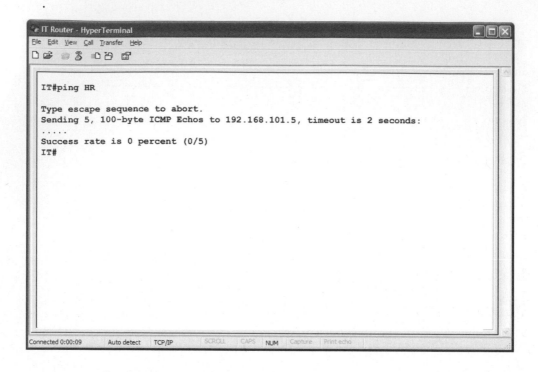

```
IT#ping HR

Type escape sequence to abort.
Sending 5, 100-byte ICMP Echos to 192.168.101.5, timeout is 2 seconds:
.....
Success rate is 0 percent (0/5)
IT#
```

## Criteria for Completion

You have completed this lab when you have identified and documented the MAC address of each LAN interface in your internetwork. If you choose to implement MAC address filtering, success is measured by confirming that unwanted devices are blocked while others are not.

# Task 1.5: Applying the OSI Model

If you've ever sat through even a single hour of network training, you've probably had your fill of the ISO's Open Systems Interconnection (OSI) reference model. While such intolerance is understood and shared by many, the ISO and others had a stroke of genius when they decided to categorize information processing into a stack of interrelated steps known as layers. By simplifying the entire data communications process through a division of labor, these groups succeeded in opening the door to many that otherwise never would have been able to grasp the concept of networking in general.

This separation of functions, each often attributable to a single protocol, or agreed-upon method of communication, has simplified software development and implementation. Additionally, it has ensured that entire systems need not be redesigned for the sake of updating a single protocol. For example, if the IETF needed to enhance the capabilities of IP, it would not need to revamp the entire TCP/IP protocol suite in order to do so. This adds an incentive to update protocols when needed instead of procrastinating until more of the suite requires attention.

What all of this means to you is that you have different levels of classification for the equipment in your internetwork. The benefit of these classifications is that you can easily concentrate your efforts on one group of components at a time, from cabling and adapters to hubs and MAUs and then on to switches, routers, and application-level entities. Furthermore, troubleshooting efforts are greatly reduced when you are not swimming in a sea of possibilities but instead have an orderly approach to what group of components is capable of producing the symptoms you witness.

# Scenario

Knowing the value of the basics of networking, you plan to arrange all the components of your internetwork by their highest level of involvement in the OSI model. As new components are implemented or existing ones malfunction, you plan to refer back to your documentation to choose the correct path to follow with the task at hand.

# Scope of Task

## Duration

This lab should take about 30 minutes.

## Setup

This task involves the categorization of not only every electronic component in your internetwork, but also of every type of cable and adapter used. You will need all devices and cables in your installation and room to spread out and group the components. Documenting the pieces you are not able to amass around you will help to include them in troubleshooting when the time comes.

## Caveat

While routers, for example, are regarded widely as Layer 3 devices, they also connect physically to the network, a Layer 1 phenomenon. Each interface of the router also contains circuitry allowing it to participate in the Layer 2 media access method and to produce the characteristic frames of the network to which it is attached. Therefore, don't get caught up in the intricacies of the device at this point, even though proper troubleshooting requires you to realize that a device that functions at multiple layers can malfunction at each layer. For this task, concern yourself with identifying the highest layer at which a component operates.

Be careful of the word *frame*. There are Layer 1 frames and Layer 2 frames. So using the concept of frame production to categorize a device may be misleading. The frames created by a T1 CSU/DSU are Layer 1 frames. They pull together a single byte from 24 different sources 8,000 times a second. Unlike an Ethernet frame, which is an example of a Layer 2 frame, T1 frames lack the ability to survive in the network on their own. Ethernet, on the other hand, installs addressing and error detection mechanisms in each frame.

T1 frames cannot enter the network on their own but instead must be collected into super-frames consisting of 12 or 24 frames. Each frame in a superframe is separated by a framing bit of a certain value. When the pattern of these framing bits is recognized by the receiving circuitry, it is then possible to pick the individual frames out of the superframe. In short, the overhead of a Layer 2 frame tells something about the data in that frame, while the overhead of a Layer 1 frame tells nothing of its eclectic data but instead serves to help synchronize the receiving clock to the transmitting clock, among other basic functions.

## Procedure

Documentation of the results of this task is beneficial both for those components you cannot bring to the table during the task and for those that you can. Eventually, each piece of your internetwork has the capability to be inconveniently positioned, such that dismantling of equipment unrelated to the problem or task at hand may be necessary to assess the situation. Being familiar with the functionality of each component will aid in including or excluding it from the list of possible suspects that could cause a particular problem or symptom.

### Equipment Used

The equipment you use will depend on the equipment you have available to you. It could include, but is not limited to, any of the following:

- Hubs
- MAUs
- Switches
- NIC cards installed or not
- Computers
- Modems (analog, DSL, cable)
- ISDN equipment
- Routers
- Wireless access points
- Wireless adapters of various system connectivity (expansion slot, USB, etc.)
- CSU/DSUs
- Cables related to any of these components

### Details

Figure 1.19 depicts the seven layers of the OSI reference model. Beside it are some of the devices that operate no higher than their corresponding layer.

**FIGURE 1.19**    The OSI model and devices

| 7 | Application | Gateways, computers |
|---|---|---|
| 6 | Presentation | |
| 5 | Session | |
| 4 | Transport | |
| 3 | Network | Routers, Layer 3 switches |
| 2 | Data link | NICs, switches, bridges, concentrators |
| 1 | Physical | Cables, adapters, interfaces, connectors, pins, repeaters, MUXs, transceivers, hubs, modems, CSU/DSUs, MAUs, terminal adapters, NT1s |

1. Choose a component from your network to categorize by layers of the OSI model.

2. Use Figure 1.19 to help categorize your component. Consult other resources, such as the Internet, for help categorizing entities not found in the lists in the diagram.

3. Document the device by name and highest layer orientation.

4. If the component currently is not attached to the network, place it with items of the same layer. This action will help solidify the component's place in the model in your mind, helping to speed future recognition as well as helping to generate ideas later of what parts of the network could be causing any given symptoms you may happen to observe.

5. Repeat steps 1 through 4 for each component.

## Criteria for Completion

You have completed this lab when you have categorized each component in your internetwork by the highest layer of the OSI model at which it operates and confirmed your choices by consulting reputable sources.

# Task 1.6: Developing an IP Addressing Scheme

One of the skills most elusive to a network administrator is the ability to effectively flesh out an IP subnet based on an address and mask. Although this lab breaks from the tradition of the book and strives to teach as much as guide, this one topic alone can make or break the career of even an otherwise talented administrator. This lab presents a more modern technique that, when mastered, allows you to perform all calculations in decimal, avoiding the cumbersome world of binary tables and charts.

Once it has delivered the pertinent information regarding IP subnetting calculations, this lab will guide you through using your own IP address space to develop a scheme that suits your particular needs and growth potential.

# Scenario

Your internetwork is ready for IP addressing design. It has fallen on you alone to design the addressing scheme for all sites in your multinational internetwork that you sketched out earlier. You have been asked to use only the private Class B address 172.16.0.0/16. All IP networks must come from this address space.

# Scope of Task

## Duration

A task like this eventually will take less than 30 minutes, but allow yourself a couple of hours while learning.

## Setup

For this task, refer back to your original sketch of the internetwork. You will use this to produce a simpler diagram on which to assign portions of the available address space. Your setup for this task will be similar, but in a slightly smaller scale, to that of Task 1.1.

## Caveat

While this lab has you make generalities for the LAN segments in your internetwork, you may not be able to do so in all cases. As a primary example, consider the situation in which your network does not use Dynamic Host Configuration Protocol (DHCP) servers. If instead you must statically configure each device with its own permanent IP address, your drawing would be more complete if every device were drawn explicitly and labeled with its corresponding address.

# Procedure

Read the following sections describing a newer method of subnet calculation and then follow the steps to apply this method to your internetwork.

## Geographical Aspects

Your internetwork drawing includes addressing for the following sites:

- New York
- Los Angeles
- London
- Tokyo
- Sydney
- Cairo

## Equipment Used

The equipment you represent in your drawing will be exactly that of Task 1.1, but the detail of your drawing will not include each device.

## Details

For this task, you need your original sketch of the internetwork from Task 1.1. Employ the following techniques to use the 172.16.0.0/16 address space to supply network and host portions to every LAN and WAN segment drawn, except for the remote access legs. Those will be supplied by the ISPs that the telecommuters use. Once they're tunneled into the network, their host count must be factored into the total number of hosts required for their local LAN.

### A Faster Way to Subnet

Traditional methods of dividing a given IP address space into subnets have you work in binary at one or almost all points in the process. Presented here is a method that allows you to work entirely in decimal. The procedure may seem a bit unorthodox at first, but continued practice will result in the ability to solve subnetting problems much more quickly than before. It is estimated that, on average, a problem that would normally take up to 5 minutes to complete can be finished in less than 30 seconds using this method. Try it the next time you take an exam with subnetting problems to increase your chance of success and of finishing the exam on time. The sidebar titled "The Two Types of Subnetting Problems" explains how to spot the type of subnetting problem you have encountered.

Before reading that sidebar, however, it is important that you understand the relationship between the number of digits in a value, the base of the numbering system (2 for binary, 10 for decimal, and 16 for hexadecimal, for example), and the number of values those digits can represent. Consider the following generic formula, which takes these factors into account.

$$\left( \begin{array}{c} \text{base of the} \\ \text{numbering} \\ \text{system} \end{array} \right)^{\text{number of digits}} = \frac{\text{total number of values}}{\begin{array}{c} - \quad 1 \\ \hline \text{largest possible value} \end{array}}$$

Using this equation, you can determine that three decimal (base-10) digits form 1,000 different values but that 999 is the largest value formed. Similarly, the following equation shows why 255 is the largest octet (8-bit) value possible in base 2, a well-known IP fact, but that counting 0 (zero), there are 256 total different binary combinations.

$$\frac{\begin{array}{c} 2^8 = 256 \\ - \quad 1 \end{array}}{255}$$

## The Two Types of Subnetting Problems

Subnetting exercises can be split into two broad categories: those that refer to the number of subnets and/or hosts per subnet are required and all others. Let's call these Type I and Type II problems, respectively.

### Type I Problems

These problems can be identified by the characteristic phrase "how many," as in "How many subnets are produced by applying a subnet mask of 255.255.192.0 to the address 10.0.0.0/8?" or "How many hosts are available on each subnet produced?" The "how many" phrase could be absent in a Type I problem, however, as in an exercise that asks, "Which subnet mask produces 512 subnets, each supporting 126 hosts, given a default Class B address?" In this case, the mere mention of the number of subnets and/or hosts per subnet implies quantity, or "how many?"

### Type II Problems

Just as the various clichés that start out "There are two types of people in the world..." define one type of person and lump everyone else into a second category, simply disqualifying an exercise as a Type I problem makes it a Type II problem. While Type II problems have no telling verbiage, they tend to pose questions such as, "Which subnet is the address a member of?" or "What's the broadcast address of the subnet?" or "What is the host range of the subnet?"

If you consider that the word *bit* is a contraction of the words *binary* and *digit*, then the base of the numbering system must always be 2 when dealing with bits. With that in mind, the following two special cases for the equation presented earlier are used in Type I problems.

Equation for subnets:

$$2^{\text{number of subnet bits}} = \text{number of subnets}$$

Equation for hosts:

$$2^{\text{number of host bits}} - 2 = \text{number of hosts per subnet}$$

Once you have identified the type of subnetting exercise you have in front of you, there are four important pieces of information that can be gleaned from any subnetting problem. The sidebar titled "The Four Important Facts" explains what these are and how they are used.

Using the definitions of the four important facts, consider an address of 192.168.10.80/26. With just this information, we can surmise the following:

- **def:** /24 (assumed, based on a Class C address)

- **non-def:** /26 (given in the problem and could have been given as 255.255.255.192)

- **all IPs:** 32 (a welcome no-brainer)
- **next mult:** 32 (careful—not the same as **all IPs** when **non-def** is less than /24)

The next step is to use these four important facts to solve Type I and Type II problems. The sidebar "Using the Four Facts" describes how to put the facts into use.

---

## The Four Important Facts

Any subnetting problem deals with up to four important pieces of information that you can ascertain easily. Two or three of these four facts can be subsequently used to solve your sub-netting exercise, depending on the type of problem with which you are dealing.

### The Default Subnet Mask (def)

This is the subnet mask that you are assigned initially. The default mask could be the classful mask when no other is given. However, let's say an administrator has four assistants, each one dedicated to the four major departments of the organization. Assume the administrator is assigned the 172.31.0.0/16 address space but needs to split it up for the departments.

Working backwards using the equation for subnets, the administrator can determine that four subnets, one for each department, will require two subnet bits because the exponent 2 in $2^2 = 4$ represents the number of subnet bits. As a result, each of the four assistants is restricted to the /18 mask, the one they are assigned initially. Therefore, when each assistant considers their default subnet mask for their own IP subnetting computations, it will be /18, not /16, because falling back to the classful default will result in infringement upon the address space of their cohorts, which would cause various problems once implemented.

### The Non-default Subnet Mask (non-def)

This is the subnet mask being considered for use. When doing a Type I subnetting problem where both the default mask and non-default mask are used, the non-default mask is the greater of the two. In Type II problems where the default mask is not used, the non-default mask is simply the mask used in your calculations.

### All IP Addresses Have 32 Bits (all IPs)

While this fact seems entirely academic, the number 32 is required whenever you wish to determine the number of host bits that are left over after subnetting turns on all the 1s in the mask that it needs.

### The Next Multiple of 8 Greater Than the Non-Default Mask (next mult)

Given that the non-default subnet mask can be anything from /9 up to /30, the next multiple will tend to be 16, 24, or 32. This value is essential in discovering the interesting octet and its incremental value.

## Using the Four Facts

The four important facts allow you to determine four things:

- The number of subnets

- The number of hosts per subnet

- The interesting octet

- The incremental value of the interesting octet

The first two solve a Type I problem, while the last two are used to flesh out subnet boundaries and host ranges, allowing the solution of Type II problems. Here's how.

### The Number of Subnets

By raising 2 to the result of subtracting **def** from **non-def**, you effectively raise 2 to the number of subnet bits, which is the equation for subnets presented earlier. The result for our example is four subnets:

$$
\begin{array}{r}
26 \\
-\ 24 \\
\hline
2^2 = 4
\end{array}
$$

### The Number of Hosts per Subnet

By raising 2 to the result of subtracting **non-def** from **all IPs**, you effectively raise 2 to the number of host bits. Subtract 2 from this result and you have the equation for hosts presented earlier. The result for our example is 62 hosts per subnet:

$$
\begin{array}{r}
32 \\
-\ 26 \\
\hline
2^6 - 2 = 62
\end{array}
$$

### The Interesting Octet and Incremental Value

The interesting octet is the one that changes with each successive subnet address, or boundary. With a dotted-decimal mask it's easy to spot the interesting octet. It's the one that is neither a 0 nor a 255. In classless inter-domain routing (CIDR) notation, it is equally easy to spot the interesting octet. You need only divide **next mult** by 8. Because **next mult** will be 16, 24, or 32, the interesting octet will be 2, 3, or 4. Raise 2 to the result of subtracting **non-def** from **next mult** and you produce the number of values in the interesting octet between subnet boundaries, that is, the incremental value of the interesting octet. Our interesting octet is the fourth, and its incremental value is 64:

$$
\begin{array}{r}
32/8 = 4 \\
-\ 26 \\
\hline
2^6 = 64
\end{array}
$$

## A Spreadsheet for Practice

The following steps detail how to create a spreadsheet you can use to check your work with this subnetting technique, allowing you to make up your own problems and check your solutions when no solutions are given.

1. Open Microsoft Excel or a compatible spreadsheet application.
2. Type **Default CIDR** in cell B3.
3. Type **Non-default CIDR** in cell C3.
4. Type **Interesting Octet** in cell D3.
5. Type **Increment** in cell E3.
6. Type **Subnet Bits** in cell F3.
7. Type **# of Subnets** in cell G3.
8. Type **Host Bits** in cell H3.
9. Type **# of Hosts** in cell I3.
10. Enter this formula, with no spaces, in cell D4:

    =IF(AND(C4<8,C4>=0),1,IF(AND(C4<16,C4>=8),2,IF(AND(C4<24,C4>=16),3,IF(AND(C4<=32,C4>=24),4))))

11. Enter this formula, with no spaces, in cell E4:

    =IF(AND(C4<8,C4>=0),POWER(2,8-C4),IF(AND(C4<16,C4>=8),POWER(2,16-C4),IF(AND(C4<24,C4>=16),POWER(2,24-C4),IF(AND(C4<32,C4>=24),POWER(2,32-C4),"N/A"))))

12. Enter this formula, with no spaces, in cell F4:

    =IF((C4-B4)>=0,C4-B4,"N/A")

13. Enter this formula, with no spaces, in cell G4:

    =IF(AND(F4>=0,F4<=32),POWER(2,F4),"N/A")

14. Enter this formula, with no spaces, in cell H4:

    =32-C4

15. Enter this formula, with no spaces, in cell I4:

    =IF(C4<32,(POWER(2,H4))-2,"N/A")

16. You can dress your spreadsheet up in Excel by choosing Tools ➢ Options ➢ View and unchecking Formula bar, Gridlines, Row & column headers, Horizontal scroll bar, and Vertical scroll bar.

## Subnetting Steps

When followed, this procedure brings resolution to even the most difficult subnetting problems. In certain cases, you may have to break the problem into its component pieces and then apply these steps to those pieces.

1. Determine if the problem is Type I or Type II or both.
2. For a Type I problem, determine **def**, **non-def**, and **all IPs**. For a Type II problem, determine **non-def** and **next mult**.

3. If the problem is Type II only, skip to step 7. Otherwise, continue with step 4.

4. Determine the number of subnets using the equation for subnets.

5. Determine the number of hosts per subnet by using the equation for hosts.

6. If the problem is Type I only, stop here.

7. Determine the interesting octet by dividing **next mult** by 8.

8. Determine the incremental value of the interesting octet by raising 2 to the result of subtracting **non-def** from **next mult**.

9. Flesh out the subnets using the following steps.

   a. Start with the original address in the problem. If not zeroed out already, substitute a 0 in the interesting octet and all octets to the right, if any. This produces the current subnet.

   b. Add the incremental value to the value of the interesting octet of the current subnet, changing no other octet, to find the next subnet.

   c. If the interesting octet of the next subnet has a value of 256 and you are not allowed to change the value of the next octet to the left, either because it is already 255 or because you do not own the next value, then the current subnet was the last. Keep the value of 256 in the interesting octet of the next subnet for the next step. After finishing step 9f, you are done. Otherwise, if you are allowed to change the value of the next octet to the left, change the 256 to a 0 and add 1 to the next octet to the left.

   d. If there is not a value of 0 in the interesting octet of the next subnet, then the broadcast address for the current subnet is 1 less than the value of the interesting octet of the next subnet and 255 in all octets to the right, if any. Otherwise, the broadcast address is 1 less than the next subnet's value in the octet to the left of the interesting octet and 255 in the interesting octet and all octets to the right, if any.

   e. Find the first valid host address in the current subnet by adding 1 to the value in the fourth octet of the current subnet address.

   f. Find the last valid host address in the current subnet by subtracting 1 from the value in the fourth octet of the current subnet's broadcast address.

   g. If step 9f was not your last step according to the instructions in step 9c, repeat the procedure from step 9b.

## Subnetting Your Internetwork

The following steps guide you to the successful completion of this lab:

1. Count the number of LANs and WANs in your internetwork, not including any remote access networks.

2. Add 10 percent to this value for future growth.

3. If the result is a whole number power of 2, go to the next step. Otherwise, find the next whole number power of 2. For example, if step 2 produced 25, the result of this step would be 32.

4. The exponent by which you raise 2 is the number of subnet bits required for your final result.

5. The subnet bits added to your original mask creates your new mask, or **non-def**.

6. The result of subtracting **non-def** from **all IPs** is the number of host bits. Make sure that subtracting 2 from the result of raising 2 to the number of host bits meets or exceeds 110 percent of the host requirements of your largest LAN segment.

7. Further subnet one of your equally sized subnets to supply addresses to all your WAN segments, using the ideal subnet mask for point-to-point networks.

While step 7 is adequate in the lab, in production you would want to find the value corresponding to your growth budget for each size LAN segment and, starting with the largest of these, take larger subnets and resubnet them to supply addresses for the smaller LANs more efficiently and with less waste than suggested here. Such an effort is not reserved only for WAN links.

## Criteria for Completion

You have completed this task when you have specified a unique subnet for each of your LAN and WAN segments using 30-bit masks for your WAN links.

# Task 1.7: Designing a VLAN Scheme

Virtual LANs (VLANs) provide a mechanism for administrators to deal with some of the increasingly prevalent trends of modern enterprise networking. It is necessary, occasionally, to post members of a highly integrated team in separate locations, closer to the personnel they support. Doing so can result in logistical issues, including how to afford secure access to the resources these team members require in collaborating with one another and performing their jobs. Fortunately, with VLANs, spatial separation is a surmountable obstacle. Furthermore, when switching over ATM backbones, VLANs can be extended geographically to a virtually limitless scope.

Another benefit of VLAN implementation is the reduction in broadcast traffic on a VLAN compared to the broadcasts present on a flat LAN. The scope of a VLAN corresponds to a discreet broadcast domain, which corresponds to a separate IP subnet. LAN switches do not pass frames, broadcast or otherwise, between VLANs. To communicate between VLANs, tagged frames must be passed to a router. Because each VLAN overlays a unique IP subnet, only a Layer 3 device is capable of understanding the IP subnet differences and changing a frame's VLAN affiliation. This router involvement provides for an added benefit: the use of access control lists to limit cross-VLAN traffic in an intelligent way.

Workgroup LAN switches generally are capable of interconnecting with each other by trunk ports in addition to attaching to end devices over access ports. Just for perspective, if a switch has only one type of interface, it's the access port, making trunk ports something of a special case. Because access ports can be members of only a single VLAN at a time, and because end devices on these ports do not understand frame tagging or even realize they are members of a VLAN (which are visible only to switches and routers for grouping end devices), frames sent out access ports must be untagged, standard frames. However, because all VLANs can be allowed across trunk ports, frames must be tagged to indicate their VLAN affiliation. Protocols that tag frames for transmission across trunks include IEEE 802.1Q and Cisco's proprietary Inter-Switch Link (ISL) as well as ATM LANE, and 802.10 for FDDI.

## Scenario

The LANs in New York, Los Angeles, London, and Tokyo are expected to experience unacceptable levels of contention for bandwidth as well as to be inundated with excessive levels of broadcast traffic. In order to avoid the undesirable utilization rates, you decide to design VLANs into the switched networks at these locations.

## Scope of Task

### Duration

This task should take about 30 minutes.

### Setup

For this task, you need your original sketch of the internetwork from Task 1.1. Using your diagram allows you to visualize the details of this task. Have access to a spreadsheet application or a word processor that allows you to create tables so you can track and document your design.

### Caveat

Not all switch models support VLANs. Furthermore, when creating trunk links between switches, care must be taken to use a frame tagging method that is compatible with both switches. Some switch manufacturers employ proprietary tagging protocols. When deploying a multivendor switched network, plan on using a standards-based tagging mechanism, such as 802.1Q. Be aware that your equipment will not allow trunks to be configured on 10Mbps ports. Only FE ports or faster can be configured as trunks.

## Procedure

This task guides you through the design process that goes into creating VLANs and implementing VLANs on a Cisco Catalyst 3550 LAN switch and 2611XM router.

## Geographical Aspects

Your internetwork drawing includes addressing for the following sites:

- New York
- Los Angeles
- London
- Tokyo

## Equipment Used

The equipment you represent in your drawing will be a subset of the switches from Task 1.1, but your drawing will include more detail for each device. You also need access to a computer and spreadsheet or word processing software.

## Details

The following points must be observed to complete this task successfully:

- Notate which links in your original diagram must be configured as trunks. These will be the links that are required to carry traffic for more than one VLAN.

- Devices originally connected to a switch or hub in Task 1.1 may need to be relocated to meet the requirements of the task, but the number of devices connected to a particular concentrating device cannot be altered. Assume that all connections go to a central equipment room, so patching to a different concentrator is not an issue.

- Be sure to redesign your IP subnets from Task 1.6 to allow the option of intercommunication between VLANs. Placing multiple VLANs in the same IP subnet prohibits them from contacting one another, but they may still pass through a common router interface to exit the local area.

### New York

- Place the servers together on their own VLAN, named Servers.
- The 15 10Base2 workstations must be placed in the same VLAN as 20 of the workstations currently attached to switch 2, named Sales.
- Ten workstations currently connected to the hub and 10 workstations connected to switch 2 must be placed in the same VLAN, named Transcription.
- The other 10 hub-attached workstations and 5 workstations connected to switch 2 must be placed in the same VLAN, called Engineering.
- The remaining 5 workstations attached to switch 2 must be placed in a separate VLAN, called IT.

### Los Angeles

The 105 workstations attached to switch 3 must be separated into 3 VLANs of 35 workstations each, named MKTG, HR, and ACCT.

### London

The 52 workstations attached to switch 10 must be evenly distributed among 4 VLANs, named FLOOR1, FLOOR2, FLOOR3, and FLOOR4.

### Tokyo

- The 35 workstations attached to switch 6 must be split into 5 VLANs with 7 workstations each, named Project1, Project2, Project3, Project4, and Project5.

- The 10 workstations attached to switch 7 should be in separate VLANs but the same IP subnet. The workstations on these VLANs will not be allowed to communicate with one another but must be able to communicate with the rest of the network through router J.

### VLANs on the Cisco 2611XM Router and Catalyst 3550 Switch

The following steps walk you through creating VLANs on a Cisco Catalyst 3550 Ethernet switch and a Cisco 2611XM router and placing interfaces in one of these VLANs on the 3550.

1. In order to group interfaces on a switch into a VLAN, you first must create the VLAN and then place interfaces in it. Before any configuration is performed on the 3550, there is only one VLAN, VLAN 1, the default management VLAN. The show vlan privileged EXEC command in the following output indicates this is the only VLAN in existence on this switch and all interfaces are members of that VLAN.

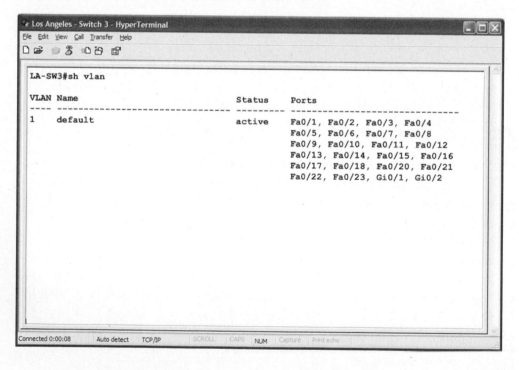

2.  The following output shows the commands necessary to create VLANs 100, 101, and 102 on the Catalyst 3550, naming them MKTG, HR, and ACCT.

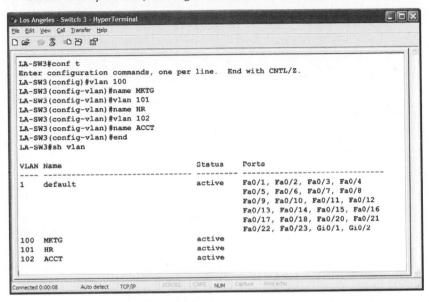

3.  The next screen shot illustrates two ways to place interfaces in VLANs after they have been created. You can use the standard interface command, with a single interface type and number, such as f0/1, or you can use the interface range command to place multiple interfaces in the same VLAN simultaneously. Note that the show vlan output indicates the four interfaces are now in the MKTG VLAN.

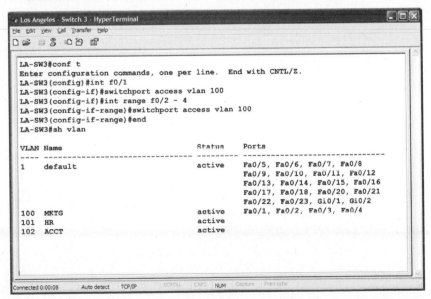

**4.** That takes care of the access ports, those that belong to a single VLAN and connect to end devices, not trunked to other switches or routers. Now, to create a trunk between switch 3 and router E, for example, it is necessary to make each device aware of this intent. Note that there are automatic settings that can result in trunk formation, but it is often best to configure the interfaces that make up the trunk to be in a trunking state all the time, thus minimizing the chance of the trunk reverting to a non-trunking state. The show interface trunk command in the following output indicates that no trunks exist currently on switch 3.

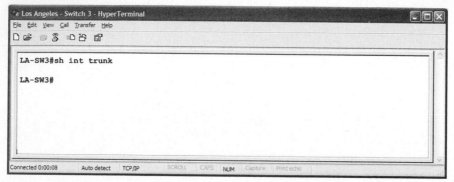

**5.** By starting out on router E and creating a subinterface for each VLAN on the physical interface you want to act as a trunk, you will be able to confirm the trunk's status on the switch in the final step. It's not a bad idea to coordinate the subinterface number (.100) with the VLAN number. This helps in identification later on.

6.  Finally, configure the corresponding interface on the 3550 to use the same frame-tagging encapsulation chosen on the router and force the status to trunking only. The output of the show interface trunk command now shows the successful formation of the trunk between switch 3 and router E, as seen in the following screen shot, as opposed to the earlier blank output of the same command.

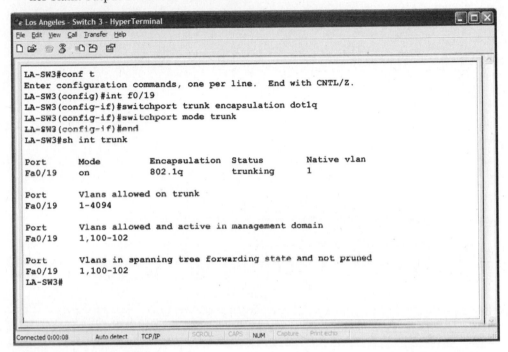

## Criteria for Completion

You have completed this task when you have designed VLAN schemes for each of the four geographic locations that support the groupings detailed earlier and adjusted your IP address scheme to support the VLANs. Your spreadsheet should have a section for each city. Each of these sections should have an entry for each VLAN, to include the name of the VLAN, a number for it, and the number of ports to be placed in the VLAN, similar to the following example.

|   | A | B | C | D | E |
|---|---|---|---|---|---|
| 1 | City: | Los Angeles | | | |
| 2 | | | | | |
| 3 | VLANs: | Number | Name | Port Count | |
| 4 | | 100 | MKTG | 35 | |
| 5 | | 101 | HR | 35 | |
| 6 | | 102 | ACCT | 35 | |
| 7 | | | | | |

# Phase

# 2

# Implementing and Configuring the Design

In this phase of the installation of your internetwork, you conduct a series of tasks aimed at perfecting and erecting the design you began in Phase 1. Here, you will configure the addressing you designed, as well as put together a naming convention for your network components. You have the opportunity in this phase to delve into the red-hot world of wireless networking, including the distant cousin to wireless networking, Bluetooth. Configuration of analog and DSL modems gives you a way to attach a non-networked device to the network through a remote-access connection. Finally a couple of tricks with Cisco routers are presented for the convenience and cost savings they can afford the network administrator.

The tasks in this phase map to all four domains in the objectives for the Comp-TIA Network+ exam.

# Task 2.1: Assigning IP Addresses

In today's internetworks, a device without an IP address is probably a piece of furniture. But the assignment of an IP address is not arbitrary and must follow a well-thought-out design. How the address makes it into the configuration of the device is a topic of interest as well. You have taken care of designing the addressing scheme. Now it is time to decide how to introduce the intended addresses into the devices.

Two broad choices exist. Static configuration involves the manual input of the address into the appropriate software interface. Dynamic configuration uses a protocol between client and server or allows a device to assign itself a pseudo-random address.

This task guides you through the static assignment of an IP address in various networking devices, as well as configuring them to assign and obtain addresses dynamically, either through the Dynamic Host Configuration Protocol (DHCP) or Automatic Private IP Addressing (APIPA).

## Scenario

After designing the IP addressing scheme for your network, you want to explore your options for IP address assignment in various devices. You may decide to use one of the address assignment methods exclusively or a combination of the methods you investigate.

## Scope of Task

### Duration

This task should take about 1 hour.

### Setup

For this task, you need the IP addressing scheme that you designed earlier. You also need various devices that you can configure with IP addresses, as well as the means you established previously to gain configuration access to the devices.

### Caveat

While all TCP/IP speaking devices have a way to configure or obtain an IP address, the methods of configuration vary substantially. Configuring one PC with an IP address, for example, will not guarantee your ability to configure another intuitively. You may have to investigate, on your own, the proper method to configure devices not presented in this task.

Note that devices not normally considered to operate at or above Layer 3, such as hubs and switches, might still allow the configuration of an IP address for management purposes. Such address assignment proves useful for Telnet and Simple Network Management Protocol (SNMP) access to the device, as well as for creating a target for ping and traceroute utilities.

## Procedure

In this task, you learn how to assign addresses to a Microsoft Windows–based PC, a Cisco router, and a Linksys wireless router. You also learn how to configure the DHCP service on a Windows-based server and a Linksys wireless router and both the service and relay agent on a Cisco router.

### Equipment Used

For this task, it is ideal for you to have access to the same type of devices presented here. Additionally, devices that can be configured with an IP address are highly recommended because familiarity with the configuration of a variety of devices extends your intuition with regard to configuring unfamiliar devices. Devices capable of IP configuration include, but are not limited to, the following.

- Hubs
- MAUs
- Switches
- Servers
- Workstations
- Routers
- Modems (DSL, cable)
- Wireless access points
- Specialty devices that offer Internet access for control or management

## Details

The following sections guide you through configuring sample devices with IP addresses in different manners, as well as setting up sample devices as DHCP servers and relay agents.

### Address Assignment on a PC Running Windows XP Professional

Choosing how an address is assigned to a computer running a Microsoft operating system, like most other Windows functions, is not a straightforward process. You must navigate your way to a specific dialog within the graphical user interface (GUI) to make the change. Your choices are static assignment and dynamic assignment of IP addresses. Depending on the method you choose, additional options vary, but static assignment, by definition, requires the most configuration.

#### STATIC ADDRESS ASSIGNMENT

Once you grasp configuring a computer with static IP information, setting it up for dynamic assignment is a breeze. Start with the more difficult of the two methods.

1.  On the Desktop, right-click My Network Places.

2.  In the shortcut menu, click Properties to bring up the Network Connections window.

3.  Right-click the adapter on which you wish to configure a static address.

4.  In the shortcut menu, click Properties to bring up the Properties dialog for your adapter.

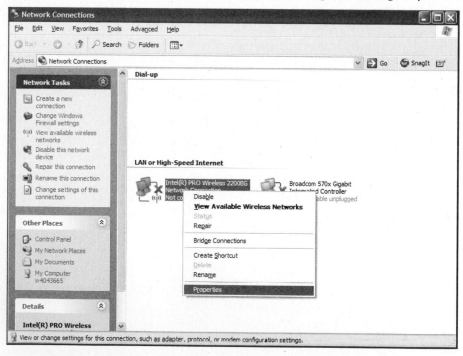

5. On the General tab of the Network Connection dialog, scroll down to Internet Protocol (TCP/IP), if necessary, and click on it.

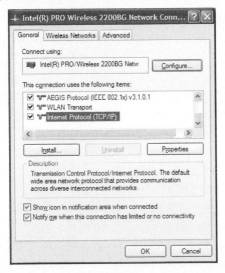

6. Click the Properties button to bring up the Internet Protocol (TCP/IP) Properties dialog.

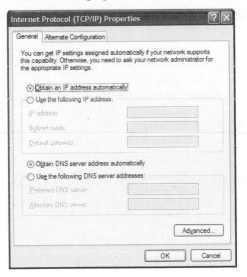

7. Fill the Use The Following IP Address radio button. The Use The Following DNS Server Addresses radio button fills in automatically.

8. Enter the device's IP address information, including address, mask, and default gateway.

9.  Supply the address for one or more DNS servers in the internetwork that are available for fully qualified domain name (FQDN) resolution.

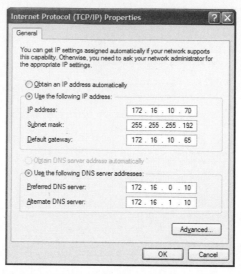

10. Click OK to save your changes and close the Internet Protocol (TCP/IP) Properties dialog.

11. Click OK to close the Properties dialog for your adapter.

12. Close the Network Connections window.

### DYNAMIC ADDRESS ASSIGNMENT WITH DHCP

Used more often in production, dynamic address assignment is fairly simple on most devices. Many hosts are set to use DHCP to obtain their IP information right out of the box.

1.  On the Desktop, right-click My Network Places.

2.  In the shortcut menu, click Properties to bring up the Network Connections window.

3.  Right-click the adapter on which you wish to configure a static address.

4.  In the shortcut menu, click Properties to bring up the Properties dialog for your adapter.

5.  On the General tab of the Network Connection dialog, scroll down to Internet Protocol (TCP/IP), if necessary, and click on it.

6.  Click the Properties button to bring up the Internet Protocol (TCP/IP) Properties dialog.

7.  Click the Obtain An IP Address Automatically radio button.

8.  If you want to dynamically learn the address of one or more DNS servers as well, click the Obtain DNS Server Address Automatically radio button. Otherwise, click the Use The

Following DNS Server Addresses radio button and supply the address for one or more DNS servers in the internetwork that are available for FQDN resolution.

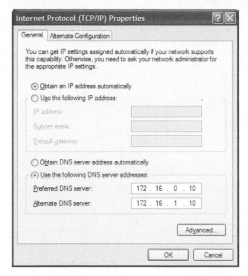

**9.**  Click OK to save your changes and close the Internet Protocol (TCP/IP) Properties dialog.

**10.**  Click OK to close the Properties dialog for your adapter.

**11.**  Close the Network Connections window.

### AUTOMATIC CONFIGURATION WITHOUT DHCP

When the Obtain An IP Address Automatically radio button is selected in the Internet Protocol (TCP/IP) Properties dialog but there is no active DHCP server available, Microsoft uses the link local block provided for in RFC 3330 and calls it APIPA. The local block is the entire Class B range 169.254.0.0/16. That means if you ever see 169.254 as the first two octets of your IP address, you have connectivity to a network. You are just unable to contact a DHCP server, which is done by broadcasting into the dark in the hopes of a response to your plea.

The following steps allow you to witness APIPA in a controlled environment. Ensure your second Ethernet device is not acting as a DHCP server and does not have access to a DHCP server.

**1.**  Use a straight-through or Ethernet crossover cable to connect the NIC on your computer to another Ethernet device, making sure you get a link light on your NIC.

**2.**  Open a command prompt. For example, click Start ➤ Run, type **cmd**, and click OK.

**3.**  Enter the command **ipconfig /release**.

**4.**  Enter the command **ipconfig /renew**.

**5.**  Note the IP address of the adapter in question. If it does not start with 169.254, it may be 0.0.0.0. Enter the command **ipconfig** and you should see the APIPA address for your adapter.

### Address Assignment on a Cisco Router

#### STATIC ADDRESS ASSIGNMENT

To assign static addresses for a Cisco router, follow these steps:

1. Enter Global Configuration mode.

   ```
   RouterE#config t
   RouterE(config)#
   ```

2. Enter Interface Configuration mode for the interface you wish to configure.

   ```
   RouterE(config)#int f0/0
   RouterE(config-if)#
   ```

3. Enter the IP address and mask you desire for the interface being configured.

   ```
   RouterE(config-if)#ip address 172.16.10.65 255.255.255.192
   RouterE(config-if)#
   ```

4. Unless that was your last interface, change to another interface and continue repeating this procedure.

   ```
   RouterE(config-if)#int f0/1
   RouterE(config-if)#
   ```

5. Exit configuration.

   ```
   RouterE(config-if)#end
   RouterE#
   ```

#### DYNAMIC ADDRESS ASSIGNMENT WITH DHCP

To assign dynamic addresses for a Cisco router, follow these steps:

1. Enter Global Configuration mode.

   ```
   RouterE#config t
   RouterE(config)#
   ```

2. Enter Interface Configuration mode for the interface you wish to configure.

   ```
   RouterE(config)#int f0/0
   RouterE(config-if)#
   ```

3. Instead of an IP address and mask, specify **dhcp** after the command ip address.

   ```
   RouterE(config-if)#ip address dhcp
   RouterE(config-if)#
   ```

**4.** Unless that was your last interface, change to another interface and continue repeating this procedure.

```
RouterE(config-if)#int f0/1
RouterE(config-if)#
```

**5.** Exit configuration.

```
RouterE(config-if)#end
RouterE#
```

## DHCP Server Configuration

The next two sections illustrate how to configure a DHCP server on a Microsoft Windows server, a Cisco router, and a Linksys wireless router. Some of Cisco's Catalyst switches and other devices can be configured in the same manner as the router shown here.

### PC RUNNING WINDOWS SERVER 2003

Just as configuring how a computer obtains its own IP information takes a bit of getting used to, configuring a DHCP server is not an intuitive process. The following steps guide you through the process using the Windows Server product.

**1.** If the DHCP server has been installed, access the Microsoft Management Console (MMC) plug-in from All Programs ➤ Administrative Tools ➤ DHCP, producing the MMC application with the DHCP plug-in.

**2.** If the server has a NIC card configured with a static IP address, the plug-in is populated already with the FQDN of the server (based on the domain associated with the NIC) as well as the corresponding IP address, as in the following graphic. A DHCP server must not have a dynamically configured address, if for no other reason than so DHCP relay agents can be configured with a set IP address to which broadcasts can be forwarded.

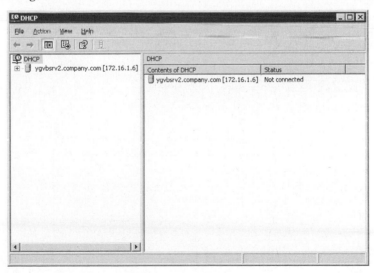

3. To put together the configuration, known as a scope, that provides DHCP clients with all the information required to function, you need to right-click on the server and select New Scope from the shortcut menu. This brings up the New Scope Wizard.

4. Click Next on the welcome screen to continue with the New Scope Wizard and bring up the Scope Name screen.

5. In the Scope Name screen, enter a name and description appropriate for the IP subnet you are configuring and click Next.

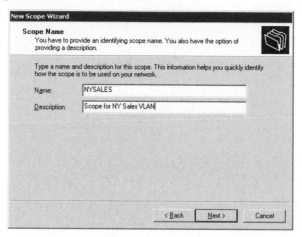

6. In the IP Address Range screen, enter the first and last IP address in the range of addresses approved for assignment to DHCP and/or Bootstrap Protocol (BootP) clients. Addresses are entered most easily by using a period (dot) between octet values and pressing Tab only to move between addresses, not octets. In this screen, you also specify the subnet mask to be used, in either prefix-length or dotted-decimal format. Click Next.

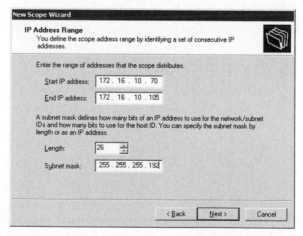

7. In the Add Exclusions screen, you can enter addresses or groups of addresses that fall within the original range created in the IP Address Range screen. Exclusions are addresses that must not be assigned to DHCP clients because they are assigned statically to other devices. By being able to design the addressing scheme from scratch, you usually avoid the need for exclusions because you can place reserved addresses at the beginning and/or end of the subnet, which keeps the assignable address in a contiguous group. Click Next.

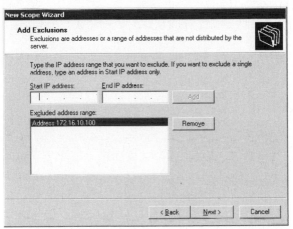

8. The Lease Duration screen advises you on how to choose an appropriate lease duration, with eight hours as the default. Basically, lease duration should be inversely proportionate to connection churn, or how frequent drops from and insertions to the network are. Click Next.

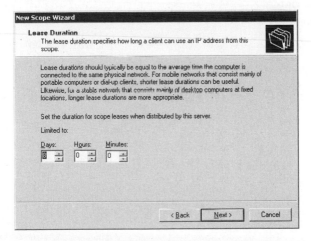

**9.**   DHCP options are the minutiae that can be assigned to clients, along with their IP address, mask, and lease duration. Options include default gateway, DNS servers, and Windows Internet Naming Service (WINS) servers, among scores of others. RFC 2132 defines all current options for DHCP. In the Configure DHCP Options screen, select Yes, I Want To Configure These Options Now and click Next to begin with configuring the most common options.

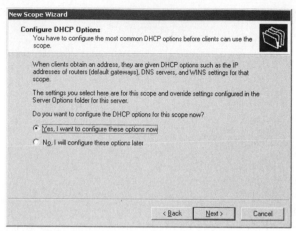

**10.**   In the Router (Default Gateway) screen, enter the IP address of the default gateway and click the Add button, making sure the correct address appears in the window below the address entry fields. Click Next.

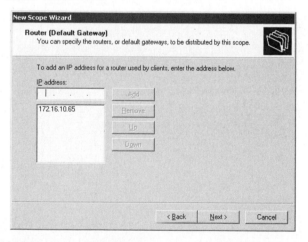

**11.**   In the Domain Name and DNS Servers screen, enter the domain name that you want associated with the local device name as well as appended, as a default, to device names that can't be resolved alone. Also enter the IP address of any DNS servers, clicking the Add button after entering each address. Alternatively, if the name of your server can be resolved locally, or by broadcasting, as with WINS, you can enter the name of the server and click the Resolve button to paste the associated address before clicking the Add button. The Up and Down buttons can be used to alter the order in which the servers are used, the first in the list being the primary server. Click Next.

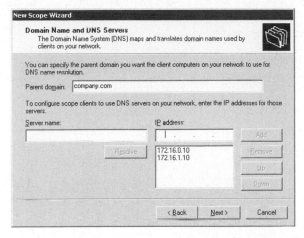

12. The WINS Servers screen is completed in the same manner as the Domain Name and DNS Servers screen. WINS is a service for NetBIOS-to-IP resolution, which works as a series of broadcasts or unicasts between WINS clients and servers. The Next button takes you to the Activate Scope dialog.

13. Selecting Yes, I Want To Activate This Scope Now in the Activate Scope screen brings up the Completing The New Scope Wizard screen.

14. Click the Finish button on the Completing The New Scope Wizard screen to end the wizard and return to the MMC and the DHCP plug-in.

15. Expanding all trees in the left pane and clicking on Address Pool under your scope produces a view similar to that in the following screen shot. In the right pane, you see your address range and any exclusions you entered.

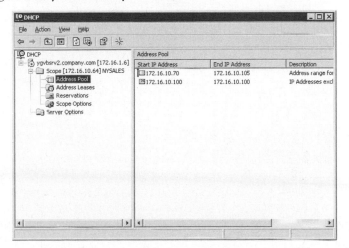

**16.** By clicking on Address Leases under your scope, you are able to monitor the leases once they have been assigned to the DHCP clients.

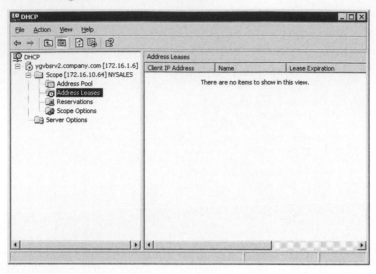

**17.** Clicking on Reservations under your scope shows a pane on the right that explains reservations and exclusions. While exclusions are entered under Address Pool, you can enter a new reservation by right-clicking Reservations and choosing New Reservation to produce the New Reservation dialog, the same way new exclusions can be entered by right-clicking Address Pool and choosing New Exclusion Range.

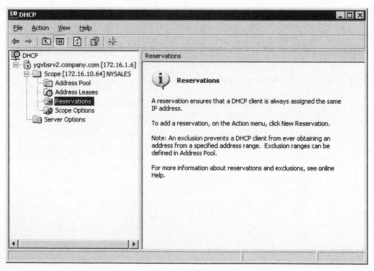

**18.** In New Reservation dialog, you enter an IP address in the range you created earlier and the MAC address of the device that should always receive the IP address. This is acceptable for servers that do not require static IP addresses to function properly. Click the Add button to create the reservation and produce another blank reservation form. Continue to click Add after completing each form until you have made your last reservation. Then click the Close button to return to the MMC.

**19.** If you click on Scope Options, the right pane displays the options you have set already. If you wish to configure additional options, it's as simple as right-clicking on Scope Options and then choosing Configure Options from the shortcut menu.

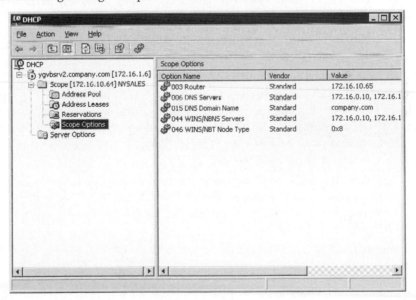

**20.** For example, the following dialog box illustrates how you can change the NetBIOS node type, assuming the default, h-node, is not desired. If you scroll down to option 046 and highlight its line, the Data Entry section of the dialog box shows the current setting of 0x8.

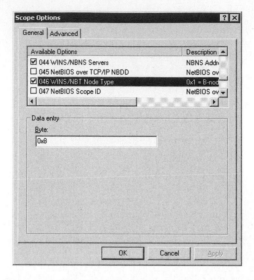

**21.** By scrolling to the right, you display the legend that defines 0x8 as h-node and shows that you can use 0x1, 0x2, and 0x4 for the other node types. Click OK when you are done changing or setting options.

**22.** Because your scope has been capable of handing out leases for some time, now, you can simply exit the MMC and check back on it later if you need to.

### CISCO 2611XM ROUTER

Doing most things on a Cisco router involves knowing generically the way a technology operates and knowing the commands to make that happen. Establishing a DHCP server is no exception. If you were able to follow the Windows configuration, creating a DHCP server on a Cisco router should present no problem. This section gives you an example to follow in configuring a Cisco router as a DHCP server.

**1.** To make sure the DHCP server service is running on the router, use the `service dhcp` global configuration command. This service runs by default, but you will not see evidence in the running configuration. If it is not running, however, the line `no service dhcp` will be in running configuration.

```
DHCP-Router#conf t
DHCP-Router(config)#service dhcp
```

**2.** It's recommended that you set up a DHCP database on an FTP, TFTP, or RCP server, using the `ip dhcp database` command in global configuration mode. If you opt not to create a database, which helps in tracking and clearing address conflicts, you need use the `no ip dhcp conflict logging` global configuration command to disable the recording of these conflicts to a server.

DHCP-Router(config)#**ip dhcp database ftp://user:password@172.16.0.10/nydhcp**

or

DHCP-Router(config)#**no ip dhcp conflict logging**

3.  Exclusions are entered globally and applied to any pool that includes the excluded addresses. Again, an exclusion is appropriate when a device such as a server must be assigned a static address in the middle of the address range of your DHCP scope, a situation avoided by conscientious planning. With Cisco's implementation of a DHCP server, however, addresses you do not want to assign that are at the beginning or end of a network or subnet still must be excluded, despite careful planning.

    In the following code, the first exclusion is the server address excluded in the Windows Server 2003 example. The second and third exclusions are the ranges of address in the 172.16.10.64/26 subnet that were not included in the Windows-based scope, by virtue of being able to specify specific beginning and end addresses in Windows.

    DHCP-Router(config)#**ip dhcp excluded-address 172.16.10.100**
    DHCP-Router(config)#**ip dhcp excluded-address 172.16.10.65**
      ➥**172.16.10.69**
    DHCP-Router(config)#**ip dhcp excluded-address 172.16.10.106 172.16.10.126**

4.  Cisco arranges the DHCP scope as a hierarchy, allowing you to apply global parameters to a pool based on a parent block and specific parameters to the pools based on each smaller block that falls within the parent block. Parameters specified in the larger pool are inherited by the subset pools, with similar parameters in the subset pools typically overriding corresponding parameters inherited from the parent pool. What is not supported is the definition of specific beginning and end addresses in the blocks; instead you specify an address and prefix length, defining the entire block, equivalent to a network or subnet, as assignable. It is for this reason that you must specify as exclusions all addresses in all pools that you do not want assigned.

    Notice how, in the following code, the main NY pool is defined first. In it, the entire 172.16.10.0/24 subnet is specified, along with the company.com domain name and the name servers and NetBIOS node type, all corresponding to those entered in the Windows Server 2003 example. Following the main pool are four smaller pools with 26-bit prefixes. The content of the second of these, NYSALES, corresponds to the remainder of the specific scope illustrated in the Windows DHCP server configuration. Leases are not inherited and default to one day, which is why eight-day leases appear in each of the four smaller pools.

    DHCP-Router(config)#**ip dhcp pool NYMAIN**
    DHCP-Router(dhcp-config)#**network 172.16.10.0 /24**
    DHCP-Router(dhcp-config)#**domain-name company.com**
    DHCP-Router(dhcp-config)#**dns-server 172.16.0.10 172.16.1.10**

```
DHCP-Router(dhcp-config)#netbios-name-server 172.16.0.10
  172.16.1.10
DHCP-Router(dhcp-config)#netbios-node-type h-node
DHCP-Router(dhcp-config)#ip dhcp pool NYTRANS
DHCP-Router(dhcp-config)#network 172.16.10.0 /26
DHCP-Router(dhcp-config)#default-router 172.16.10.1
DHCP-Router(dhcp-config)#lease 8
DHCP-Router(dhcp-config)#ip dhcp pool NYSALES
DHCP-Router(dhcp-config)#network 172.16.10.64 /26
DHCP-Router(dhcp-config)#default-router 172.16.10.65
DHCP-Router(dhcp-config)#lease 8
DHCP-Router(dhcp-config)#ip dhcp pool NYENG
DHCP-Router(dhcp-config)#network 172.16.10.128 /26
DHCP-Router(dhcp-config)#default-router 172.16.10.129
DHCP-Router(dhcp-config)#lease 8
DHCP-Router(dhcp-config)#ip dhcp pool NYIT
DHCP-Router(dhcp-config)#network 172.16.10.192 /26
DHCP-Router(dhcp-config)#default-router 172.16.10.193
DHCP-Router(dhcp-config)#lease 8
```

5.  In order to perform the reservation you performed earlier on the Windows Server 2003, you must enter the following commands. Cisco calls reservations *manual bindings*.

```
DHCP-Router(dhcp-config)#exit
DHCP-Router(config)#ip dhcp pool NYWEB
DHCP-Router(dhcp-config)#host 172.16.10.95
DHCP-Router(dhcp-config)#hardware-address 000f.1fbd.76a5 ieee802
DHCP-Router(dhcp-config)#client-name NYWEB
```

**LINKSYS WIRELESS ROUTER**

The Linksys wireless router is capable of handing out an IP address and subnet mask, as well as DNS and WINS server addresses, to DHCP clients. To set up the wireless router, you need to access the configuration interface using HTTP and a browser. The default IP address of most models is 192.168.1.1, but it can be changed to suit your needs. Perform the following steps to access the router and configure its DHCP server:

1.  Connect your computer to the Linksys wireless router.

2.  Open a command prompt. For example, choose Start ➢ Run, enter **cmd**, and click OK.

3.  Enter the command **ipconfig**.

4.  Note the IP address of the default gateway for the interface connected to the router.

5.  Open your web browser.

6.  Enter **http://A.B.C.D** into the address line, where *A.B.C.D* is the IP address of the default gateway noted earlier.

**7.** In the Connect To dialog, leave User Name blank and enter the password for your router. The default is admin.

**8.** The initial page displayed is the Basic Setup page under the Setup tab. This is where you configure the DHCP server settings. If you would like to alter the IP address of the router, do so in the Local IP Address field, as shown in the following graphic. If you change the address, save the change with the Save Settings button at the bottom of the page so the Starting IP Address field will reflect your change.

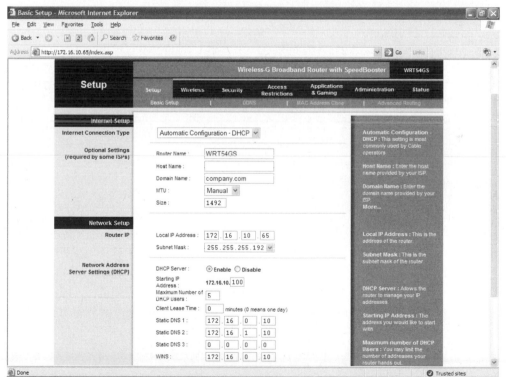

9.  The Subnet Mask field should match the mask of the local subnet to which the router is attached.

10. DHCP Server should be set to Enable.

11. The starting IP address will begin with the same three octets as your local IP address. You can change the last octet to one of your choosing, but be careful to make sure it is within the same subnet as your local IP address, which is advertised to clients as the default gateway, and make sure enough addresses are left afterward for the devices you expect to be on the local network, which you can limit with the Maximum Number Of DHCP Users field next.

12. Set the Maximum Number Of DHCP Users field to the maximum number of addresses you wish to hand out. Setting this field too high increases the risk of unauthorized hackers getting onto your network.

13. The Client Lease Time option can be set as high as 9,999 minutes, which is just shy of 7 days. The default is 0, which corresponds to 1 day and is equivalent to a setting of 1,440.

14. Enter the addresses of up to three DNS servers and one WINS server in the appropriate fields.

15. Click the Save Settings button at the bottom of the page to finalize your configuration, and then wait for the confirmation page to display.

16. Click the Continue button on the confirmation page to return to the configuration pages.

17. Close the router's configuration window by exiting your browser.

### DHCP Relay Agent on a Cisco Router

When you do not want to configure a Cisco router as a DHCP server, you can configure the router as a DHCP relay agent. A relay agent watches for the DHCPDISCOVER broadcast on the interface acting as the agent and forwards it as a unicast to a proper DHCP server, which could be anywhere in the internetwork. The DHCP server must have a scope or pool corresponding to the subnet in which the interface acting as relay agent resides. The DHCP server will mask this interface address with the masks in each pool until it has a complete configuration to assign to the client. Note that DHCP is not the only broadcast type that the relay agent supports. A number of set UDP-based broadcasts, such as DNS queries, in addition to many others you can configure with the `ip forward-protocol` command, are supported by this function.

The following procedure assumes there is a DHCP service running on the DNS server at 172.16.0.10 but the router is attached to the subnet 172.16.10.64/26 and must act as a relay agent for the DHCP requests the clients on that subnet submit:

1.  Go to the interface attached to the subnet in need of DHCP services and place it in the subnet.

```
DHCP-Relay-Rtr(config)#int f0/0
DHCP-Relay-Rtr(config-if)#ip address 172.16.10.65 255.255.255.192
```

2.  On the same interface, which will have to watch for the DHCPDISCOVER broadcasts from the clients on that attached subnet, issue the `ip helper-address` command to give the router the DHCP server's address to unicast to when it receives the requests.

```
DHCP-Relay-Rtr(config-if)#ip helper-address 172.16.0.10
```

Note that you can configure more than one helper address on the interface, but the overall procedure is a very simple one to perform. If a DHCP server already exists on the internetwork, this may be the easiest solution to implement.

## Criteria for Completion

You have completed this task when you have configured all addresses on all desired devices in the manner you wish to employ and tested for appropriate connectivity, using utilities such as ping and traceroute.

# Task 2.2: Naming Network Devices

Each device worth accessing in your network has an address that must be known. Network devices can also be named, so finding them is a more intuitive process, just like being able to look up a phone number by using a name. A name can be linked with an IP address, and this association can be logged in a database that can then be accessed by others. As a result, you can contact the device by using its name without ever knowing its address, because name resolution occurs automatically and behind the scenes. All you have to know is the name of the device.

Device names need to make sense to those that access the resources the devices serve. Often the name is found by searching an index of devices by type. So names that mean something, instead of random or serialized codes, add efficiencies to daily network usage. As the PC world moves closer to an all-IP existence, device names more and more frequently fall into a domain naming hierarchy, such as server.company.com. But until pre-XP operating systems are completely phased out, names based on the Network Basic Input Output System (NetBIOS) application programming interface remain on the scene.

DNS is the service that resolves FQDNs to IP addresses, and WINS resolves NetBIOS names to IP addresses. Either system can be deployed in the local enterprise, but DNS is woven into the global Internet as well, allowing us to contact devices all around the world using their domain names instead of IP addresses. NetBIOS names are not hierarchical, while DNS names, or FQDNs, are. For example, a device might have the very one-dimensional NetBIOS name of server1, but the same device in the DNS world might be named server1.company.com, after the global commercial domain, the company name, and the device name. Furthermore, WINS is a dynamic service, but unless you use Dynamic DNS (DDNS), currently available only in the enterprise, DNS requires manual administrative additions to its database in order to include names for lookup.

# Scenario

All your devices have default names, which you find nearly worthless for resource management. You decide to name a few of the devices most likely to be accessed from across the network, such as servers.

# Scope of Task

## Duration

This task should take about 30 minutes.

## Setup

For this task, you should have your internetwork diagram to update with names or to copy for naming, if need be. You also need various devices that you can configure with names, as well as the means established previously to gain configuration access to the devices.

## Caveat

While names can be reused in a hierarchical system, as in the case of server1.ny.company.com and server1.tokyo.company.com, where the domain names differentiate the names, care should be exercised when using NetBIOS and other non-hierarchical naming systems if the identically named devices are in the same broadcast domain. Devices in such an environment must be named uniquely.

# Procedure

In this task, you assign names to Windows-based PCs, Cisco routers, and Linksys devices.

## Equipment Used

For this task, it is ideal for you to have access to the same types of devices presented here. Additionally, devices able to be configured with a name are recommended. Devices capable of being named include, but are not limited to, the following:

- Switches
- Servers
- Workstations
- Routers
- Specialty devices that offer Internet access for control or management

## Details

The following sections guide you through configuring sample devices with names. Consult Task 2.1, "Assigning IP Addresses," for how to enter DNS server information into a Windows-based PC.

### Naming a PC Running Windows XP Professional

1.  On the Desktop, right-click My Computer.

2.  In the shortcut menu, click Properties to bring up the General tab of the System Properties window.

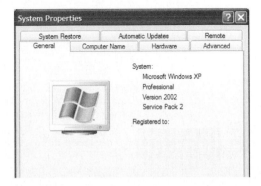

3.  Click the Computer Name tab.

4.  Optionally, enter a nonfunctional description for your computer that will show up in various informational screens.

5.   Click the Change button to bring up the Computer Name Changes dialog.

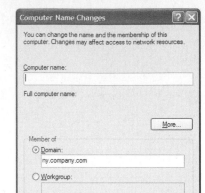

6.   Enter the desired name for the computer in the Computer Name field.

7.   Check the Member Of section of this dialog to make sure the settings are correct.

8.   Click OK to accept the changes to this dialog.

9.   Click OK to leave the System Properties window.

**NAMING A CISCO ROUTER AND SETTING A DEFAULT DOMAIN**

1.   Enter Global Configuration mode.

     ```
     Router#config t
     Router(config)#
     ```

2.   To name the router, use the hostname command.

     ```
     Router(config)#hostname RouterE
     RouterE(config)#
     ```

3.   (Optional) If you intend to specify a DNS server for name resolution, use the ip domain lookup (formerly ip domain-lookup) command to make sure name lookup is enabled.

     ```
     RouterE(config)#ip domain lookup
     RouterE(config)#
     ```

4.   (Optional) Use the ip name-server command to specify the addresses of up to six DNS servers.

     ```
     RouterE(config)#ip name-server 172.16.0.10 172.16.1.10
     RouterE(config)#
     ```

5.   (Optional) Use one of the following two methods to help resolve unqualified, or short-name, references.

Use the `ip domain name` (formerly `ip domain-name`) command to have a single default domain name to use in unqualified resolutions. For example, pinging ny1 would attempt to resolve ny1 first and then, if unsuccessful, ny1.company.com.

```
RouterE(config)#ip domain name company.com
RouterE(config)#
```

Use the `ip domain list` (formerly `ip domain-list`) command to have one or more domain names appended, in the order entered, to unqualified names until a resolution is found. For example, pinging ny1 would attempt to resolve ny1 first, and then, if unsuccessful, ny1.company.com, and then, if unsuccessful, ny1.ny.company.com.

```
RouterE(config)#ip domain list company.com
RouterE(config)#ip domain list ny.company.com
RouterE(config)#
```

6. Exit configuration.

```
RouterE(config)#end
RouterE#
```

### LINKSYS WIRELESS ROUTER

1. Connect your computer to the Linksys wireless router.
2. Open a Command Prompt. For example, choose Start ➢ Run, type **cmd**, and click OK.
3. Enter the command **ipconfig**.
4. Note the IP address of the default gateway for the interface connected to the router.
5. Open your web browser.
6. Enter **http://A.B.C.D** into the address line, where *A.B.C.D* is the IP address of the default gateway noted earlier.
7. In the Connect To dialog, leave User Name blank and enter the password for your router. The default is admin.

8.  The initial page displayed is the Basic Setup page of the Setup tab. This is where you configure the device name and domain name. Enter the name in the Host Name field and the domain name in the Domain Name field.

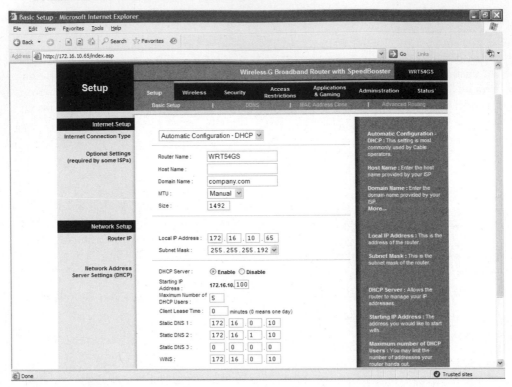

9.  Click the Save Settings button at the bottom of the page to finalize your configuration, and then wait for the confirmation page to display.

10. Click the Continue button on the confirmation page to return to the configuration pages.

11. Close the router's configuration window by exiting your browser.

## Criteria for Completion

You have completed this task when you have configured all names on all desired devices and tested for appropriate connectivity using utilities such as ping and traceroute or a WINS management interface, which will show your configured names registered with WINS.

# Task 2.3: Installing Wireless NICs

Sometimes, limitations imposed by the physical location of a workstation preclude a wired network attachment. Other times, owing to the efficiencies afforded by unfettered mobility, it makes more sense to equip a workstation with a wireless adapter.

Many newer laptop computers come with built-in wireless network interface cards (NICs), but those that do not are easily modified for wireless network attachment. Without much additional effort, you can add wireless NICs to newer desktop and tower systems as well. And for the undaunted, any system with available internal slots can be upgraded for wireless attachment. Furthermore, you can avoid almost all angst by using a Universal Serial Bus (USB) NIC, as long as there is an available USB interface. If not, it's easy and affordable to add a USB hub, supplying your system with plenty of additional interfaces.

## Scenario

You have a desktop workstation that is not cost efficient to wire to the network. You also have two laptops that you wish to equip with wireless NICs. You have one Peripheral Component Interconnect (PCI) NIC for the desktop and two NICs—one a PC Card and the other a USB—for the laptops. You have other workstations that you might be interested in outfitting with wireless NICs, based on how well these work out.

## Scope of Task

### Duration

This task should take about 90 minutes.

### Setup

For this task, you need at least one desktop computer and a laptop. The same laptop can be used twice, if necessary. You also need three NICs: a PCI, a PC Card, and a USB. Set up where you have room to work and access to a source of ground. A static mat to perform work over is preferable. Use an antistatic wrist strap, if possible, while handling electronic devices.

### Caveat

Some desktop workstations do not have available internal expansion slots. If these same machines have no USB interfaces at all, your options for wireless attachment are extremely limited, if they exist at all. Always keep in mind that 1 USB subsystem can handle more than 100 interfaces through daisy-chained USB hubs. So, even if there are no available USB interfaces, as long as one exists, it can be expanded to offer availability, although power considerations may come into play as the number of devices increases. USB hubs come in active and passive varieties, the active hubs powering the peripherals with their USB interfaces instead of placing this requirement on the computer's USB interface.

If a full-size workstation has a nonintegrated wired NIC card and you will not require the wired attachment in the future, you have the option of replacing the wired NIC with a wireless NIC. What this means is that you are not necessarily out of expansion options in those systems with no free expansion slots and no USB interfaces.

# Procedure

In this task, you open a desktop system and install a PCI NIC card. Additionally, you expand laptop systems with PC Card and USB adapters. Each of these adapters converts an otherwise wired-only workstation to wireless attachment.

## Equipment Used

For this task, you must have at least one desktop or tower system and at least one laptop computer. You need one each of the following NICs:

- PCI (ISA is acceptable if the full-size workstation has no available PCI slots)
- PC Card (formerly known as PCMCIA)
- USB

## Details

The following sections guide you through installing the hardware and software of three types of wireless NICs in Windows-based desktop or laptop PCs.

### PCI Wireless NIC in a Full-Size System

#### HARDWARE INSTALLATION

1. Remove the NIC from any packaging it may be in.

2. Unscrew the antenna from the card, if so equipped. Figure 2.1 shows a Linksys Wireless-G PCI Adapter with the antenna detached.

3. Connect the clip on your antistatic wrist strap to a designated ground point at your workbench. If no such ground point exists, connect your antistatic wrist strap to an unpainted metal location on your case's chassis. If you can't find an unpainted metal location with the cover of the case on, find one at your earliest opportunity after removing the cover (which you'll do in step 5). Put the strap on your wrist. If you do not have a wrist strap, follow the static dissipation techniques in the sidebar "Electrostatic Discharge (ESD)."

4. If using the chassis for ground, make sure the case is plugged into an AC outlet with a third-prong ground.

5. Remove or open the cover of the case, noting that removal methods vary by case. Some require you to remove four or five screws on the back and slide the cover, in one or two pieces, toward the front of the case. Others have a very simple push-button mechanism on one or both sides that releases the cover and allows removal or opening, similar to the hood of a car.

6. Recognize that not all slots in your motherboard are PCI. In fact, you may find out you have no PCI slots, or at least none available. If you have none, then check for ISA slots and complete this procedure substituting ISA for PCI. Compare the card you have with the available slots in your motherboard, choosing one for installation or targeting one for replacement, if necessary. Figure 2.2 shows how a PCI card matches up with a corresponding PCI slot in a motherboard.

Figure 2.3 shows an existing wired PCI NIC that may have to be removed to provide a point of insertion for the wireless NIC.

**FIGURE 2.1**    Linksys Wireless-G PCI Adapter

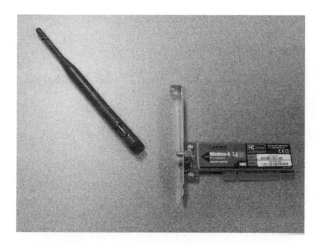

**FIGURE 2.2**    NIC matched to an expansion slot

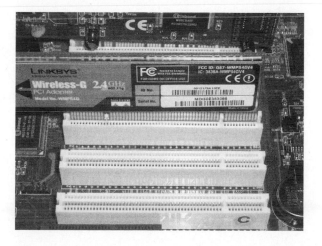

7.  (Optional) Remove the existing card if necessary, paying attention to the fact that the card is likely secured, at the bracket, to the backplane. Note that there are various ways to secure cards. Sometimes screws are used, and sometimes mechanical clips. Pull the card firmly and evenly and make sure it's perpendicular to the board in which it is inserted.

8.  Insert the wireless NIC into the appropriate slot, using firm, even pressure on the edge of the card opposite the edge with the electrical contacts. Use two hands and apply pressure until you hear and/or feel the insertion and visually confirm that the contacts are evenly and completely inserted into the slot. Figure 2.4 shows a properly inserted PCI adapter.

**FIGURE 2.3**    Existing wired NIC

**FIGURE 2.4**    Properly inserted adapter

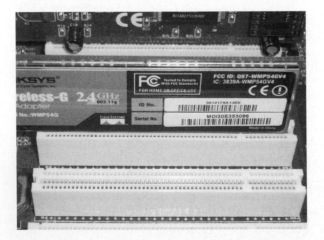

9.  Secure the card to the backplane using the method for your case. Figure 2.5 shows the backplane of a computer that uses screws to secure adapters.

10. Close or replace the cover and secure it, making sure to remove your static strap's clip before doing so, if it is clipped to an inside ground point.

11. Attach the screw-on antenna, if you have one, from the outside at the back of the system. Figure 2.6 shows the antenna before screwing it onto the installed wireless NIC.

**FIGURE 2.5**   Screw-type backplane attachment

**FIGURE 2.6**   Attaching the antenna

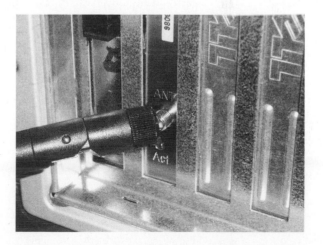

Regardless of how you attend to the issue of ESD, attend to it. Your hands must be at the same voltage as the electronic components with which you are working. You need not be able to perceive the effects of ESD—whether by touch, sight, or sound—for them to destroy sensitive electronic equipment. To make matters worse, the effect they have on the delicate circuitry may manifest as intermittent faults that cannot be duplicated reliably, making troubleshooting more difficult.

If you do not have an antistatic wrist strap available, a common effective workaround is to open the case and, with the power off, touch the shell of the power supply with both hands while it is plugged into an AC outlet. Make sure you don't move around while working on the equipment without again neutralizing your body's static charge through the power-supply case. Of course, working on static-prone surfaces, such as shag carpeting, is not recommended.

If the power supply has a toggle switch, make sure it is off. Do not trust the front power switch. The case might have the soft-power feature, meaning the operating system turns off the system, and the power button must be held for some duration before the computer turns off. If this is the case, and there is also no toggle switch, do not leave the power cord plugged into the power supply after you touch the shell to dissipate your body's static charge, but plug it back in each time you need to neutralize your static again.

One sure indication that you must remove the power cord before touching the internal electrical components of the system is the existence of one or more LEDs on the motherboard or daughter cards, indicating the presence of potentially dangerous voltages. Note that the absence of such LEDs does not indicate that the system is safe without removing the power cord.

## SOFTWARE INSTALLATION

If you are running a Plug and Play operating system, simply powering up and logging on might result in the system recognizing and preparing the software for installation. Just provide the driver disk if requested and point the system to the drive in which it is inserted. Otherwise, make sure you have the driver disk for your adapter and follow the steps in this section to attempt to get your card recognized and functional. As you make your way through these steps, keep an eye out for any specific requirements for your device or card that cause a necessary deviation from this procedure and follow the appropriate steps in your case.

1.  Open Control Panel (Start ➤ Control Panel).

**2.** Double-click Add Hardware. The Add Hardware Wizard window opens.

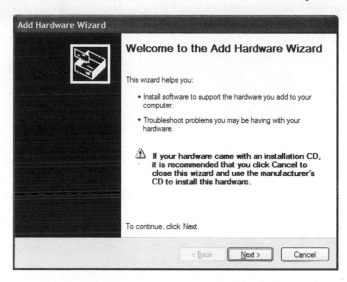

**3.** The wizard first searches for any hardware for which software has not been installed.

**4.** If the adapter was not discovered automatically, then after a few moments, the wizard likely will produce the following screen, which asks if the hardware is connected.

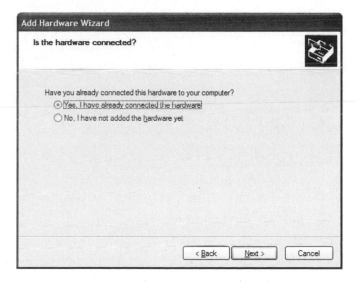

**5.** If you have not installed the adapter yet, click the No radio button and click the Next button, which takes you to the final screen of the wizard, shown next. Checking the box so your computer powers down and clicking the Finish button allows you to install your adapter. Proceed from the beginning of the hardware installation section.

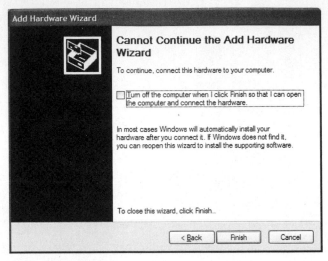

Otherwise, if you have installed the adapter, filling in the Yes radio button and clicking the Next button in the Is The Hardware Connected screen produces the next screen, which shows you the hardware that the operating system already knows about.

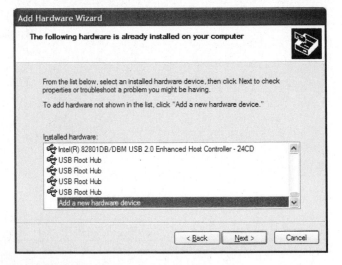

**6.** Scroll to the bottom of the list, looking for your new hardware along the way. If you find it, the system already knows about it. No further setup needs to be performed. Otherwise, click on the final entry in the list, Add A New Hardware Device, and click the Next button. This brings up the following screen.

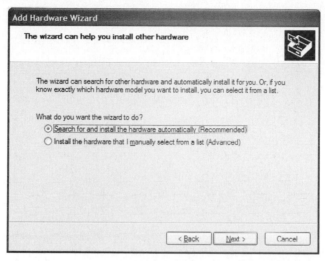

**7.** Let the wizard search for your hardware by leaving the Recommended radio button filled and clicking the Next button. The following screen is an example of what you see next, while you wait for the search to complete.

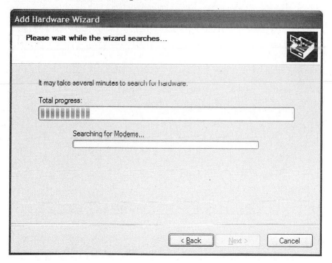

**8.** If the wizard finds your hardware, follow the wizard to complete its setup. Otherwise, if you are presented with the following screen, indicating that your hardware could not be found, click the Next button to bring up a list of possible devices that can be installed.

**9.** In the screen that appears, find Network Adapters in the list and click on it. Click the Next button to bring up the Select Network Adapter screen.

**10.** Don't worry about trying to find your adapter in the list. Click the Have Disk button to go to the Install From Disk screen.

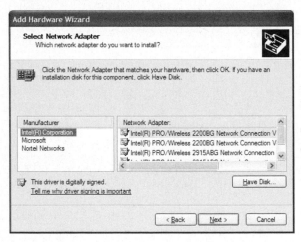

**11.** Insert your driver disk and click the Browse button to find the driver files that match your hardware and operating system.

12. Once you locate and select the driver file, ending in `.inf`, for your adapter, click on the filename and click the Open button. Doing so brings you back to the Install From Disk screen with the complete path filled in.

13. Click the OK button to continue the installation, clicking the Finish button in the Completing the Add Hardware Wizard screen.

Now your adapter should be ready for use. In some cases, rebooting your system is required to complete the installation. Additionally, follow the manufacturer's instructions for installing any applications you want to use to control your hardware and to attach to a wireless network, noting that Windows XP prefers its built-in application for control.

## PC Card Wireless NIC in a Laptop

### HARDWARE INSTALLATION

1. Remove the NIC from any packaging it may be in. The following picture shows a Linksys wireless NIC ready for installation.

2. Find the PC Bus slot in your mobile computer. For example, note the appearance of the slot in the laptop shown in the following picture.

3. Insert the PC Card into the slot with the labeling up. Push the card until you feel a final resistance followed by a faint release, indicating full insertion into the slot. The following picture shows the PC Card fully inserted into the slot.

4. If the computer is powered off, power it on at this time. Once you log into the operating system, or if the computer is already on, you are ready to begin the software installation process.

### SOFTWARE INSTALLATION

The installation of a PC Card device is generally a non-issue, as Plug and Play takes you through the entire process painlessly. Just be sure to have your driver disk in case you are asked for it by the installation process. If you must follow a manual installation process, use the steps for software installation presented earlier in the section "PCI Wireless NIC in a Full-Size System" to install the drivers for your adapter. Also install any utilities from the manufacturer at this time, keeping in mind that Windows XP prefers to manage its own wireless networks.

## USB-Attached Wireless NIC on Any Computer

### HARDWARE INSTALLATION

1. Remove the NIC from any packaging it may be in. The following picture shows a Linksys wireless USB NIC adapter ready for installation. The interface at the bottom left of the picture is the USB interface.

2.  Your operating system may require the installation of the adapter's software before you connect the adapter to the computer. Read the documentation that came with your adapter to see what the manufacturer suggests. If software installation is required before hardware attachment, follow the procedure outlined in the instructions included with your adapter.

3.  Plug the included USB cable into the adapter and plug the other end into your computer, powered on or off. The following picture shows the USB cable before insertion into a laptop.

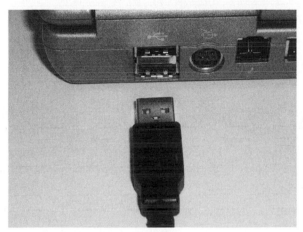

4.  If the system is powered up, or once it is and you log into the operating system, the computer should recognize the adapter automatically.

5.  If the drivers have not been installed already, you may be required to install them now. If the operating system detects this situation, it will alert you to whatever it needs. Simply follow the prompts to complete the installation.

**SOFTWARE INSTALLATION**

USB devices generally install themselves, occasionally asking for software from a distribution disk that comes with the device. On the off chance manual driver installation becomes necessary, the manual software installation procedure outlined earlier is likely to take care of your needs here.

## Criteria for Completion

You have completed this task when you have installed the hardware and software for your adapters and confirmed the proper installation of the adapters from Device Manager, accessible in Windows XP, as follows:

1.  Click Start ➤ Control Panel ➤ System to bring up the System Properties applet.

**2.** Click the Hardware tab to bring up the Hardware page.

**3.** Click the Device Manager button to open the Device Manager.

**4.** If it's not already expanded, click the plus sign beside Network Adapters to expand the category.

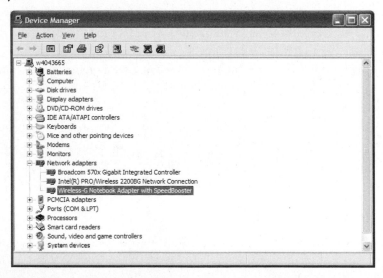

A yellow triangle associated with the adapter indicates a problem with the adapter and the likelihood of its malfunction. The lack of all abnormal icons indicates the correct installation of the device.

# Task 2.4: Measuring Wireless Signal Strength

Various factors influence the signal strength in your wireless LAN, including proximity to the wireless access point (WAP), output capability of the access point, interference from other wireless/cordless devices and electronics operating on a similar frequency, and physical obstructions.

This task suggests various scenarios that you can duplicate while you note the effect on wireless signal strength using your own equipment.

## Scenario

You are interested in positioning your access point in the best place possible for overall reception. You must consider sources of signal interference and blockage, as well as how far away wireless clients are expected to be.

## Scope of Task

### Duration

This task should take 1 to 2 hours.

### Setup

For this task, you need a computer with a wireless NIC installed. Any computer will do, but a portable unit, such as a laptop, is preferable because you'll need to change position readily. An application that allows you to measure signal strength must be installed on the computer. Windows XP includes this utility out of the box. You also need a wireless access point, which could be any of a number of device types, such as a dedicated access point or a wireless router.

The facility you use for your experiment should have a variety of physical obstructions, such as walls and objects of varying density. The existence of cordless phones operating at the same frequency as your wireless LAN (often 2.4GHz) and certain microwave ovens (look inside the door for the operating frequency), especially older ones, is a plus.

### Caveat

Some interferers completely mask the signal from the access point, leading you to believe you are out of range when simply removing the source of interference, all other things being equal, might result in a measurable signal.

Different utilities measure signal strength with different scales. Some indicate strength by a percentage of original transmission strength, while others simply show strength by multiple bars, more bars indicating more strength. Still others use a sequence of descriptions, such as poor and excellent. A combination of these methods may be employed, but comparing results from one utility to another may be difficult.

## Procedure

In this task, you use a wireless NIC and a wireless access point to gauge the signal strength to various locations, taking various factors into account.

### Equipment Used

For this lab, you need the following equipment:

- At least one computer system, preferably a laptop computer, with wireless access and utility
- Wireless access point
- Source(s) of interference (cordless phone, microwave oven, etc.)
- Microwave-safe mug or cup and a water source

### Details

Conduct this task as you would conduct an experiment. Document your results and analyze why the results are what they are and if it is possible that the results are transient due to some unknown cause. If there is anything you can think of that adds depth to your experience as you follow these steps, feel free to try it out, documenting the results for later reference and validation. Be careful to prove your results instead of drawing final conclusions too early and risk misinterpretation.

1. Position the computer as close to the WAP as possible.

2. Open the utility you use to show wireless signal strength. The following screen shot shows excellent signal strength to a WAP in close proximity.

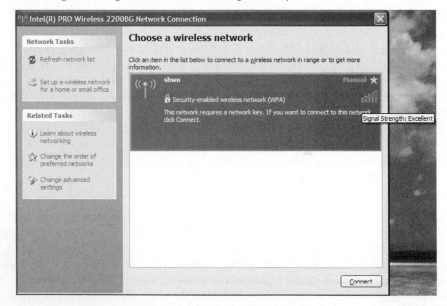

3.   Move the computer in a straight line (with no obstructions in between) and in equal increments, say 10 feet each, checking signal strength after each move. Continue until you can no longer move or you lose the signal.

4.   Moving back to the access point, take the computer to the other side of the nearest wall and check signal strength. Put additional walls between the computer and WAP until no more walls exist or you lose the signal.

5.   Move the computer to the next floor up, staying as close as possible to the same position on each floor with respect to the WAP (preferably directly above it). Check the signal strength and then continue to move up floor by floor, checking signal strength on each floor, until you are out of floors or signal. Perform the same procedure floor by floor in the opposite direction.

6.   Place a microwave oven rated to operate at the a frequency similar to your wireless LAN between your computer and WAP. Using a microwave-safe mug or cup, fill the vessel to about a third of its capacity. Run the microwave on high for 1 or 2 minutes or however long it takes to see if you lose your signal or measure its strength.

7.   Using a cordless phone of the same operating frequency as your wireless LAN, plug the base into an electrical outlet, but also into the phone line if possible. You really only need for the handset to be able to communicate with the base. The ability to call out is not necessary. Use the following permutations, check signal strength and availability with each configuration. You might notice more a lack of measurable signal than mere signal loss with this step. In the following arrangements, note that the reference to *phone* means that the handset is operational in the position noted and *base* refers to the cordless phone base that plugs into power and phone line.

WAP →base →phone →computer (this means base and operational phone between computer and WAP)

WAP→base→computer→phone

WAP→computer→base→phone

## Criteria for Completion

You have completed this task when you have documented the results from each scenario you were able to duplicate. Use your findings to judge the best location for all WAPs in your installation as well as the location of all sources of interference.

# Task 2.5: Implementing Bluetooth

Bluetooth technology is ideal for "cutting the cord" between peripherals and their host computers as long as the two remain in close proximity with one another; in the case of products that fall into Class 2 or 3, the maximum distance should be 10 meters and 1 meter, respectively. This same model works for many other pairings, such as cell phones and wireless headsets. Newer applications continue to emerge and include, but are not limited to, the following:

- Low-bandwidth networking between computers, personal digital assistants (PDAs), cell phones, MP3 players, and digital cameras
- Wireless in-car phones
- Replacement for infrared in remote controls
- Hearing aid attachments
- Wireless gaming controllers
- Data transfer from medical and testing equipment

However, there is a more industrial class of Bluetooth, known as Class 1, that uses more power but extends to distances of 100 meters, opening the door for an entirely different category of Bluetooth usage.

Because Bluetooth remains a technology that few know very much about, more space than usual is dedicated here to introduce it. Bluetooth is the internal codename that was turned into the official public name for a cable replacement technology, the key features of which are robustness, ease of use, low power consumption, and low cost. Bluetooth was created in 1998 by a consortium composed of Intel, IBM, Ericsson, Nokia, and Toshiba (and later joined by Microsoft) and known as the Bluetooth Special Interest Group (Bluetooth SIG). Bluetooth has always been proposed as an open specification. IEEE agrees that the specification should be nonproprietary and adopted an early Bluetooth standard called 802.15.1; it continues to develop the standard independently of the Bluetooth SIG.

Bluetooth uses the same license-free frequency range, 2.4GHz, as many wireless LAN standards and other household electronics. However, unlike wireless LAN technologies, which can be disrupted by common sources of interference, Bluetooth employs a frequency-hopping technology that divides the band into 79 channels and can hop from channel to channel 1,600 times per second, avoiding disruption of its service by sources of interference.

Bluetooth version 1.0 was plagued with certain issues that inhibited stable interoperability among vendors. Versions 1.1 and 1.2 fixed these issues and even added features, such as an adaptive form of frequency hopping to avoid crowded frequencies. The data rate of versions 1.$x$ did not exceed 723.1Kbps. Version 2.0 of the specification adds Enhanced Data Rate (EDR) and boasts bit rates of 2.1Mbps, with 3Mbps as a theoretical maximum. Version 2 is backward compatible with 1.$x$.

On March 28, 2006, the Bluetooth SIG announced it would be teaming with the WiMedia Alliance to use its version of ultra-wideband (UWB) in a version of Bluetooth with a much higher bit rate than earlier versions. This new version is intended to remain compatible with current applications, as well as meet the high-speed demands of large data transfers and high-quality video and audio in portable devices, multimedia projectors, and televisions.

The key difference between Bluetooth and wireless LANs is that the latter use more power, making batteries less likely as a power source. The ability to use batteries is one of the benefits of Bluetooth, offering true stand-alone freedom from cables or a powered host. Of course wireless LANs need the extra power, resulting in more expensive hardware, to be able to span greater distances than Bluetooth.

# Scenario

One of your computer system units must be placed directly beside a relay-control unit that connects by an extremely short cable to a specialized adapter installed in the computer. The relay-control unit must be positioned in the corner of the office nearest the shop floor, which is on the opposite side of the office from the desk. The problem is that while you have installed a video extension cable behind the wall, resulting in an interface for the monitor in the wall directly behind the desk, you do not wish to run keyboard and mouse extension cables the same way. Instead, you decide to utilize a Bluetooth keyboard and mouse.

# Scope of Task

## Duration

This task should take about 15 minutes.

## Setup

For this task, you need a computer and a Bluetooth-compatible keyboard and mouse. If you have additional Bluetooth devices, this is a good time to consult their documentation for instructions on how to interface them with your other Bluetooth components. You need to have all related driver and application disks available during this procedure. Set up in an area that gives you ample room to spread out during installation and enough room to move away from your Bluetooth receiver to test distance limitations.

## Caveat

Not all cordless peripherals use Bluetooth technology. Not to discourage the purchase and use of such devices, but there is something to be said for following an open standard. Non-Bluetooth cordless devices generally must stand on their own, while peripherals that are compatible with Bluetooth are able to work together in most circumstances. It just depends on whether their functions are complementary or exclusive or even unrelated.

# Procedure

In this task, you connect a Bluetooth device to a computer. The example uses a Logitech Cordless Desktop MX 5000 Laser for Bluetooth.

## Equipment Used

For this task, you must have at least a computer and a Bluetooth peripheral. While it would be helpful to have the same equipment noted here, practically any Bluetooth-compatible device, or even a non-Bluetooth device, will provide nearly equivalent benefit.

## Details

The following steps guide you through installation and setup of the Logitech Cordless Desktop MX 5000 Laser.

1. Remove the device from any packaging it might be in. Figure 2.7 shows two of the components of the Logitech Cordless Desktop. The third component is the keyboard.

2. Insert the Bluetooth receiver into a USB interface.

3. If the computer is powered off, power it on at this time. Once you log into the operating system, or if the computer is already on, the operating system will detect the new device. You should see one of three messages similar to the one shown here.

4. Open Device Manager by choosing Start ≻ Control Panel and double-clicking System to bring up the System Properties applet.

5. Click the Hardware tab to bring up the Hardware page.

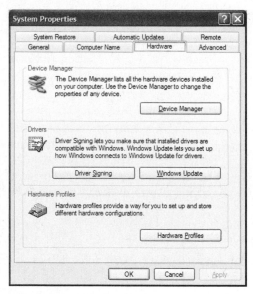

6. Click the Device Manager button to open the Device Manager.

**7.**  If it's not already expanded, click the plus sign beside Human Interface Devices to expand the category, as shown in the following screen shot.

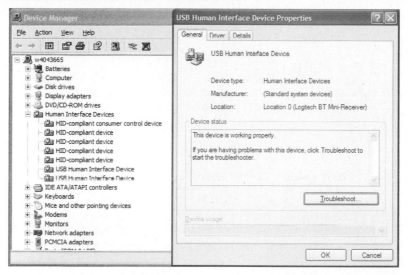

Double-clicking one of the USB Human Interface Device entries brings up the properties page shown in the preceding screen shot. Note the reference to Logitech in the Location field. If you double-click any of the other entries in the Human Interface Devices group, you will find that they are more generic and do not specify Logitech but instead reference Microsoft, because they are common to all such devices.

**F I G U R E   2 . 7**    Bluetooth hub/receiver and mouse

8.  Many stand-alone peripherals require batteries for power, as shown in the following picture of the bottom of the keyboard. Note also in the picture the unique Bluetooth address that all peripherals have. The mouse has one too.

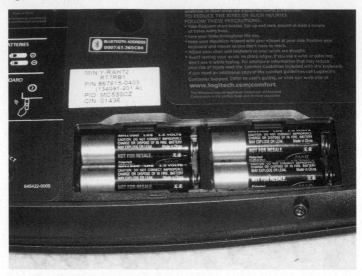

9.  If your device has a power switch and it is off, as with the mouse and keyboard in Figure 2.8, switch it on. This might cause your device to connect automatically.

10. All Device Manager can tell you is whether the Bluetooth receiver has been detected. If your devices do not connect to the receiver automatically you might have to press the Connect buttons on both the peripheral and the receiver, usually found on the underside of the device, within moments of each other. If your device does not have such a button, consult the product's documentation for its method of manual connectivity. Figure 2.8 shows the Connect buttons on the bottom side of the Logitech devices.

Be aware that, based on the device being installed, you might need to install application software to enhance its capabilities to match those advertised. Otherwise, the peripheral might have only basic functionality, lacking certain expected features.

## Criteria for Completion

You have completed this task when you have installed the hardware and used Device Manager to confirm the proper installation of its drivers, as well as tested the peripherals for proper function.

Remember that in Device Manager, a yellow triangle associated with the hardware indicates a problem with the driver and the likelihood that the device will not function properly. The lack of all abnormal icons indicates the correct installation of the device.

**FIGURE 2.8**    Component power switches and connect buttons

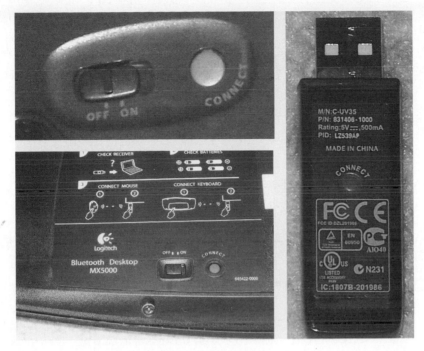

# Task 2.6: Implementing Ad Hoc Wireless Networking

When one or more wireless-attached devices connect to the network through a wireless access point (WAP), the arrangement is referred to as infrastructure mode. Sometimes it's necessary for two or more devices to communicate with one another without the use of a wireless access point. Such an arrangement is referred to as ad hoc mode. Situations such as this arise when it is not feasible to place an access point near the devices but the devices still need to communicate with one another.

Perhaps there is no need for the added expense of an access point. Normally, an access point is a gateway to the rest of the network or the Internet. If one of the ad hoc members has a connection to such resources, you can simply share that connection and obtain access where you need it without a WAP.

## Scenario

Two employees of your company have regular meetings in a new conference room in a wing of the building that has not been set up yet for network access. As a result, there is no way for them to collaborate electronically, using methods such as file sharing. They both have wireless NICs for their laptops and have requested that their machines be set up for ad hoc wireless networking.

## Scope of Task

### Duration

This task should take about 30 minutes.

### Setup

For this task, you need two or more computers with wireless NIC adapters installed. Make sure the computers are no farther from one another than the distance allowable between a wireless client and a WAP.

### Caveat

While some wireless access points are compatible with multiple wireless standards (such as IEEE 802.11b and 802.11g), allowing them to interoperate through the WAP, interconnecting devices in an ad hoc arrangement most often results in the use of client-side adapters that support only one standard. In this case, all adapters must adhere to the same standard or you will not be able to communicate among all devices.

Currently, there is no way to use the same wireless NIC to connect to one wireless LAN running in infrastructure mode at the same time it is connected to other devices running in ad hoc mode. It is possible, however, to share a network connection on another wireless or wired adapter with a different wireless adapter running in ad hoc mode, offering the connectivity of the other network to the ad hoc members.

## Procedure

In this task, you use ad hoc wireless networking to connect two or more computers together and test their connectivity.

### Equipment Used

For this task, you must have at least two computers capable of wireless network attachment and an operating system or separate application capable of wireless network administration.

## Details

### Creating the Ad Hoc Network

The following steps guide you through the setup of an ad hoc wireless network between two devices. Afterward, you can use the steps in this task to enable additional devices to join the ad hoc network. This task assumes the use of Windows XP.

1.  On the computer's Desktop, right-click My Network Places and choose Properties. This produces the Network Connections window.

2.  In the Network Connections window, find the icon for the wireless NIC you wish to set up for ad hoc connectivity. Right-clicking the NIC's icon and choosing Properties generates the Network Connections pages for the specific adapter.

3.  On the Wireless Networks tab, click the Advanced button (not the Advanced tab).

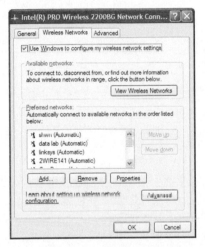

4.  In the Advanced dialog, shown in the following screen shot with the proper selection for this task, Access Point (Infrastructure) Networks Only is the only radio button that cannot be selected for ad hoc mode to work properly. However, for this task, because you might have an access point within range, fill the radio button beside Computer-To-Computer (Ad Hoc) Networks Only, and then click the Close button to return to the Wireless Networks tab.

In production, it is alright to select the first item in this list as long as no access points are within range when you want to connect systems as an ad hoc network.

**5.**   In the Wireless Networks tab, click the Add button to bring up the Association tab of the Wireless Network Properties pages.

**6.**   Following the details of the next image, enter a service set identifier (SSID) that does not conflict with the name of any of your other wireless networks. Disable data encryption, although in production you might establish encryption. Also, make sure the check box labeled This Is A Computer-To-Computer (Ad Hoc) Network; Wireless Access Points Are Not Used is checked. Click the OK button.

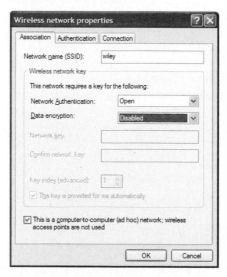

**7.**   Had you kept or returned to the default action of accessing any available network, you would need to scroll to the bottom of your preferred networks, if enough exist to make doing so necessary, to reveal the newly added ad hoc network. Having chosen to access ad hoc networks only, and assuming no other ad hoc networks existed already, your ad hoc network appears alone in the list.

8. Click the OK button and then return to the Wireless Networks tab where you might notice that the icon for your ad hoc connection now has a circle associated with it, indicating that your wireless adapter is transmitting for the ad hoc network and is receptive to others that would like to join.

9. (Optional) If you would like to set up Internet Connection Sharing (ICS) over this ad hoc network connection, click the Advanced tab (not the Advanced button). All you need to do to share your default gateway through another NIC with others in the ad hoc network is put a check in the box labeled Allow Other Network Users To Connect Through This Computer's Internet Connection.

**10.** Click the OK button to return to the Network Connections window.

**11.** You are now finished with the Network Connections window and can close it if you wish.

### Testing the Ad Hoc Network

Once you have the ad hoc network set up on at least two devices, it is time to test your configuration. The following steps can assure you that your design is successful.

**1.** Right-click My Network Places on the Desktop and select Properties.

**2.** Right-click your wireless adapter and select View Available Wireless Networks. This brings up a list of the wireless networks of which you are currently in range, as well as all ad hoc networks you have set up. Because of the current settings, you see only the ad hoc network you just configured and any other ad hoc networks previously configured.

**3.** Note that the ad hoc network you configured is not connected currently. Compare your results to the following screen shot. This is to be expected if you used an SSID that is unique and not used by anyone else.

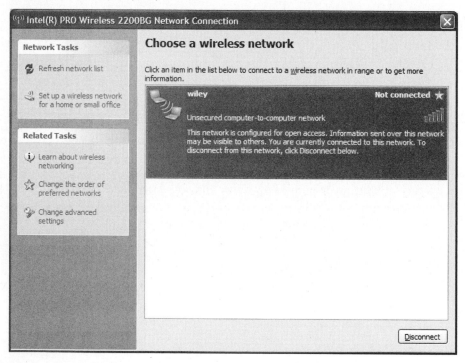

4. Perform the earlier steps to create an ad hoc wireless network on another wireless system. Notice that when the two systems detect one another, the status for the ad hoc network changes, as shown next.

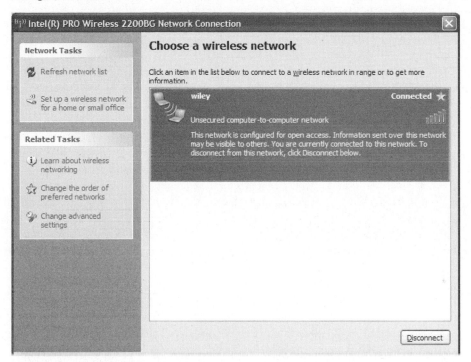

5. Check the IP addresses on the two systems. If APIPA kicked in, both machines are on the same IP subnet automatically. Otherwise, statically configure the wireless adapters of both systems with IP addresses on the same subnet. Ping one system from the other, thus proving successful ad hoc configuration.

## Criteria for Completion

You have completed this task when you complete the steps for testing the ad hoc network with successful results.

# Task 2.7: Using an Analog Modem

Once, in the still blossoming age of personal computing, analog modems, devices that connect through a normal phone line to the Public Switched Telephone Network (PSTN), were our only way of accessing remote networks. Since those days, the industry has offered various other solutions, from the ISDN terminal adapters of the '90s to the DSL and cable modems of today. Nevertheless, an analog modem can be a surprisingly welcome and convenient resource when you're away from your normal surroundings. It takes practically nothing to run a line cord from the RJ-11 modem interface of your laptop to the wall jack in order to access the Internet and download a driver for a NIC you just pulled out of storage. One alternative is to contact the manufacturer for a distribution disk and wait for it to be delivered. A better option, although still not favorable, is to use another computer, if available, to download the driver and copy it to removable media that will work in your computer.

While this is just one example, there is no doubt that keeping an analog modem around for emergencies, such as power outages, is a fairly decent idea. In such a case, you can use the batteries of your laptop to power up, and because a standard phone line is not affected by power outages, unlike DSL and cable modems, an analog modem can still be used to contact an ISP in the event of lost power.

## Scenario

You have an outlying computer in your site that would benefit from immediate Internet access. However, the nearest WAP is too far away for connectivity. The cabling crews are days away from getting a drop to the computer's location. There is an analog phone jack in the cube next door, which will remain unoccupied for the foreseeable future. You decide to run a line cord from the computer's analog modem to the jack in the next cube and gain temporary Internet access that way.

## Scope of Task

### Duration

This task should take about 20 minutes.

### Setup

For this task, you need one computer in cable range of an analog phone jack.

### Caveat

The word *modem*, a concatenation of *modulator/demodulator*, has become fairly overused. If you've ever heard the term *ISDN modem*, you've witnessed a misuse of the word. The modulation portion of the process involves taking the digital computer information and placing it on an analog carrier. Demodulation, then, is the removal of the information from the analog carrier and the generation of the corresponding digital bit stream. ISDN, however, is digital across the service provider's line, meaning that modulation and demodulation never occur.

Additionally, be careful that you do not confuse an external DSL or cable modem for an analog modem. These devices are not interchangeable. This task requires an analog modem, whether internal or external.

Be aware that phone lines other than classic analog lines are not likely to stay live during power outages. For this reason, even in corporate enterprise environments where millions of dollars can be spent on digital private branch exchange (PBX) systems, it is still wise to keep a few strategically placed analog phone lines in service for the situation in which all other equipment not powered by generators has failed.

## Procedure

In this task, you use an analog modem to gain access to a remote network, installing the modem beforehand, if necessary.

### Equipment Used

For this task, you need one computer with an analog modem. The modem may be built in, as in the case of most laptops manufactured in the last few years, or it may be an internal modem that currently is or is not installed. It must be installed before the task can be verified. Alternatively, you may use an external analog modem, which means you will require an available serial port on the computer.

### Details

If you have an internal modem that needs to be installed before beginning, refer back to Task 2.3 for ESD recommendations and general adapter installation procedure.

#### Starting the New Connection Wizard

The following steps get you started with the establishment of a dial-up connection, after which point, the next two sections diverge based on your individual needs.

1.  On the computer's Desktop, right-click My Network Places and choose Properties. This produces the Network Connections window.

2.  In the Network Connections window, click Create A New Connection in the left frame under Network Tasks. This brings up the New Connection Wizard.

3.  On the New Connection Wizard welcome screen, click Next, which takes you to the Network Connection Type screen.

**4.** In the Network Connection Type screen, select Connect To The Internet and click the Next button.

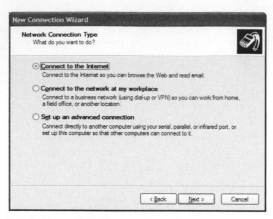

Because the Set Up An Advanced Connection setting concentrates on direct connection between computers (which is not our goal) or allowing other devices to dial into the local computer (also not our goal), ignore that selection, but feel free to explore it on your own. Because the skills you learn here can be ported to the second option, Connect To The Network At My Workplace, you can ignore that selection for now, as well.

Selecting Connect To The Internet and clicking the Next button takes you to the Getting Ready screen. The remaining steps for both options deviate here. Examine the following procedures to ascertain which of the final steps are appropriate for you.

## Continuing with an Existing Dial-Up Account

Perform the steps in this section after first completing the steps in the section titled "Starting the New Connection Wizard" earlier in this task. You must have an existing dial-up account with an ISP or corporate RAS server.

**1.** In the Getting Ready screen, fill in the Set Up My Connection Manually radio button and click the Next button.

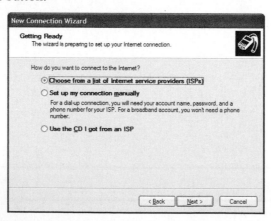

2.  In the Internet Connection screen, the selection Connect Using A Dial-Up Modem refers to an analog modem and is the option you want in this case. Fill in that radio button and click the Next button.

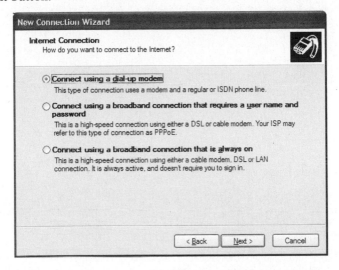

3.  In the Connection Name screen, enter a friendly name for the connection to be displayed anytime the connection is referenced, whether in the Network Connections window or in the system tray. Click Next.

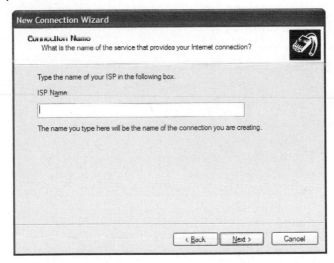

**4.** In the Phone Number To Dial screen, enter the numerical string to be dialed. It is best if you enter any preceding digits that must be dialed when calling from this location. One or more commas (,) may be entered for delay between any two numbers. Click Next.

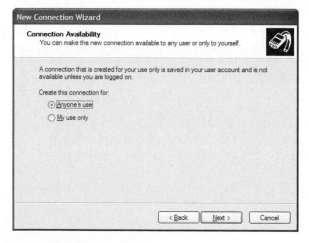

**5.** In the Connection Availability screen, choose whether to make this connection available to everyone that logs onto the computer or just to your account. Click Next.

**6.** The Internet Account Information screen, shown in the following image, is the key to efficient access to the remote network. The more efficiency you choose, the less security you enjoy, however. For example, leaving the User Name and Password fields blank and disabling Use This Account Name And Password When Anyone Connects To The Internet From This Computer results in the imposition of the requirement to supply this

information every time you connect. Enter the information you desire and select or dese-
lect the options you wish. Click the Next button.

7.  In the Completing The New Connection Wizard screen, choose to add a shortcut to your
    connection to your Desktop if you want one there and click the Finish button to exit the
    wizard. This automatically brings up the Connect dialog for your connection, which you
    can access in the future from the Network Connections window or from the Desktop
    shortcut, if you chose to make one.

Make sure your modem is connected to an analog phone jack and then enter any pertinent
information, make any adjustments desired to the Connect dialog, and click the Dial button
to contact the remote network. Figure 2.9 shows the Connect dialog.

By opening your Network Connections window, you are able to confirm the existence of the new connection you just made, as seen in the next image.

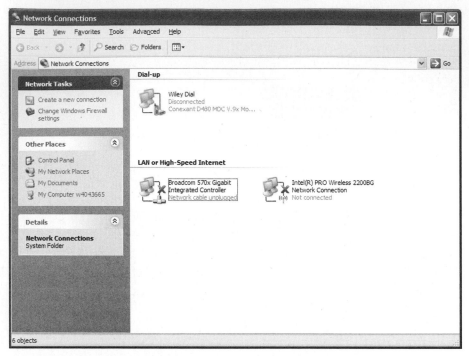

**FIGURE 2.9**    The Connect dialog

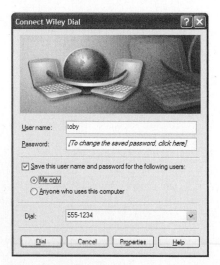

## Continuing without an Existing Dial-Up Account

Perform the steps in this section after first completing the steps in the section titled "Starting the New Connection Wizard" earlier in this task. These steps assume you do not have an existing dial-up account.

1.  In the Getting Ready screen, fill in the radio button beside Choose From A List Of Internet Service Providers and click the Next button to go straight to the Completing The New Connection Wizard screen. You jump straight to the Completing The New Connection Wizard window because you must leave the wizard so that the operating system can take you to a folder under `Program Files` named `Online Services`.

2.  Make sure your modem is connected to an analog phone jack, and then in the `Online Services` folder, run the shortcut Refer Me To More Internet Service Providers.

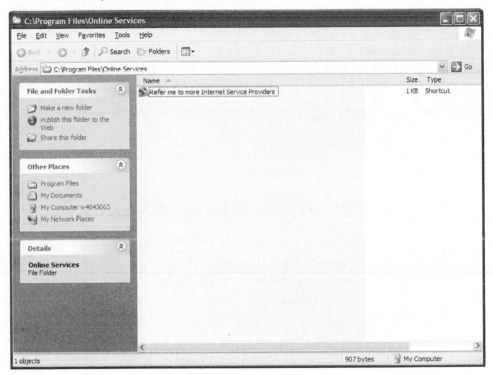

3.  This brings up the Internet Connection Wizard and a three-step process to getting you connected with an ISP. Figure 2.10 shows the wizard dialing the Microsoft Internet Referral Service to request a lit of ISPs local to where you originated your call.

**4.** Finally, the service finishes sending you the ISPs with a local or toll-free presence, as shown in the subsequent screen shot. Choose an ISP and click the Next button to move on to step 2, entering your contact information to begin setting up your service.

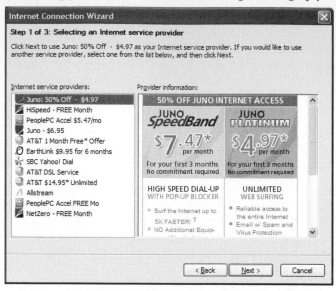

**FIGURE 2.10**    Dialing the Microsoft Internet Referral Service

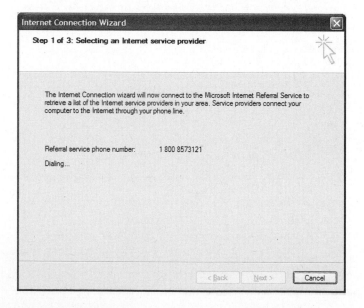

**5.**   Enter the requested information into the screen labeled Signing Up With An Internet Service Provider, and then click Next.

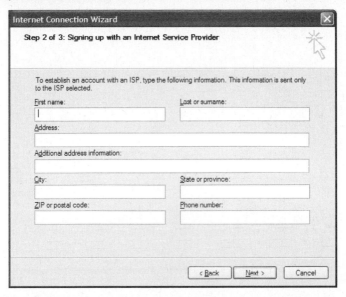

**6.**   Depending on the service you choose, you might be required to specify to which packages you wish to subscribe to.

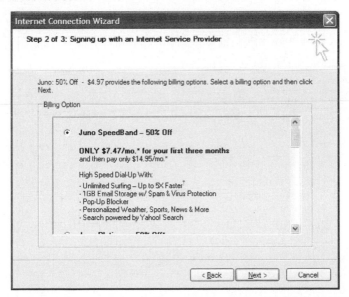

**7.** Then, enter your billing information so that the service provider can charge you for the service. Enter your information and click the Next button.

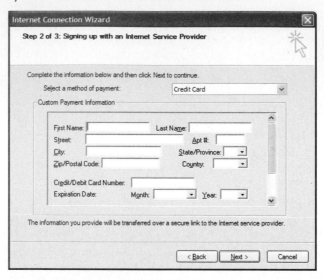

What happens next depends on the service provider you chose, but the general idea can be derived from the following image, showing the ISP being contacted and the promise of receiving credentials that will allow you to access the Internet.

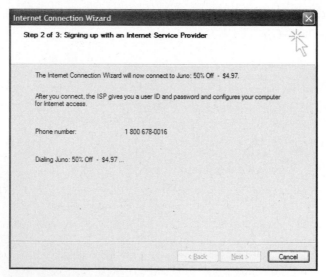

## Criteria for Completion

You have completed this task when you are able to use your new dial-up connection(s) to access one or more remote networks.

# Task 2.8: Using a DSL Modem

For the most part, a DSL modem comes to you from your service provider already configured and ready to go. But devices that are configured become unconfigured. Situations for which a configuration works are subject to change. It is for these reasons that it's good to know about the inner workings of a DSL modem.

How a DSL modem is interconnected with other devices has a bearing on how it should be configured. The modem can act as a transparent traffic conductor or it can be a highly integral part of the local area. It can hand out IP addresses to LAN clients or not. Depending on the way the DSL circuit is provisioned by the service provider, one modem configuration might work while another does not.

## Scenario

One of your telecommuters has reset his DSL modem at home. He is having trouble following the instructions from his provider's technical support group. You have some tasks that you need to perform on his mobile computer, so you plan to take a look at the modem while you are at his home in an effort to get him up and running and minimize his loss of productivity.

## Scope of Task

### Duration

This task should take about 45 minutes.

### Setup

For this task, you need a DSL modem and line and the space to set up a computer for configuration and verification.

### Caveat

There are many brands of DSL modems, known as remote ADSL terminal units (ATU-Rs). Among these brands, there are different models. The method for configuration can be unique for each model. While this task seeks to give you the confidence to investigate the configuration of any DSL modem, you might find configuring your particular device more challenging due to such differences. For example, access to the menu for configuration might be through HTTP instead of Telnet.

Your service provider might have secured the unit with a non-default password. This is not intended to keep you from configuring your modem, just to keep malicious or accidental activity to a minimum. The fact is, the ATU-R is customer premise equipment (CPE), meaning it belongs to the customer. Gaining access to the device is as easy as going through the reset procedure, usually just holding down a reset button until the LEDs cycle off and then back on. Mere power cycling is designed not to disrupt the configuration, for obvious reasons. No one wants to deploy equipment that causes a service call every time there is a power outage. The only downfall to resetting one of these devices to break in and experiment is that you lose the original configuration and have no reference to what it was.

So be aware that experimenting with your working DSL modem can result in a modem that no longer works for your particular situation. Although practically any DSL modem can be configured by the user back to the state in which it was found, be sure to have a contact available through your service provider just in case the water gets too deep or you do not have the time or patience to return your modem to service.

# Procedure

This task guides you through configuring a ZyXEL (pronounced zī-cell) 645-R DSL routing modem for various modes of service.

## Equipment Used

For this task, you need a DSL modem and a single computer to configure the modem and test its proper configuration. An Ethernet patch cable is generally used for connectivity between the computer and modem. A standard line cord, like the one used between a phone and the wall, is used to connect the modem to the provider's network.

## Details

This task guides you through the specific menu structure of the ZyXEL 645-R DSL modem.

1. Connect the Ethernet interface of your computer to your DSL modem's LAN port by a patch cable, preferably the one supplied with the DSL modem.

 Many of today's ATU-Rs are intelligent enough to allow the connection to be made with a straight-through 8-pin modular patch cable or an Ethernet crossover cable, performing the necessary electrical adaptation on-the-fly. However, the ATU-R is Ethernet DCE, just like a hub or switch. So, the textbook cable is a straight-through patch cable between the ATU-R and a computer or router, a crossover cable if the ATU-R connects to a hub or switch.

2. Make sure the DSL modem is powered on and LEDs labeled such things as "power" and "system" are lit steady. The important consideration is that the LED that represents a solid connection with your computer or LAN must be in its final state, in order for you to continue. Note that some LEDs blink as the unit is coming up and go steady after bootup is complete. Other LEDs that indicate LAN or WAN activity tend to blink erratically with passing data. A constant blink rate, however, generally means that part of the unit is still becoming ready.

3. Open a command prompt by choosing Start ➢ All Programs ➢ Accessories ➢ Command Prompt.

4. Enter the command **ipconfig**, as shown in the following screen shot. Note the value of the Default Gateway field.

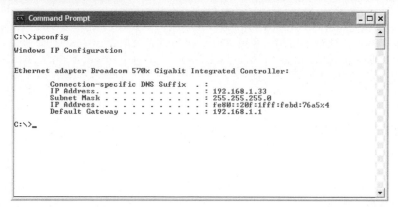

5. At the prompt, try entering the command **telnet *gateway_address***, as in the next screen shot. If this produces an error, try **http://*gateway_address*** in a web browser. In these examples, *gateway_address* is the IP address in the Default Gateway field from the output of the **ipconfig** command.

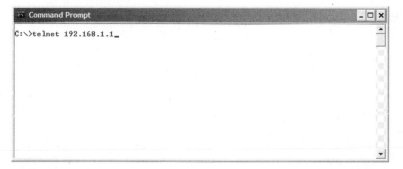

6. The ZyXEL asks for a password to telnet into its menu. The default is 1234. Once the correct password is entered, you are presented with a menu similar to the following. Obviously, there are too many selections to discuss at once, so the following steps help you navigate through the most important ones.

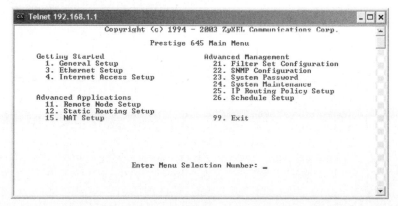

7. It is highly recommended, if you have a ZyXEL product that is currently in service, that you start in menu 24.5, seen in the following screen shot and opened by entering 24 and then 5 from the main menu. This menu walks you through backing up the configuration. Menu 24.6 guides you through restoring the configuration, should that ever become necessary. Return to the main menu when the backup is complete.

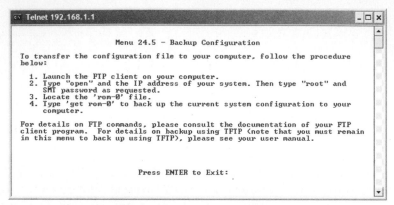

8. By entering the number **1** from the main menu, you bring up the following menu.

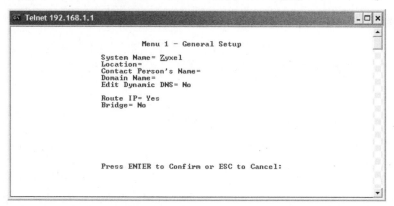

Besides entering general information for the unit, here is one of the places where you switch the unit from a visible intermediate device to a transparent bridging component. To do so, you need to set Route IP to No and Bridge to Yes. You also would need to make similar adjustments in menu 11.1—more later—as well as turn off DHCP to the LAN in menu 3.2 and switch to RFC 1483 encapsulation in menu 4.

**NOTE** Traversing these menus can be tricky at first. Press Enter to cycle through the entries and to save the settings for a particular page. Press Escape to return to a previous menu without saving changes. If you already did so by pressing Enter at the bottom prompt, Escape simply takes you back one level, keeping the changes you just saved. The spacebar cycles through the values of each entry unless the entry calls for variable input, such as an IP address.

9. From the main menu, entering **3** and then **2** displays the following page. Note this menu is called 3.2 for the sequence of numerical entries needed from the main menu to display it.

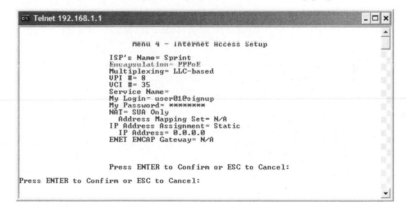

It is here that you are able to turn on and off the built-in DHCP server that hands addresses out to local devices requesting them. Additionally, you can limit the number of leases handed out, as well as specify the starting address for the scope. DSL accounts with static IP addresses need to have the DNS servers entered on this menu. Dynamic services need these entries left at their defaults of 0.0.0.0.

10. From the main menu, entering **4** brings you to the following page.

Following are the four encapsulation types and the reason to use each one.

**PPPoE (Point-to-Point over Ethernet)**   PPPoE and PPPoA both require user information in the form of the user's email account and password in order to authenticate against a RADIUS server before network access is granted. These services are rapidly being replaced by a DHCP offering, requiring no such authentication. Ethernet frames are sent across the DSL line to the DSL access multiplexer (DSLAM).

**PPPoA (Point-to-Point over ATM)**   ATM cells are sent over the DSL line to the DSLAM.

**RFC 1483**   Simply encapsulates user data in ATM AAL5 cells without otherwise communicating with the network. This encapsulation creates an "open pipe" to the DSL network, providing data transport only, no intelligence. Any required authentication takes place farther back in the user network, such as on a router or individual computer, through a PPPoE client, for example.

**ENET ENCAP (Ethernet encapsulation)**   This encapsulation is required for two different service provider offerings:

**DHCP-based DSL circuits**   The service provider offers non-authenticated DHCP services over the WAN. In this exchange, the DSL modem is the DHCP client for public IP addressing from the service provider. In an unrelated function, the modem is still a DHCP server of private IP addressing for the LAN. Only one IP lease is given out per DHCP DSL line. Any theft of this very insecure DSL line, although easy to perpetrate, results in loss of connectivity for the subscriber because of the one DHCP lease being taken, which leads to a service call and the discovery of the thief.

**Static IP offerings**   All IP information must be entered in the ZyXEL for static lines, unlike leaving all information blank or at zeroed-out defaults when using the same encapsulation type for DHCP offerings. These entries are made in menus 3.2 and 11.3.

1.   From the main menu, entering **11** and then **1** brings you to menu 11.1.

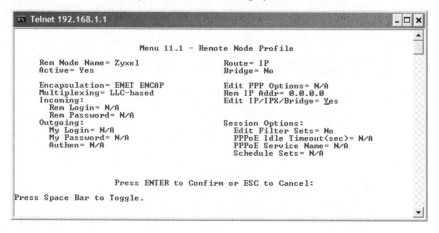

Two main functions bear mentioning here. The first involves the immediately visible Route and Bridge fields. These must be manipulated, based on whether you use RFC 1483 encapsulation, as mentioned earlier. The second is the field labeled Edit IP/IPX/Bridge. By pressing the spacebar, you change this entry from No to Yes. However, this is not a permanent change. Pressing Enter after changing the value to Yes takes you to the following menu, 11.3, even though the number 3 was never entered.

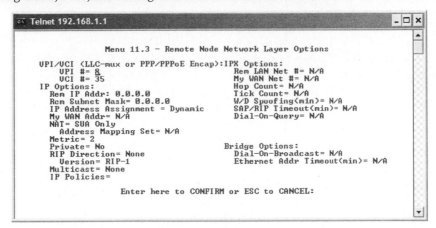

When you exit menu 11.3, the Yes value returns to No. This is normal, and it should not be changed back to Yes unless you wish to go back into menu 11.3. It is in menu 11.3 that the default gateway and subnet mask are entered for static IP offerings. Menu 11.3 is not used for the other three service offerings.

2. From the main menu, entering **99** exits back to the Windows command prompt.

Other useful menus are as follows:

**23**   Change modem password. Be careful. Lost passwords are easily circumvented but at the cost of the current system configuration, unless it has been backed up at menu 24.5.

**24.1**   Shows LAN and WAN (DSL circuit) bit rates and packet statistics.

**24.2.1**   Shows the modem's MAC address.

**24.4**   A menu of utilities, including ping, reboot, and reset DSL line.

## Criteria for Completion

You have completed this task when you have performed the steps on a ZyXEL 645-R DSL modem or investigated similar settings and utilities on your own model of DSL modem. The true test of success is to open a web browser and surf the Internet across the DSL line with the modem used in this task.

# Task 2.9: Using a Router as a Frame Relay Switch

Granted, it is not always the best solution to configure a Cisco router as a Frame Relay switch, but sometimes you have to do what is necessary with what you have. While Cisco may not optimize its routers for Frame Relay switching, it is certainly no slouch when it comes to providing an efficient mechanism over an unlikely device.

This task shows you the general approach to configuring a Cisco router to act as a Frame Relay switch. This is not to say that the same router cannot route as well as switch, but it is not possible to route packets and switch Frame Relay frames over the same interface simultaneously because an IP address is not configured on an interface used for Frame Relay switching. The foregoing discussion presents one of the reasons that you need an additional router, beyond those diagramed in your lab drawing, to perform this task.

## Scenario

You are having issues with Voice over IP (VoIP) traffic from Sydney to LA. You would like to give voice packets preferential treatment over data packets. You decide to implement Frame Relay across the WAN links between Tokyo and LA and between Tokyo and Sydney so that you are able to use the built-in traffic shaping inherent in Frame Relay. Your plan is to build a full mesh—each endpoint connects to every other endpoint—of virtual circuits between Tokyo's router J, LA's router D, and Sydney's router L. None of the three routers is capable of being a Frame Relay endpoint as well as a Frame Relay switch, so a fourth router, router X, must be brought in to act as the switch.

## Scope of Task

### Duration

This task should take about 90 minutes.

### Setup

For this task, you need to be able to attach a computer to a craft interface (for example, the console port) of a Cisco router to configure the device as a Frame Relay switch. It is ideal if you have access to four such devices and the CSU/DSUs or comparable cabling to interconnect the routers.

## Caveat

Keep in mind that this solution is ideal only in certain situations, such as when you cannot afford additional equipment and a Cisco router is available or when you have a modest WAN topology with a somewhat limited traffic flow. Specialized Frame Relay switching equipment is available from Cisco and other vendors for those situations where a bit more muscle is indicated.

# Procedure

In this task, you configure a router as a Frame Relay switch. Optionally, to test your configuration, you can configure three other routers to send Frame Relay traffic through the router acting as a switch.

## Equipment Used

For this task, you need one computer and one Cisco router capable of Frame Relay switching. Optionally, you can use three additional routers to test your configuration. If you configure three additional routers, you need a method of connecting these routers to the router acting as a Frame Relay switch, either CSU/DSUs or back-to-back cabling.

See Task 2.10, "Simulating T1 CSU/DSUs," if you decide to use cables to simulate your T1 circuits.

## Details

Figure 2.11 illustrates the topology and Frame Relay configuration that this task seeks to construct.

Note that fewer T1 circuits are required, only three in comparison to the redundant set of four T1s in the original topology. Because this example configures Frame Relay on the physical interface of each endpoint router, the Frame Relay interfaces of all three routers must be configured in the same IP subnet.

Optionally, you can stretch beyond the goals of this task, using the skills you learn here to add redundancy back in. To do so, make up your own additional Frame Relay configuration to accommodate your redundancy. Note that you need a total of six T1 circuits for the equivalent redundancy in this Frame Relay environment. The three additional endpoints, from an IP-addressing perspective, need to be in the same subnet with one another, which must be a different subnet from the one presented in this task.

Each T1 circuit from each endpoint router carries traffic for two permanent virtual circuits (PVCs), one to each remote endpoint. Consider Tokyo as endpoint number 1, LA as endpoint number 2, and Sydney as endpoint number 3. Table 2.1 lists the data-link connection identifiers (DLCIs) for these virtual circuits (VCs) using the endpoint numbers to fabricate the DLCIs.

**TABLE 2.1**    Frame Relay DLCIs

| VC # | VC Source | VC Destination | DLCI |
|------|-----------|----------------|------|
| 1 | Tokyo | LA | 102 |
| 1 | LA | Tokyo | 201 |
| 2 | Tokyo | Sydney | 103 |
| 2 | Sydney | Tokyo | 301 |
| 3 | LA | Sydney | 203 |
| 3 | Sydney | LA | 302 |

**FIGURE 2.11**    Frame Relay topology

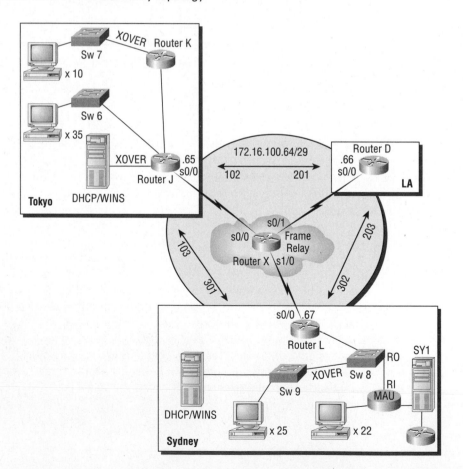

### Configuring the Frame Relay Switch

The following steps configure router X as a Frame Relay switch with the proper port/DLCI mappings to interconnect Tokyo, LA, and Sydney in a full mesh topology.

1. Enter Global Configuration mode.

```
RouterX#config t
RouterX(config)#
```

2. Turn on Frame Relay switching, turning router X into a Frame relay switch.

```
RouterX(config)#frame-relay switching
RouterX(config)#
```

3. Remove the IP address from each interface involved in switching and configure each interface for standards-based Frame Relay encapsulation and standards-based Local Management Interface (LMI) format. The switch's interfaces need to act as Frame Relay data circuit-terminating equipment (DCE) so they can communicate properly with the endpoints, which act, by default, as data terminal equipment (DTE) over the access line with the switch. The DCE designation has nothing to do with the V.35 clocking of the serial interface.

```
RouterX(config)#int s0/0
RouterX(config-if)#no ip address
RouterX(config-if)#encapsulation frame-relay ietf
RouterX(config-if)#frame-relay lmi-type q933a
RouterX(config-if)#frame-relay intf-type dce
RouterX(config-if)#int s0/1
RouterX(config-if)#no ip address
RouterX(config-if)#encapsulation frame-relay ietf
RouterX(config-if)#frame-relay lmi-type q933a
RouterX(config-if)#frame-relay intf-type dce
RouterX(config-if)#int s1/0
RouterX(config-if)#no ip address
RouterX(config-if)#encapsulation frame-relay ietf
RouterX(config-if)#frame-relay lmi-type q933a
RouterX(config-if)#frame-relay intf-type dce
```

4. Create Frame Relay switching routes for the PVCs, paying attention to inbound and outbound interfaces as they relate to each DLCI. Consult Figure 2.11 for details. The frame-relay route command lists the inbound DLCI first, relating it to the interface on which the command is executed. The outbound interface and DLCI are listed last. The effect is to switch the inbound frame from one port to another, swapping the DLCI as indicated in the command if it's numerically different, which by the way, is not mandatory. Inbound and outbound DLCIs could be the same.

```
RouterX(config-if)#int s0/0
RouterX(config-if)#frame-relay route 102 int s0/1 201
RouterX(config-if)#frame-relay route 103 int s1/0 301
RouterX(config-if)#int s0/1
RouterX(config-if)#frame-relay route 201 int s0/0 102
RouterX(config-if)#frame-relay route 203 int s1/0 302
RouterX(config-if)#int s1/0
RouterX(config-if)#frame-relay route 301 int s0/0 103
RouterX(config-if)#frame-relay route 302 int s0/1 203
```

**5.**  Exit configuration.

```
RouterX(config-if)#end
RouterX#
```

## Configuring Frame Relay on the Endpoints

To test your switch configuration, you can configure two or three of the endpoints for Frame Relay as the WAN encapsulation. This section shows you the steps to configure each of the three endpoints in Figure 2.11.

### TOKYO'S ROUTER J

**1.**  Enter Global Configuration mode.

```
RouterJ#config t
RouterJ(config)#
```

**2.**  On the Frame Relay interface, disable the interface, configure the IP address, and set the encapsulation and LMI format. You disable the interface to prevent the router from learning incorrect information, which may cause you to have to go through a lengthy reboot of the router to get rid of the information.

```
RouterJ(config)#int s0/0
RouterJ(config-if)#shutdown
RouterJ(config-if)#ip address 172.16.100.65 255.255.255.248
RouterJ(config-if)#encapsulation frame-relay ietf
RouterJ(config-if)#frame-relay lmi-type q933a
```

**3.**  So the interface does not learn any improper IP information through inverse ARP when you bring it back up, turn this feature off.

```
RouterJ(config-if)#no frame-relay inverse-arp
RouterJ(config-if)#
```

**4.**  To be a good neighbor, so the interface does not respond to inverse ARP requests from others when you bring it back up, turn this feature off.

```
RouterJ(config-if)#no arp frame-relay
RouterJ(config-if)#
```

**5.** Now that all functions of inverse ARP have been turned off, you need to tell the router manually which remote IP address can be found at the other end of which PVC by specifying the PVC's local DLCI. The router hears about the DLCIs from the switch but has no way of resolving these to IP addresses automatically now that the inverse ARP service has been disabled.

```
RouterJ(config-if)#frame-relay map ip 172.16.100.66 102
RouterJ(config-if)#frame-relay map ip 172.16.100.67 103
RouterJ(config-if)#
```

**6.** At this point, it is perfectly safe to bring the interface back up.

```
RouterJ(config-if)#no shutdown
RouterJ(config-if)#
```

**7.** Exit configuration.

```
RouterJ(config-if)#end
RouterJ#
```

### LA'S ROUTER D

**1.** Enter Global Configuration mode.

```
RouterD#config t
RouterD(config)#
```

**2.** On the Frame Relay interface, disable the interface, configure the IP address, and set the encapsulation and LMI format.

```
RouterD(config)#int s0/0
RouterD(config-if)#shutdown
RouterD(config-if)#ip address 172.16.100.66 255.255.255.248
RouterD(config-if)#encapsulation frame-relay ietf
RouterD(config-if)#frame-relay lmi-type q933a
```

**3.** Turn off inverse ARP requests.

```
RouterD(config-if)#no frame-relay inverse-arp
RouterD(config-if)#
```

**4.** Turn off inverse ARP responses.

```
RouterD(config-if)#no arp frame-relay
RouterD(config-if)#
```

**5.** Map each remote IP address to its corresponding local DLCI.

```
RouterD(config-if)#frame-relay map ip 172.16.100.65 201
RouterD(config-if)#frame-relay map ip 172.16.100.67 203
RouterD(config-if)#
```

6.  Bring the interface back up.

```
RouterD(config-if)#no shutdown
RouterD(config-if)#
```

7.  Exit configuration.

```
RouterD(config-if)#end
RouterD#
```

**SYDNEY'S ROUTER L**

1.  Enter Global Configuration mode.

```
RouterL#config t
RouterL(config)#
```

2.  On the Frame Relay interface, disable the interface, configure the IP address, and set the encapsulation and LMI format.

```
RouterL(config)#int s0/0
RouterL(config-if)#shutdown
RouterL(config-if)#ip address 172.16.100.67 255.255.255.248
RouterL(config-if)#encapsulation frame-relay ietf
RouterL(config-if)#frame-relay lmi-type q933a
```

3.  Turn off inverse ARP requests.

```
RouterL(config-if)#no frame-relay inverse-arp
RouterL(config-if)#
```

4.  Turn off inverse ARP responses.

```
RouterL(config-if)#no arp frame-relay
RouterL(config-if)#
```

5.  Map each remote IP address to its corresponding local DLCI.

```
RouterL(config-if)#frame-relay map ip 172.16.100.65 301
RouterL(config-if)#frame-relay map ip 172.16.100.66 302
RouterL(config-if)#
```

6.  Bring the interface back up.

```
RouterL(config-if)#no shutdown
RouterL(config-if)#
```

7.  Exit configuration.

```
RouterL(config-if)#end
RouterL#
```

## Criteria for Completion

You have completed this task when your Frame Relay switch's configuration matches the configuration given in this task. Where possible, it advised that you validate your configuration with two or more other routers using the configuration for the endpoints given in this task.

# Task 2.10: Simulating T1 CSU/DSUs

Occasionally, it becomes necessary to use serial interfaces between routers when no actual circuit exists. Suppose you're testing a theory in a lab environment. You don't need to pay for a T1 just to confirm that part of your design will work. Or maybe you are caught in need of a router with two LAN interfaces, one for multi-access and the other as a backbone to another router, but the spare you have has only one such interface. It does, however, have at least one serial interface that you do not need for anything else, as does the router at the other end of the backbone. If it is not prohibitive to place these routers in close proximity until you acquire another router or a module for your router, you can use a serial connection between routers to accomplish the same effect as using an Ethernet-based backbone.

CSU/DSUs are not negligible in price, especially when you only need to fill a gap temporarily. Of course, if you already have two lying around, it's a small feat to make a crossover T1 network cable. Using 8-pin modular plugs, simply cross pins 1 and 2 on one end of a cable to pins 4 and 5 on the other end, respectively, and you have a cable that can be relatively long compared to the solution in this task. Plugging the ends of the cable in to the network interfaces of the CSU/DSUs simulates a T1 circuit from a service provider, without the expense. If you don't have a pair of CSU/DSUs, however, your options are even more limited.

Cisco routers use the ITU-T V.35 specification for serial interfaces, much as the slower EIA/TIA-232 (formerly RS-232) is used on serial interfaces or COM ports on a computer. You can use a null modem cable with EIA/TIA-232 interfaces, which crosses over pins with complementary functions, mating transmit with receive, RTS with CTS, and so on to connect two computers directly to one another. Cisco specifies a solution that works in a similar fashion: a male V.35 DTE cable for normal connection to a CSU/DSU and a female DCE version to eliminate the CSU/DSU by connecting directly to the male DTE end. Minimal configuration is required on the router with the DCE cable, while no additional configuration is required on the router with the DTE cable.

## Scenario

Two of the departments in one of your larger sites are isolated by design. No network traffic has been allowed to cross between departments. Now there is a need for information to flow between the departments, but you do not want them to be part of the same IP subnet. Your preference is to be able to interconnect the departments yet control what information passes between them. You decide to use the existing routers, which connect the departments to other parts of the internetwork, and make a connection between them so that you can use access control lists (ACLs) to filter traffic between the departments. However, the only interfaces common to the routers are serial. Having only one available CSU/DSU, you are forced to use a V.35 DCE cable on one of the routers. Fortunately, the two routers are in the same rack in one of the equipment rooms.

## Scope of Task

### Duration

This task should take about 30 minutes.

### Setup

For this task, you need to set up two Cisco routers and a computer on which to configure them. Only the back-to-back V.35 cabling is needed on the routers for network connectivity.

### Caveat

Although this method of connectivity is as effective as an actual T1, the range is drastically reduced—only a few feet, down from halfway around the world in the case of an actual T1 circuit. (If you go farther than halfway, you went the wrong direction!) This is not a way to obviate service-provider T1 circuits. Furthermore, Cisco cables, even those assembled by third parties, are not known for their value. Because not many shops have V.35 DCE cables lying around, the expense of implementing this solution might well be a disincentive, especially in volume installations where a discount is enjoyed for circuits but not for cables.

## Procedure

In this task, you simulate a T1 with no CSU/DSUs, using back-to-back V.35 cables.

### Equipment Used

For this task, you need two Cisco routers. The example uses 2611XMs. You also need one V.35 male DTE cable and a mating V.35 female DCE cable. Additionally, you need a computer to access the command-line interface (CLI) of the routers, as well as cabling and adapters to do so.

### Details

Figure 2.12 shows a standard male end of a DTE V.35 cable. Figure 2.13 shows the female end of a DCE V.35 cable that mates with the standard male.

**FIGURE 2.12**    Male V.35 connector

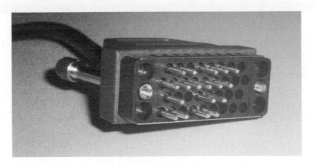

**FIGURE 2.13**    Female V.35 connector

It does not matter to which of the two routers you attach the DCE cable. However, you need to know which router has the DCE cable because it will be the one with the additional configuration. Fortunately, Cisco's IOS has a method of discovering where the DCE cable is attached.

1. After connecting the cables between routers, issue the show ip interface brief EXEC command on each one to observe the state of the serial interfaces before configuration.

```
DTERouter#sh ip interface brief
Interface      IP-Address      OK? Method Status        Protocol
Serial0/0      unassigned      YES unset  up            down
DTERouter#
```

```
DCERouter#sh ip interface brief
Interface      IP-Address      OK? Method Status        Protocol
Serial0/0      unassigned      YES unset  up            down
DCERouter#
```

Note that Layer 1 is up but Layer 2 is down. This is because the cable creates line synchronization between the routers, but frame synchronization, which relies on a plesiochronous clock source, cannot be established. For that to occur, one of the routers must be set to produce a clock signal that the other end can recover from the data.

2. To confirm that the routers detect the cable you have attached as what you expect it to be, enter the command show controllers on each router for the interface with the V.35 cable attached.

```
DCERouter#show controllers s0/0
Interface Serial0/0
Hardware is PowerQUICC MPC860
DCE V.35, no clock


DTERouter#show controllers s0/0
Interface Serial0/0
Hardware is PowerQUICC MPC860
DTE V.35 clocks stopped.
```

The routers detect the type of cable attached and report this to you, as well as the fact that there is no clock established, resulting in the up/down state.

3. Enter Interface Configuration mode on the DCE router for the interface with the DCE V.35 cable attached.

```
DCERouter#config t
DCERouter(config)#interface s0/0
DCERouter(config-if)#
```

4. Use the clock rate interface command, only on the DCE router, to set the bit rate in bits per second for the connection between the routers. Doing so brings up the connection almost immediately.

```
DCERouter(config-if)#clock rate 2000000
%LINEPROTO-5-UPDOWN: Line protocol on Interface Serial0/0, changed state to up
DCERouter(config-if)#end
DCERouter#
```

5. The results of the show controllers command now indicates that each end acknowledges the existence of the clock signal.

```
DCERouter#show controllers s0/0
Interface Serial0/0
Hardware is PowerQUICC MPC860
DCE V.35, clock rate 2000000
```

```
DTERouter#show controllers s0/0
Interface Serial0/0
Hardware is PowerQUICC MPC860
DTE V.35 TX and RX clocks detected.
```

6.   Again issue the show ip interface brief command on each router and notice that after configuration, the interfaces are in an up/up state.

```
DTERouter#sh ip interface brief
Interface     IP-Address     OK? Method Status          Protocol
Serial0/0     unassigned     YES unset  up              up
DTERouter#

DCERouter#sh ip interface brief
Interface     IP-Address     OK? Method Status          Protocol
Serial0/0     unassigned     YES unset  up              up
DTERouter#
```

## Criteria for Completion

You have completed this task when you have connected two routers with back-to-back V.35 cables and brought both interfaces to an up/up state.

# Phase

# 3

# Maintaining and Securing The Network

Phase 3 comprises many tasks that an administrator performs during the life of an established internetwork, including securing the infrastructure against active assaults, as well as more passive issues, such as spyware infiltration. In addition to spyware mitigation, this phase treats the issue of scanning for viruses and keeping your operating system current with the latest updates. Some of the tasks in this phase concentrate on authorizing users and their administrative groups for access to services and resources, denying others implicitly or outright.

Attacks on networks and their resources vary widely. This phase gives you some methods to combat the most popular attacks, in addition to ways to guard against such attacks in the first place by encrypting your data. Because accidents can compromise data every bit as much as malicious deeds, one of the tasks in this phase presents a strategy and method to back up your information, in preparation for just such an accident.

The tasks in this phase map to domains 2 and 3 in the objectives for the CompTIA Network+ exam.

# Task 3.1: Creating Local User Accounts

To be able to manage access to resources, you must create user accounts. A user account is a security object in an operating system that uses authentication to verify the identity of the user attempting to gain access to resources. If the user does not authenticate properly, whether by password, smart card, biometrics, or other means, the user account cannot be used to gain access to network resources.

Granting or denying access to resources sometimes involves great strategy. Perhaps you wish to list all the groups and individuals you want to have access to all of your network's resources. Perhaps, instead, you would rather do so for some resources, but because the list of those you want to deny access to some resources is shorter than the list of those you want to grant access, the best strategy might be to deny the short list instead of allowing the longer one.

Another strategy worth mentioning is how to come up with the user account names. One of the best-known and simplest methods is to use a person's first initial and last name concatenated to make a single string of letters, such as jjones for Jonathan Jones. The method you use is entirely up to you, but the best methods create a meaningful username that is not easy to guess, such as a user's three initials and the last four digits of their Social Security number. For example, jdj6789 might be the username for Jonathan D. Jones, whose Social Security number is 123-45-6789. This method is at once elegant in its security, with a middle initial no one really knows and the last four numbers of the Social Security, which even fewer know, and sensible in its use of personal information, not spelling out the name or using the entire Social Security number.

This task walks you through the steps necessary to create a local user account—one that exists only for the resources local to a particular computer, not across a domain—without delving any deeper than the foregoing discussion into the process of developing a naming convention. Later tasks test the access rights of such an account. If your network is made up of one or more domains, you may or may not have the necessary rights to manage users and groups. It is much more likely, however, that you have access to these objects on your own computer. Furthermore, local user accounts are all you need to master this concept on a small cadre of machines, porting what you learn to a larger, domain-based environment later in your studies or practice.

# Scenario

You have a computer on the network that you want to use to house collaborative folders for three company associates. At this point, you need to create user accounts for these individuals so that later you can exercise granular control over their access to the various resources you intend to create.

# Scope of Task

## Duration

This task should take about 20 minutes.

## Setup

For this task, you need to have room to set up two computers with a network connection to one another.

## Caveat

Local user accounts do not follow the user to other computers. For that type of central account repository, you must have a user domain as opposed to the simpler workgroup model, as well as some type of directory service, such as Microsoft's Active Directory. Additionally, you need some form of domain controller system to hold the user account objects and handle requests for authentication from domain member devices as users attempt to access their resources. Such a model is much more complex and beyond the scope of this book. This task and the related tasks in this phase seek only to convey the concept of secure accounts and resources, not to turn you into a domain administrator.

# Procedure

In this task, you create three local user accounts in preparation for resource access control.

## Equipment Used

For this task, you'll use only one of the two computers to create three local user accounts. In a later task, to test these accounts, you will use the other one. These computers require network access to each other.

## Details

You will need only one of the networked computers, the one that is to house the shared folders and the user accounts. The following steps guide you through the process of creating three user accounts, one for Ann Kaminski, one for Bob Underhill, and one for Cathy Sullivan.

1. On the computer's Desktop, right-click My Computer and choose Manage.

2. In the left pane of Computer Management, click the plus sign beside Local Users And Groups under System Tools to expand the category.

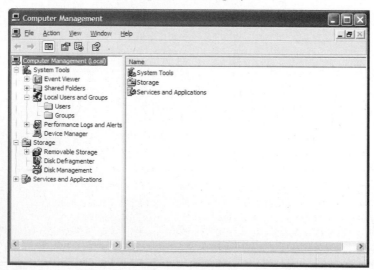

3.  Under Local Users And Groups, click the Users folder to produce the current list of user accounts that have been created on this computer.

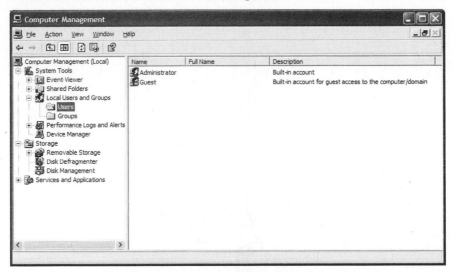

4.  Right-click in an unaffiliated (blank) portion of the right pane of the Computer Management window and then click New User on the shortcut menu.

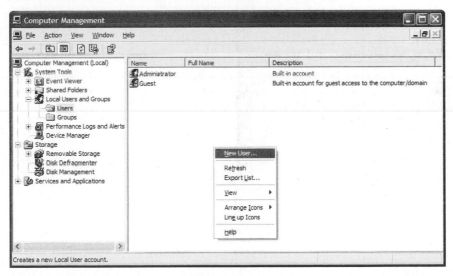

5.  In the New User dialog, the two most important and functional pieces of information are the User Name and Password fields (and, of course, the Confirm Password field, which must be the same as the Password field). Enter the username for Ann Kaminski

in accordance with your company's naming convention, as well as her initial password, which should be difficult to guess.

Optionally, include the full name of the user and a meaningful description of the account or the user.

6.  Because local accounts will not be used to log onto this computer's graphical interface but instead to simply control access to its resources, it is not advisable to make the user change their password at next logon. Conceivably, the user might never log on to the computer locally, but any access to the computer's resources will be restricted until the password is changed. Instead, remove the check mark from the top check box, which makes the second and third check boxes selectable. Place a check mark in the Password Never Expires box.

7.  Click the Create button to finalize the establishment of the account. The New User dialog clears and is ready for the second account. Enter similar information for Bob and Cathy, clicking the Create button after each one, and then click the Close button when you are finished.

8.  Note that in the following screen, all three new accounts are listed, along with their full names and descriptions.

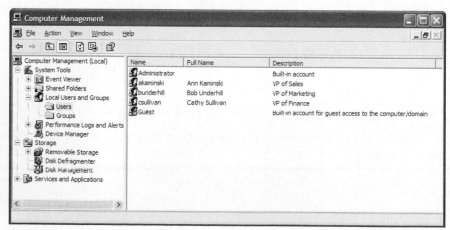

## Criteria for Completion

You have completed this task when you confirm that the three accounts are visible in the right pane of the Computer Management window while Users is selected in the left pane.

# Task 3.2: Creating Local User Groups

While creating user accounts is the first step toward assigning rights to users, user accounts alone leave a bit to be desired when it comes to actually assigning rights. Imagine hundreds, even thousands, of resources that must be guarded against unauthorized access. For each resource, you need to list each user granted access, with others being denied access, by default. Once you multiply the number of users by the number of resources, you begin to understand the sheer magnitude of the task at hand. The number of entries easily approaches the number you calculate. Such numbers are daunting even on the local level; envision the same scenario in a domain-wide setting.

Clearly, a solution is needed. Since the first networked operating systems, one solution has been to place user accounts into user groups that bind the member accounts by function or simply by general access policy. For example, instead of adding 20 user accounts to a resource, applying the exact same permissions for each user, why not build a user group that contains each user account and apply the permissions once to the group?

A single user account can be a member of multiple groups. Generally, the user enjoys a composite of all positive rights to a resource if their account is a member of multiple groups with varying rights. The user is granted all mutually exclusive rights and the best of all related rights. However, any denial of access to a resource for the members of a group trumps their positive access to the same resource by means of any other group. Such a priority placed on negative access makes it effortless to blacklist any user account. Simply place the "blacklist" group in every resource's access control list (ACL) with full denial of access associated with the group and then add individual user accounts to the group as needed and you have an efficient mechanism to deny radically anyone's access to all resources at any time. It is no difficult task to develop other strategies, as well, to limit individual access to certain resources through group membership on a more granular level.

## Scenario

You have a computer on the network that you want to use to house collaborative folders for three company associates. At this point, you need to create user groups to interrelate the user accounts of these individuals so that later you can exercise more efficient control over access to the various resources you intend to create compared with assigning rights to the actual user accounts individually.

## Scope of Task

### Duration

This task should take about 20 minutes.

### Setup

For this task, you need to have room to set up two computers with a network connection to one another.

### Caveat

Assigning rights and permissions to users, regardless of the method used, occasionally results in conflicts that can be rather difficult to troubleshoot. Furthermore, the same user accounts and groups are used to assign rights to resources shared across the network and to assign permissions to actual folders, files, and other resources. These rights and permissions combine or conflict, as mentioned earlier, causing sometimes unforeseen results that can take a bit of time to resolve.

## Procedure

In this task, you create three local user groups in preparation for resource access control.

### Equipment Used

For this task, you'll use one of the computers to create three local user groups. In a later task, to test these groups, you will use the other computer. These computers require network access to each other.

### Details

You will need only the first computer, the one that will house the shared folders and the user accounts and groups. The following steps guide you through the process of creating three user groups, one called Sales Planning, one called Advertising, and one called Receivables. Table 3.1 details the membership of these groups.

**TABLE 3.1**   Group Membership

| Group Name | Members |
| --- | --- |
| Sales Planning | akaminski (Sales), bunderhill (Mktg) |
| Advertising | bunderhill (Mktg), csullivan (Fin) |
| Receivables | akaminski (Sales), csullivan (Fin) |

1. On the computer's Desktop, right-click My Computer and choose Manage. This produces the Computer Management plug-in for the Microsoft Management Console (MMC).

2. In the left pane of the Computer Management window, click the plus sign beside Local Users And Groups under System Tools to expand this category.

3. Under Local Users And Groups, click the Groups folder to produce the current list of user groups that have been created on this computer, as seen in the following image.

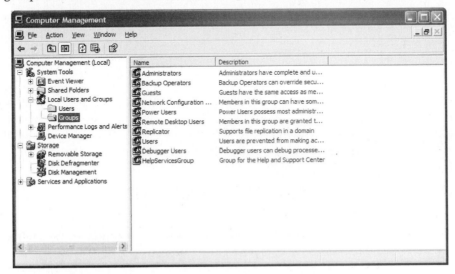

4. Right-click in an unaffiliated (blank) portion of the right pane of the Computer Management display to bring up a shortcut menu and then click New Group. This starts the New Group dialog, allowing you to enter the details for a new user group.

5. In the New Group dialog, shown next, start by giving the group a meaningful name and optionally supplying a potentially helpful description.

**6.** Click the Add button to begin the process of adding users to the group. The next image shows the Select Users dialog that pops up when you do.

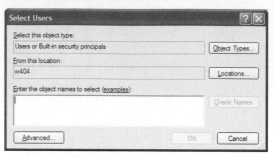

**7.** Type in the user account names for this group separated by semicolons (;) and click the OK button to go back to the New Group dialog. The following image shows the Select Users dialog with the akaminski and bunderhill user accounts typed in.

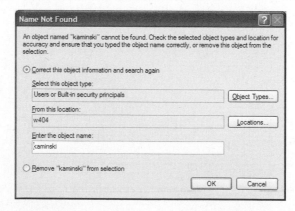

Optionally, to check your accuracy, you may elect to click the Check Names button, which will confirm your selections or give you the opportunity to correct those that are incorrect. The next image shows an example of the Check Names feature catching the omission of Ann Kaminski's first initial in her username.

**8.** As you can see in the following screen shot, which once again shows the New Group dialog, Ann and Bob's user accounts have been added to the Sales Planning group. Click the Create button to finalize the establishment of the Sales Planning group.

**9.** The New Group dialog stays open and clears out so you can create another group. Create all three groups as described in this task, following the detail in Table 3.1 and clicking the Create button after each one.

**10.** Finally, click the Close button to return to the Computer Management plug-in, where the three groups can be seen in the list of groups in the right pane.

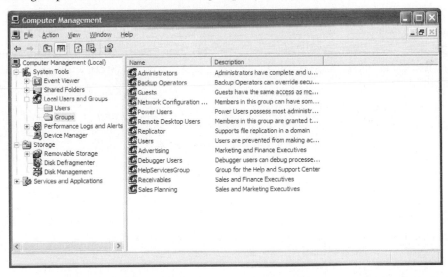

## Criteria for Completion

You have completed this task when you confirm that the three groups are visible in the right pane of the Computer Management display while Groups is selected in the left pane and you confirm that each group's membership matches the details in Table 3.1.

# Task 3.3: Managing Access to Resources

Once you have created user accounts and built groups with those accounts as members, you are ready to begin protecting your resources with access control lists (ACLs). There is a difference between protecting them from network access and protecting them from local access. You can allow access to a resource for those that are authorized to log on to the computer and at the same time deny access to anyone attempting to get to the resource from the network.

However, keep in mind that a user account can belong to two or more groups, and denial of access to a resource for one of the groups overrides permission for access to the same resource by another group. By the same token, if a user has the rights to access a resource from across the network but their user account is denied permission to access the local file, the net effect is that they have no access. Therefore, great care must be taken when securing resources. Otherwise, time might have to be spent investigating why Norm from Accounting can't access the server containing the company books.

## Scenario

You have a computer on the network that you want to use to house collaborative folders for three company associates. At this point, you need to create the folders and assign the rights and permissions to allow the appropriate groups access to the resources without allowing unauthorized access.

## Scope of Task

### Duration

This task should take about 30 minutes.

### Setup

For this task, you need to have room to set up two computers with a network connection to one another.

### Caveat

Even though you might follow this task to the letter, you may find that resources remain inaccessible despite your best effort to the contrary. This could be due to domain-level Group Policy settings that you might not have access to change. Consult your network administrator if you suspect such a restriction on the machine you are using to practice with.

## Procedure

In this task, you create three shared folders and restrict access to only two out of three executive user accounts per folder, using the groups you created for Task 3.2, "Creating Local User Groups."

## Equipment Used

For this task, you'll use one computer to create three local folders. If you use another computer to test access, the two computers require network access to each other.

## Details

The folders will be created on the computer that contains the local user accounts and groups. The following steps guide you through the process of creating and sharing three folders, one called Sales and Marketing, one called Marketing and Finance, and one called Sales and Finance. Table 3.2 details the initial access that is to be granted to each of these shares.

**TABLE 3.2**   Resource Access

| Resource Name | Group with Access |
| --- | --- |
| Sales and Marketing | Sales Planning |
| Marketing and Finance | Advertising |
| Sales and Finance | Receivables |

1.  On the computer's Desktop, right-click any unaffiliated area and choose New ➢ Folder. This creates a new folder on the Desktop.

2.  The default name for the folder you created is New Folder. Rename the folder Sales and Marketing.

3.  Right-click your new folder and choose Sharing And Security. This takes you to the Sharing tab of the Sales And Marketing Properties dialog.

4. By default, your folder is not shared. Fill in the radio button beside Share This Folder to activate the bottom portion of the page, automatically reproducing the folder name as the share name, as shown in the next screen shot.

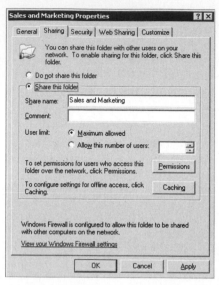

5. Click the Permissions button to generate the Share Permissions tab of the Permissions dialog for your folder. The following image shows that the built-in Everyone group, which includes all users, has Read access across the network to this resource by default.

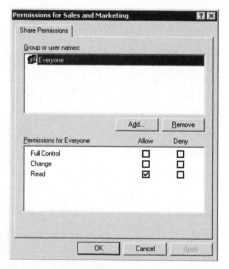

6. Click the Add button to spawn the Select Users Or Groups dialog. Type in the groups that you want to give or deny access to the resource and press Enter. The following image shows the Select Users Or Groups dialog with the Sales Planning user group typed in. Click the OK button.

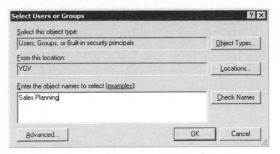

7. With Sales Planning selected on the Share Permissions tab, click the check box for Full Control in the Allow column.

8. It is too permissive to leave the Everyone group with access, so click the Everyone entry in the Group Or User Names pane and then click the Remove button. This results in the complete removal of the Everyone group from the ACL. Click the OK button to return to the Sharing tab of the Sales and Marketing Properties dialog.

Note that because all user accounts are in the Everyone group, its removal from the ACL tacitly denies anyone who is not explicitly permitted. Only members of the Sales Planning group are explicitly permitted. There is a subtle difference between this passive denial and the explicit denial that occurs when an account is in a group that is denied access overtly. If you explicitly deny the Everyone group, you shut down the resource for every account regardless of what other positive access a user has by virtue of their own account or other group membership. However, in this case, only those members of Everyone not also in the Sales Planning group get denied access to the resource—subtle, indeed.

9. Now, click on the Security tab. This is where you provide local access rights to the resource. These rights are combined with the share-level permissions to provide the effective rights for the object when it's accessed from the network. If you have specific reasons not to allow local access to anyone logged on to the computer—keep in mind you can limit who is allowed to log on to a computer, if that's an issue—adjust this step to include only those accounts or groups to be permitted access. Go through the same process you went through earlier and add the Everyone group. Again, using what you learned earlier,

remove every other account. Give the Everyone group Full Control permission over the local resource. Doing so makes certain that the individuals you intend to have access from across the network are not stymied by a restrictive local policy. The following screen shot shows the end result. Click the OK button to complete the share.

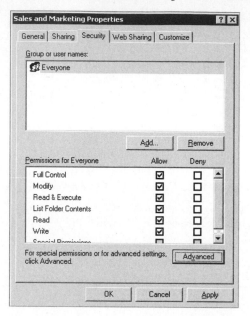

Most administrators reverse the logic of this step. The industry preference is to open shares completely to the Everyone group while restricting more specifically at the NTFS file level. That way, the rights are kept with the object, not with the share, which only points to the object. This makes troubleshooting access issues easier later. One catch: this strategy only works with NTFS filesystems. The strategy used here provides decent security for non-NTFS filesystems that have no file-level security.

**10.** It is possible, depending on the group policy implemented on your network, to check the shared resource you just created right on the same computer. If you wish to try this, open the Run dialog by choosing Start ➤ Run. Type **\\localhost** in the Open field and then click the OK button to try to bring up your own machine's list of shares. If this does not work, you might have to substitute your computer's IP address for the name localhost.

**11.** Once you produce the list of shares for your computer, right-click Sales and Markcting and select Map Network Drive. This begins the Map Network Drive dialog.

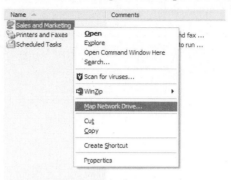

**12.** Go with the default drive letter (N in the screen shot that follows) or change to another available one. The folder name is filled in for you automatically.

**13.** Click the Different User Name link to open the Connect As dialog. The example here shows Ann Kaminski's username entered, along with her password. Once the dialog is filled out, click the OK button to negotiate the connection to the share.

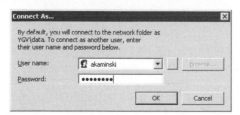

**14.** Open My Computer and note the existence of a network drive under the drive letter you assigned to this resource. The fact that total size and free space measurements are given for your mapped drive indicates that you have attached to the share successfully.

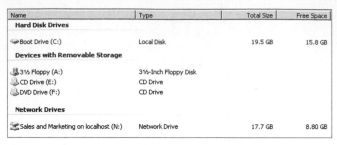

| Name | Type | Total Size | Free Space |
|---|---|---|---|
| **Hard Disk Drives** | | | |
| Boot Drive (C:) | Local Disk | 19.5 GB | 15.8 GB |
| **Devices with Removable Storage** | | | |
| 3½ Floppy (A:) | 3½-Inch Floppy Disk | | |
| CD Drive (E:) | CD Drive | | |
| DVD Drive (F:) | CD Drive | | |
| **Network Drives** | | | |
| Sales and Marketing on localhost (N:) | Network Drive | 17.7 GB | 8.80 GB |

**15.** If double-clicking the entry in My Computer brings up a window similar to the following, then you have proven further that you have created a network-accessible share. This window pops up automatically when you check connectivity by mapping a drive to a network share remotely.

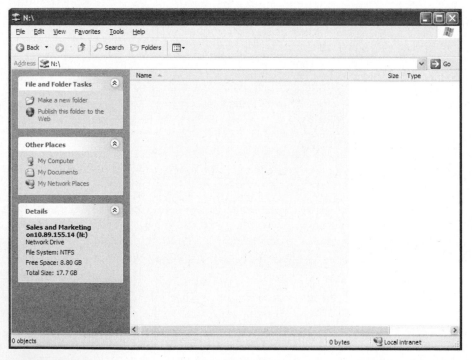

**16.** If you would like to see what happens when you try to access a resource without being authorized to do so, first disconnect from the network drive, which can be done by right-clicking its entry in My Computer and clicking Disconnect in the shortcut menu. Then enter Cathy Sullivan's credentials in an attempt to gain unauthorized access to the Sales and Marketing share.

When you try to access the share remotely, the status indicator is displayed. An error display similar to the following eventually pops up, indicating that Cathy could not be positively authenticated as Ann was and Bob would have been.

17. Notice that the entry returns to the My Computer output but that there are no drive-size specifications listed this time. That's because Cathy was denied access to the share, so the server did not bother to return these statistics.

Make sure to repeat this task for the other two shares and test to see whether the two appropriate executives can access each one while the unauthorized executive for each one cannot.

## Criteria for Completion

You have completed this task when you confirm that the two appropriate executives can access each folder while the unauthorized executive for each one cannot, based on the details of Table 3.2.

# Task 3.4: Disabling Local User Accounts

Inevitably, all companies experience churn; employees come, employees go. Overall, however, barring a major reorganization, the corporate structure tends to remain constant. In other words, in larger organizations, there is always a CEO, always a head of HR, always one or more IT folks running around like the proverbial headless chicken. If any of these employees move on to other pursuits, it is highly likely that someone will come along to take their place.

A user account is named for the individual that uses its credentials, but the value is not in the name. The true identity associated with a user account is in the rarely seen, fairly unattractive alphanumeric code associated with it. Microsoft, for example, calls this code a security identifier (SID). Every object in the directory has one. By virtue of the SID, you can change the account's name and password, and hence the logon characteristics of the account, without altering the SID. Because the access privileges are associated with the SID and not with the name of the account, when a secretary leaves the company and you know a replacement will be hired, you can simply deactivate the account and wait for the replacement to start work. At that time, changing the name and password for the account personalizes it for the new employee but keeps the job-related access the way it was so you don't have to figure it out again.

This is a very simple task to walk you through the process of disabling an existing user account, testing the result, and then re-enabling the account with new user information, again testing the result.

## Scenario

Ann Kaminski, VP of sales, has left the company. You need to rescind her access to network resources immediately but realize her position will be filled in the coming weeks. You want Ann's replacement to have access to the `Sales and Marketing` and the `Sales and Finance` shares. You decide to deactivate Ann's user account, leaving it in the Sales Planning and Receivables groups, so that the new VP of sales can be given immediate access when the time comes.

## Scope of Task

### Duration

This task should take about 20 minutes.

### Setup

For this task, you need to have room to set up two computers with a network connection to one another.

### Caveat

Disabling an account is only one step toward preventing access by a former associate. You also, to the extent of your abilities and influence, must make sure no administrative console remains open (that is, someone has logged onto it) at the same time it is left unattended. In such a case, the console becomes a potential security risk. Anyone wishing to re-enable the account or to create a new account with even greater privileges needs only to know how to do so—no hacking required.

Deactivation of accounts for departing personnel and then reactivating them when replacements are hired is a shortcut not all organizations condone. While the majority of enterprises might well allow such a practice, you might be in violation of a strict policy that states that all new personnel must begin with a security template that is to be added to for additional access rights, regardless of the position they hold.

## Procedure

In this task, you first disable the user account of Ann Kaminski. After testing the effects of disabling her account, you change the name on the account to David Elliot and subsequently prove that David is capable of accessing the same resources that Ann once could.

## Equipment Used

For this task, you need the computer with the user accounts and groups and the Sales and Marketing share. To test remote access, you will need at least one more computer. These computers require network access to each other.

## Details

The following steps guide you through the process of disabling the user account of Ann Kaminski and converting it to that of David Elliot.

1. On the computer's Desktop, right-click My Computer and choose Manage. This produces the Computer Management plug-in for the Microsoft Management Console (MMC).

2. In the left pane of the Computer Management window, click the plus sign beside Local Users And Groups under System Tools to expand this category.

3. Under Local Users And Groups, click the Users folder to produce the current list of user accounts that have been created on this computer.

4. In the right pane, double-click the akaminski account name to bring up the akaminski Properties page. Click the check box next to Account Is Disabled.

**5.** It might be necessary to manually sever all of Ann Kaminski's ties to the server. To do so, in Computer Management, expand the `Shared Folders` entry in the left pane. Then click the `Sessions` entry and right-click in the right pane on the entry AKAMINSKI, if it exists. Select Close Session from the shortcut menu, as displayed in the next image.

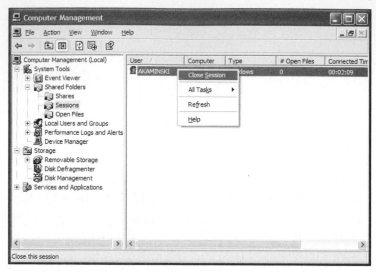

Also, you might need to sever the network connection on the computer you have been using to test Ann Kaminski's access to her resources. This can be done by simply logging off of the computer and then back on.

**6.** Using Ann's credentials, attempt to map a network drive to the `Sales and Marketing` share, as before. You are met with the following denial of access message.

**7.** In Computer Management, under Local Users And Groups, click the `Users` folder to bring back up the current list of user accounts that have been created on this computer. In the right pane, right-click the akaminski user account name and select Rename from the shortcut menu, making the user name editable. Change the name to delliot, for David Elliot, and press Enter.

**8.** (Optional) Right-click on the new name and click Set Password in the shortcut menu if you would like to change Ann's old password to something new for David.

**9.** Double-click the delliot account name to open the delliot Properties dialog. Remove the check mark from the box labeled Account Is Disabled. Note that the rest of Ann's information followed David. Note also, by clicking the Member Of tab, that David retained Ann's membership in the Sales Planning group, as shown in the next screen shot.

10. Map a network drive to the `Sales and Marketing` share, using David Elliot's new credentials.

11. Note that in the following screen shot, DELLIOT shows up in the Sessions display of Computer Management, indicating successful use of his recycled credentials.

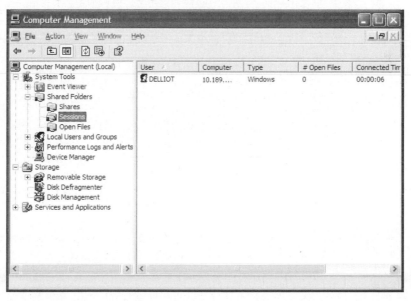

## Criteria for Completion

You have completed this task when you have disabled Ann Kaminski's account, confirmed lack of authorization, and then re-enabled the account for use by David Elliot, confirming authorization under his credentials.

# Task 3.5: Setting Password Restrictions

In the lab, simple passwords with no restrictions are great. If you choose to leave a password blank by not setting one, less effort is required to log on the dozens of times you might need to in order to carry out the various experiments you set out to perform. However, in production, the complexity of passwords and restrictions you place on them provide more security for your network than any well-thought-out user account naming convention. Theoretically, passwords are never seen by anyone, unlike usernames. In fact, you rarely see your own passwords; all you see is just a series of asterisks or bullets, each one representing a character of your password.

Due to the hassle associated with remembering new passwords, most users would never change their passwords if left to their own devices. As a result, it's incumbent upon the network administrator to set password policy requirements for the user population. Configurable requirements include how often a password can be reused, how often passwords expire, how often a user can change their password, the minimum number of characters a password must have, and the minimum complexity allowed in choosing a password.

This task explores each one of these parameters, getting you to test restrictions where possible.

## Scenario

You have had reports of resources on the network changing mysteriously, sometimes when only one associate has had authorization to access the resource. Some cases result in a complete and permanent loss of critical information. When you consult system logs, you realize that access to the resource sometimes occurred at times during the day or night when the owner of the credentials was not at their station. Your interpretation of this information is that account passwords have been compromised. Your solution is to begin enforcing password restrictions that will force all users to choose stronger passwords, and you will hold users to a stricter password policy, making this type of crime harder to commit.

## Scope of Task

### Duration

This task should take about 30 minutes.

## Setup

For this task, you need a single computer on which you can create user accounts or change the passwords of existing accounts so you can test some of the restrictions.

## Caveat

It is possible to overdo the password restrictions for your network. There is a fine line between the perfect password policy and going overboard. The line is not always easily defined and it varies, but the administrator tends to know when the users feel the line has been crossed. Just be careful not to trust this mechanism solely, and keep in mind that users tend to prefer more lax policies, even to their own detriment.

This task adjusts local Group Policy on a computer. Domain-level group policy trumps local-level group policy, sometimes making local policy adjustment impossible. When possible, an administrator is advised to adjust domain-level group policies, which are strikingly similar to the local policy settings, just farther reaching in scope.

One last note: don't use your regular account to change passwords. Start with your account, but follow the procedure to make David Elliot an administrator. Then use his account, just in case you lock him out. That way, you can always get back into your regular administrator account and set David back up properly without ever having to use his lost password.

# Procedure

In this task, you adjust five separate password restrictions, testing the effect of those that you can.

## Equipment Used

For this task, you only need a single computer, but you must have administrative privileges on the computer and the effective rights to make the adjustments set forth in this task.

## Details

The following steps instruct you on how to access the local security policy for a computer and how to adjust password restrictions.

### Preparation

1.  To keep from locking yourself out of your own administrative account (by forgetting passwords), place David Elliot's account in the local Administrators group, and then log off as yourself and back on as David. Earlier tasks can assist you with this task.

**2.** Open Control Panel and double-click the Administrative Tools applet to display the list of tools available to you.

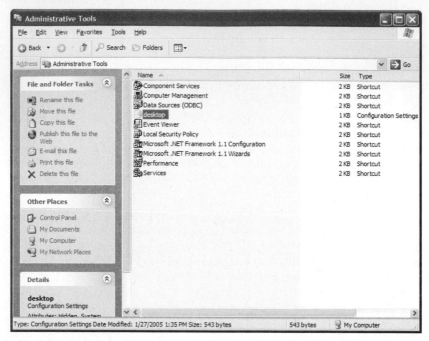

**3.** Double-click the Local Security Policy shortcut in the list to bring up the MMC with the Security Settings plug-in.

If you were able to complete these first three steps, proceed to step 11. If you see no Administrative Tools applet in Control Panel or if Local Security Policy is not one of the shortcuts that you see, you can follow this alternative procedure, starting with step 4.

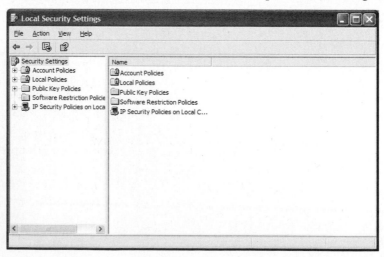

**4.**  Click Start ➤ Run and enter **mmc** in the Open field to bring up a generic MMC console and then maximize the Console Root floating window to produce a display similar to the following image.

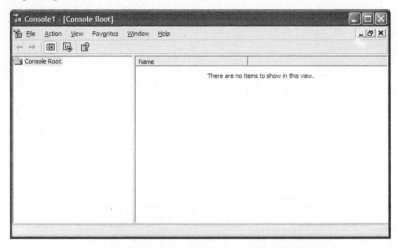

**5.**  Click File ➤ Add/Remove Snap-In to bring up a dialog that allows you to choose your own MMC snap-ins, as shown next.

**6.** Click the Add button to spawn the Add Standalone Snap-In dialog. Scroll down, if necessary, and click Group Policy Object Editor, which you see highlighted in the following screen shot.

**7.** Click the Add button to bring up the Select Group Policy Object Wizard.

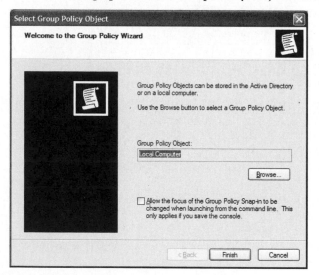

**8.** Click the Finish button to keep your configuration on the local computer. Doing so takes you back to the Add Standalone Snap-In dialog, but if you can see the Standalone tab of the Add/Remove Snap-In dialog, you might notice that there is a Local Computer Policy entry in the previously empty snap-in list.

**9.** Click the Close button in the Add Standalone Snap-In dialog to go back to the Add/Remove Snap-In dialog, which now looks like the following. Click the OK button to leave the Add/Remove Snap-In dialog.

**10.** Click the OK button to leave the Add/Remove Snap-In dialog and then expand Local Computer Policy ➢ Computer Configuration ➢ Windows Settings ➢ Security Settings, finally clicking Security Settings, as seen next, which brings you to the same display that Local Security Policy in Administrative Tools would have.

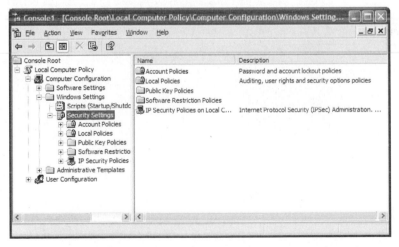

**11.** Regardless of the method used to get to this point, expand `Account Policies` and click `Password Policy` to produce the following display.

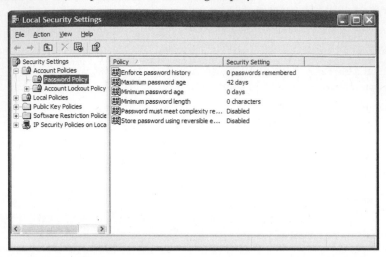

**12.** In the right pane, make sure all settings match settings in the previous screen shot. For the ones that do not, double-click the entry in the Policy column to adjust the setting. You will be setting only one of these at a time in the following steps, returning to the setting shown here before changing any other setting.

### Enforce Password History

**1.** In the right pane, double-click Enforce Password History to bring up its Properties dialog. Use the spinner buttons (arrows) to change the value to 2. Then click the Apply button, leaving the Properties dialog open because you will need it again shortly.

**2.** Press Ctrl+Alt+Delete to bring up the Windows Security display and click the Change Password button to enter the Change Password dialog. Change the password to something different, but be sure to remember this password because it will be the one you stay with for the time being. Forgetting it could lock you out. It is for this reason you should not be using an important account for this task.

3. Repeat the previous step again and try to change the password back to the previous setting. You receive the error message "Your password must be at least 0 characters and cannot repeat any of your previous 2 passwords...."

4. Click the OK button to clear the message.

5. Press the Esc key to return to Windows without changing your password.

6. Change Enforce Password History back to 0, which indicates that a password history will not be kept. Then click the OK button.

Note that a value of 0 is not advisable, and the default value of 1 is designed to avoid accidental entry of the same password during a change, not necessarily to prohibit early reuse of a password. Setting the minimum password age, coming up shortly, to greater than 0 tends to discourage rifling through dummy passwords in one sitting to get back to the current password during a mandatory change.

## Maximum Password Age

Back at the Security Settings plug-in, double-click Maximum Password Age in the right pane to display the Maximum Password Age dialog, which shows that the default length of time a user may have the same password is 42 days.

Changing the setting to 0 indicates that the password will never expire, which is not a wise choice for a secure network. Individual accounts can still be set to never expire even though you set the password to expire after a certain number of days by default. Furthermore, be careful not to set this value too low or you may have dissention in the ranks. If you set the number too high, you might as well be setting the password to never expire. A happy medium, such as the default of 42, is advised.

Even setting this control to 1 day is difficult to test, so feel free to experiment with this setting as your situation permits.

## Minimum Password Age

1. At the Security Settings plug-in, double-click Minimum Password Age in the right pane. Note that a setting of 0 days means that you can change your password with no delay from the previous change. Such freedom defeats the purpose of enforcing a password history because users are able to rotate through enough passwords, practically instantaneously, until they are once again allowed to use an old favorite. However, leaving this value at the default of 0 enables an administrator to set a user's password and then force the user to change the password to one of their own choosing the next time they log on.

2. Change the value to 1 day, and click the Apply button.

3. Press Ctrl+Alt+Delete to bring up the Windows Security display and click the Change Password button to enter the Change Password dialog. Change the password to something different, but be sure to remember it.

4. Repeat the previous step again and try to change the password to anything else. You receive the error message "The password on this account cannot be changed at this time."

5. Click the OK button to clear the message.

6. Press the Esc key to return to Windows without changing your password. Change Minimum Password Age back to 0 days and click the OK button.

### Minimum Password Length

1. At the Security Settings plug-in, double-click Minimum Password Length in the right pane. This brings up the Minimum Password Length Properties page. Note that a setting of 0 characters means that you are not required to enter a password; you can leave it blank and just press Enter to log on after supplying the username. Such a setting defeats the concept of security almost single-handedly.

2. Change the value to 9 characters and click the Apply button.

3. Press Ctrl+Alt+Delete to bring up the Windows Security display and click the Change Password button to enter the Change Password dialog. Attempt to change the password to something with eight or fewer characters. You receive the error message "Your password must be at least 9 characters and cannot repeat any of your previous 0 passwords...."

4. Click the OK button to clear the message.

5. Press the Esc key to return to Windows without changing your password. Change Minimum Password Length back to 0 characters and click the OK button.

### Password Must Meet Complexity Requirements

1. At the Security Settings plug-in, double-click Password Must Meet Complexity Requirements in the right pane. This produces this restriction's Properties page, as shown next with the Enable radio button filled in already.

2. Make sure the Enable button is filled in and click the Apply button. This enforces the following complexity requirements:

   - The password cannot contain any part of the user's account name.

   - The password must exhibit three of the following four characteristics: uppercase English letters, lowercase English letters, digits 0 through 9, and special characters, such as punctuation.

3. Press Ctrl+Alt+Delete to bring up the Windows Security display and click the Change Password button to enter the Change Password dialog. Assuming a minimum password length of 6, examples of violations are password, passw0rd, pa$$word, Pa$$, and Password. Examples of legal passwords are Passw0rd, pa$$w0rd, and Pass;!. Attempt to

change the password to something that violates any of the complexity requirements. You receive the error message "Your password must be at least 0 characters; cannot repeat any of your previous 0 passwords; must contain capitals, numerals, or punctuation; and cannot contain your account or full name."

**4.** Click the OK button to clear the message.

**5.** Press the Esc key to return to Windows without changing your password. Disable this feature and click the OK button.

## Criteria for Completion

You have completed this task when you have made the recommended password settings and tested the changes where possible.

# Task 3.6: Mitigating the Ping of Death

As a general rule, the ping utility is a valuable tool for validating remote IP host availability, confirming local node connectivity in the same instant. However, in the wrong hands, the ping utility can become a destructive force of mammoth proportions. In fact, when wielded maliciously, the ping utility can generate the "ping of death," a seemingly incessant barrage on one or more key hosts that can bring a network (including its primary resources) to its knees. Administrators often go to great lengths to match network bandwidth and equipment throughput to the projected needs of their infrastructure. It doesn't take much outside of the original plan to throw this delicate balance into a death spiral.

While the very act of intercepting Internet Control Message Protocol (ICMP) echo request packets is resource consuming in itself, some devices are better equipped to act as a lone bastion so that others need not endure what may prove, in their case, to be an intolerable level of extraneous traffic. Although it might seem that one interface on your router is being asked to take the brunt of the attack, realize that it would anyway if it's the only path into your internetwork. The same interface also would have to undergo the added strain of return traffic because CPU-involving echo replies are generally sent back out the interface on which the echo requests arrived, compounding the lack of availability for legitimate traffic.

By establishing an inbound ACL on the ingress interface, you lessen the loss of resources, such as using router CPU cycles to continue processing bogus traffic rather than blocking it at the door to begin with. Resources in the form of router backplane bandwidth and outbound interface queues can be preserved to a greater degree as well. Even bandwidth external to the router and the other host resources that are able to remain dedicated to their original intent must be considered as part of your victory over one of the simplest yet most egregious denial of service (DoS) attacks known.

This task shows you how to establish an ACL on a Cisco 2611XM router that watches for and denies access to inbound ICMP echo requests, thereby possibly improving the overall performance of your enterprise network.

# Scenario

The administrator of a principal file server in your internetwork has reported to you that an excessive amount of ICMP traffic has been detected inbound to the server. As the administrator of the router that leads to the Internet, it is in your power to restrict the number of ICMP packets that make their way into your network. You wish to make sure that associates attached through a RAS server external to the router are still allowed to test connectivity to the LAN interface on the router. You want every other ICMP echo request packet sourced on the Internet side of the router to be denied access through the router, thus relieving the malicious ICMP load on the file server. You intend to allow all other ICMP traffic so that normal network operation is not compromised.

# Scope of Task

## Duration

This task should take about 45 minutes.

## Setup

For this task, you need space to set up a Cisco router and the computer to configure it, as well as any optional equipment to create the scenario presented here.

## Caveat

Access lists can be employed in many ways and in many locations, but there are general recommendations to guide you to choose the best method. The interface to which you apply the access list and the direction in which you apply it to that interface affect how the access list will perform. This task uses an extended IP access list, which is best placed inbound as close to the source of the traffic as allowable. Therefore, it would be less efficient, and possibly ineffective, to place the access list anywhere but inbound on the router interface closest to the Internet. Furthermore, when any two ACL statements overlap, the more specific of the two must be placed before the other or the less specific statement will block the more specific one from ever being matched.

   Not all ICMP traffic is bad or malicious. In fact, sometimes, in the proper hands, all ICMP traffic is favorable. As a result, when one type of ICMP traffic is targeted for restriction, be careful not to lump all ICMP traffic together, leading to undesirable situations. For example, stopping all ICMP traffic to prevent inbound echo requests also restricts pings and trace routes sourced from inside the local network, ensuring that replies to messages sent out are blocked as they return.

# Procedure

In this task, you create an IP access list on a Cisco router to control a certain type of ICMP traffic known as echo requests while allowing certain such requests as well as all other ICMP traffic.

## Equipment Used

For this task, you need a single Cisco router with at least three Ethernet interfaces. Optionally, any pairing of interface types can be made to work, in theory, with at least one additional router necessary if serial interfaces are used. If testing the task's results is desired, three computers, as well as hubs, switches, or crossover cables, are necessary.

## Details

The following steps guide you through the process of securing assets against the threat of an ICMP attack. Figure 3.1 shows a sample portion of an internetwork that will be referenced throughout this task.

1.  Enter Global Configuration mode.

    ```
    noPoD#config t
    noPoD(config)#
    ```

2.  The first line of the access list for the VPN subnet is the most specific line of the three overlapping lines to be entered. Therefore, it must come first. This line states that any ICMP traffic coming from any device in the 172.16.50.128 subnet destined for the host at address 172.16.50.65 is allowed to pass. This makes sure that pinging the internal interface on router noPoD from a VPN connection through the RAS server is allowed but pinging any other LAN interface is not.

    ```
    noPoD(config)#access-list 100 permit icmp 172.16.50.128
    ➥0.0.0.31 host 172.16.50.65
    noPoD(config)#
    ```

**FIGURE 3.1**    Sample network

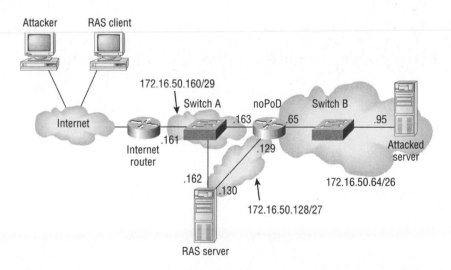

3. The second line is more specific than the third line but less so than the first. If you specify this line first, pinging the router interface at address 172.16.50.65 from a RAS client fails. If you specify it last, unwanted ICMP traffic over the VPN is not deterred.

```
noPoD(config)#access-list 100 deny icmp any 172.16.50.64
➥0.0.0.63 echo
noPoD(config)#
```

4. The last line of the access list ensures that all other traffic based on IP is allowed to pass normally, which includes all other ICMP traffic.

```
noPoD(config)#access-list 100 permit ip any any
noPoD(config)#
```

5. The access list for the public interface of the noPoD router is a bit simpler. All echo requests coming in on this interface must be blocked, but all other ICMP traffic must be allowed. The first line filters all ping requests, while the second one allows all other IP-based traffic to pass, including any other ICMP traffic.

```
noPoD(config)#access-list 150 deny icmp any 172.16.50.64
➥0.0.0.63 echo
noPoD(config)#access-list 150 permit ip any any
noPoD(config)#
```

6. Applying the access lists to the proper interfaces is that final step in securing the LAN against malicious ICMP traffic. The following lines of configuration establish the IP identities of the interfaces as well as apply the appropriate access lists where they belong. Note that the internal LAN interface of the router does not have an access list applied to it. There is no need.

```
noPoD(config)#interface f0/0
noPoD(config-if)#ip address 172.16.50.129 255.255.255.224
noPoD(config-if)#ip access-group 100 in
noPoD(config-if)#interface f0/1
noPoD(config-if)#ip address 172.16.50.163 255.255.255.248
noPoD(config-if)#ip access-group 150 in
noPoD(config-if)#interface f1/0
noPoD(config-if)#ip address 172.16.50.65 255.255.255.192
noPoD(config-if)#
```

7. Exit configuration.

```
noPoD(config-if)#end
noPoD#
```

## Criteria for Completion

You have completed this task when you have configured your router as noted and optionally tested access restrictions using equipment and connections similar to those outlined in Figure 3.1. You may substitute two computers, one for the entire public connection and one for the RAS server, in order to test your configuration more easily. Keep in mind that crossover Ethernet cables are required when connecting computers to routers.

# Task 3.7: Securing Links between Routers

Two of the most commonly secured types of communication between routers are at a low level over the link itself, using the Point-to-Point Protocol (PPP) and, at higher levels through a dynamic routing protocol, such as OSPF, using MD5 encrypted authentication, for example. Without interrouter security, you open your network to man-in-the-middle attacks. Such attacks are perpetrated by connecting to a common network with the target router and influencing routing decisions with unauthorized advertisements. Additionally, legitimate advertisements can be intercepted transparently by others, thus giving attackers information about your private network to which they should not be privileged.

If PPP authentication fails, the two routers will sync up at the Physical layer but fail to connect at Layer 2. A shared password is used for the authentication. Depending on the authentication method you choose, additional security comes from never sending the password over the link between routers, as is the case with the Challenge Handshake Authentication Protocol (CHAP).

When MD5 encrypted authentication is used in routing updates, your router will refuse any unencrypted or improperly encrypted advertisements. Furthermore, advertisements with the incorrect authentication are refused as well. Additionally, those sent out by your router will be illegible to others that are not also set up to authenticate the same encrypted credentials as your router is.

This task guides you through securing your network using PPP authentication as well as MD5 encrypted authentication for OSPF advertisements.

## Scenario

The routers connecting Tokyo and LA carry mission-critical information that is also highly confidential. In an effort to minimize espionage and erroneous routing advertisements, you have decided to implement CHAP authentication over PPP between the sites as well as MD5 encrypted authentication between their OSPF processes.

## Scope of Task

### Duration

This task should take about 1 hour.

### Setup

For this task, you need space to set up two Cisco routers and a computer or another method to configure them.

### Caveat

As with other protocols, make sure that whatever methods you choose for authentication and encryption you use the same method at both ends of the link. Certain pairings, such as Microsoft's MS-CHAP and RFC-based CHAP, are compatible, but without testing these pairings, the best solution is to match protocols at both ends where possible. Additionally, matching passwords across a link is imperative. Not all passwords in the routing domain need to match, but across any given link, they must.

## Procedure

In this task, you establish connectivity between two routers using PPP and CHAP as well as OSPF and MD5.

### Equipment Used

For this task, you need two Cisco routers with at least one serial interface each. Optionally, if testing the task's results is desired, an Ethernet interface on each router and a device connected and synced up with the routers is ideal, but a single software loopback interface on each router can supply a network for advertisement to the other router.

### Details

The following steps guide you through the individual processes of securing routers against man-in-the-middle attacks. Figure 3.2 shows a sample portion of the internetwork referenced in this task.

#### PPP Authentication

This section of the task establishes strong authentication so that the link stays down until matching authentication is used at both ends.

1.  Enter Global Configuration mode on one of the routers. Start with Tokyo's router J in this example.

    ```
    RouterJ#config t
    RouterJ(config)#
    ```

**FIGURE 3.2** Task sample network

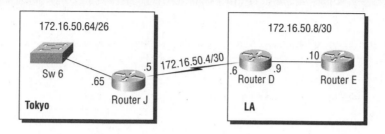

2. Establish login credentials for the remote device, router D. In the following command, the name after the `username` keyword is case sensitive and must match the remote device's hostname or the name configured with the `ppp chap hostname` interface configuration command on router D's opposing interface. The password must match the password configured in router D's `username` command or with the `ppp chap password` interface configuration command on router D's opposing interface.

```
RouterJ(config)#username RouterD password wiley
RouterJ(config)#
```

3. On the serial interface leading to router D, enter interface configuration mode and set the encapsulation to PPP.

```
RouterJ(config)#interface s0/0
RouterJ(config-if)#encapsulation ppp
RouterJ(config-if)#
```

4. Now that PPP is set as the interface's encapsulation method, PPP-specific commands become available. Set the authentication protocol to CHAP. If changing the encapsulation did not bring the link down and the interface was in an up/up condition, it switches to up/down, pending proper authentication, for which router D is not yet ready.

```
RouterJ(config-if)#ppp authentication chap
RouterJ(config-if)#
%LINEPROTO-5-UPDOWN: Line protocol on Interface Serial0/0, changed state to
down
RouterJ(config-if)#
```

5. Exit configuration.

```
RouterJ(config-if)#end
RouterJ#
```

6. With the exception of the `username` command, enter all corresponding commands for router D.

```
RouterD#config t
RouterD(config)#interface s0/0
```

```
RouterD(config-if)#encapsulation ppp
RouterD(config-if)#ppp authentication chap
RouterD(config-if)#
```

7.  Upon execution of the username command, note that the link is reestablished almost immediately.

```
RouterD(config-if)#exit
RouterD(config)#username RouterJ password wiley
RouterD(config)#
%LINEPROTO-5-UPDOWN: Line protocol on Interface Serial0/0,
    changed state to up
RouterD(config)#
```

8.  Exit configuration.

```
RouterD(config)#end
RouterD#
```

## OSPF with MD5 Encrypted Authentication

Although the link may be authenticated and in an up/up condition, OSPF might refuse to send advertisements across the PPP link until additional authentication is performed between both ends of the OSPF adjacency.

1.  Enter Global Configuration mode on one of the routers. Start with Tokyo's router J.

```
RouterJ#config t
RouterJ(config)#
```

2.  (Optional) Create a loopback interface and give it the identity of the Gigabit Ethernet interface in Figure 3.2. This aids in simulating the network without added equipment. If you have the additional equipment, feel free to configure the Ethernet address on the physical interface.

```
RouterJ(config)#interface loopback0
RouterJ(config-if)#ip address 172.16.50.65 255.255.255.192
RouterJ(config-if)#
```

3.  Enter Interface Configuration mode on the OSPF interface that connects to router D and ensure that its IP address is entered.

```
RouterJ(config)#interface s0/0
RouterJ(config-if)#ip address 172.16.50.5 255.255.255.252
RouterJ(config-if)#
```

4.  Set the password for authentication and set the password encryption type to MD5.

```
RouterJ(config-if)#ip ospf message-digest-key 1 md5 wiley
RouterJ(config-if)#
```

5.  Add all OSPF interfaces to the OSPF routing process under area 0 and require MD5 authentication for all interfaces in area 0.

```
RouterJ(config-if)#router ospf 1
RouterJ(config-router)#network 172.16.50.4 0.0.0.3 area 0
RouterJ(config-router)#network 172.16.50.64 0.0.0.63 area 0
RouterJ(config-router)#area 0 authentication message-digest
RouterJ(config-router)#
```

6.  Exit configuration.

```
RouterJ(config-router)#end
RouterJ#
```

7.  (Optional) Create a loopback interface on router D and give it the identity of the Gigabit Ethernet interface in Figure 3.2.

```
RouterD#config t
RouterD(config)#interface loopback0
RouterD(config-if)#ip address 172.16.50.9 255.255.255.252
RouterD(config-if)#
```

8.  With the exception of the ip ospf command on the serial interface, enter all corresponding commands for router D.

```
RouterD#config t
RouterD(config)#interface s0/0
RouterD(config-if)#ip address 172.16.50.6 255.255.255.252
RouterD(config-if)#router ospf 10
RouterD(config-router)#network 172.16.50.4 0.0.0.3 area 0
RouterD(config-router)#network 172.16.50.8 0.0.0.3 area 0
RouterD(config-router)#area 0 authentication message-digest
RouterD(config-router)#
```

9.  Exit configuration.

```
RouterD(config-router)#end
RouterD#
```

10. Issuing the show ip route command, note that only local interfaces exist in the routing table on both routers. The following output is from router J.

```
RouterJ#sh ip rout

[output omitted]

Gateway of last resort is not set
```

```
        172.16.0.0/16 is variably subnetted, 3 subnets, 3 masks
C       172.16.50.6/32 is directly connected, Serial0/0
C       172.16.50.4/30 is directly connected, Serial0/0
C       172.16.50.64/26 is directly connected, Loopback0
RouterJ#
```

11. Upon execution of the ip ospf command on router D's serial interface, using the same key ID (1) and password as on router J, note that the adjacency is formed almost immediately.

```
RouterD#config t
RouterD(config)#interface s0/0
RouterD(config-if)#ip ospf message-digest-key 1 md5 wiley
RouterD(config-if)#
%OSPF-5-ADJCHG: Process 10, Nbr 172.16.50.65 on Serial0/0 from
    LOADING to FULL, Loading Done
RouterD(config-if)#
```

12. Exit configuration.

```
RouterD(config-if)#end
RouterD#
```

13. Note that both routers now have complete routing tables. The following output is from router J.

```
RouterJ#sh ip rout

[output omitted]

Gateway of last resort is not set

        172.16.0.0/16 is variably subnetted, 4 subnets, 3 masks
O       172.16.50.9/32 [110/65] via 172.16.50.6, 00:01:56, Se0/1
C       172.16.50.6/32 is directly connected, Serial0/1
C       172.16.50.4/30 is directly connected, Serial0/1
C       172.16.50.64/26 is directly connected, Loopback0
RouterJ#
```

## Criteria for Completion

You have completed this task when you have configured your routers as described in the steps of the task. Optional confirmation of your configuration is encouraged.

# Task 3.8: Guarding against SYN Flood Attacks

Denial of service attacks are not limited to ICMP-based "ping of death" assaults. In fact, there are various other methods to impair network performance intentionally. One example is the "smurf" attack, where the source addresses of ping packets are falsified, thus affecting the initial target and an ultimate target, whose source address was used falsely, that receives the responses to these requests. Another example, known as a "fraggle" attack, uses UDP-based directed broadcasts, or UDP echoes, to achieve the same result, but usually on a smaller scale.

The topic of this task, however, is the SYN flood attack, in which the targeted machine is inundated with TCP segments requesting connections. These TCP segments are characterized by having only the SYN bit set in the TCP header, not the ACK bit. Recall that a TCP virtual connection is established using a three-way handshake. The device requesting the connection sends a TCP message to the intended target device with the SYN bit set in the TCP header. If the recipient is prepared to communicate, it returns a message with both the ACK and SYN bits set in the TCP header. The final step is for the original requester to return a TCP message with only the ACK bit set in the header.

Using this procedure, attackers tie up target devices by randomizing the source address of the packets and flooding the targets with initial SYN messages. When a target device responds to these messages, further tying up its own resources, it tends to compromise intermediate systems as they attempt to deliver the undeliverable, overflowing caches and exhausting resources. Your weapon against such an attack is to prohibit inbound messages seeking to establish a new TCP session. Only TCP connections sourced from the protected network are allowed to form.

## Scenario

Having taken care of the ICMP problem with the file server by making adjustments to the edge router, you realize that there is still something amiss. Suspecting other forms of attack, you decide to test for the existence of a SYN flood attack from the public network and, if necessary, take measures to control the attack.

## Scope of Task

### Duration

This task should take about 30 minutes.

### Setup

For this task, you need space to set up a Cisco router and the computer to configure it as well as any optional equipment to create the scenario presented here.

## Caveat

Denying the establishment of TCP connections from outside hosts is not, by itself, an effective method of attack mitigation if Internet-accessible servers exist on the internal network. In such cases, you might need additional tools and utilities to allow connections to be formed from the outside and still control malicious activity. One such solution involves VPNs, the use of a public network to form a private connection. Other methods scrutinize traffic more intently to avoid certain flows while allowing less-threatening ones. These more advanced methods are beyond the scope of this book.

# Procedure

In this task, you create an IP access list on a Cisco router to control SYN floods while allowing VPN TCP connections to be established by external hosts.

## Equipment Used

For this task, you need a single Cisco router with at least three Ethernet interfaces. Optionally, any pairing of interface types can be made to work, in theory, with at least one additional router being necessary if serial interfaces are used. If testing the task's results is desired, three computers, as well as hubs, switches, or crossover cables, are necessary.

## Details

The following steps guide you through the process of securing assets against a SYN flood attack. Figure 3.3 shows a sample portion of an internetwork that will be referenced throughout this task.

**FIGURE 3.3**    Task sample network

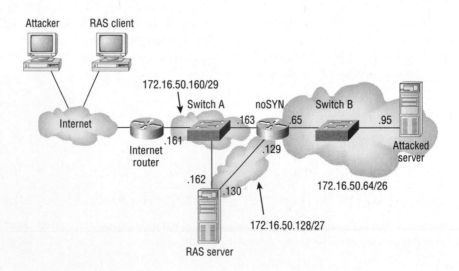

## Testing for SYN Flooding

The first step is to determine if SYN flooding appears to be occurring. There is no need to combat a problem that does not exist. The cure can be challenging enough to warrant avoiding when unnecessary. The method for accomplishing this is to set up an access list that permits the specific types of traffic that you are studying and to monitor the matches against each type.

1.  Enter Global Configuration mode.

    ```
    noSYN#config t
    noSYN(config)#
    ```

2.  Create an access list that tests for TCP segments to the attacked server that have and do not have only the SYN bit set in the header (not the ACK bit as well). Because this is a binary condition, either it is set or not, and because you cannot test first for just the SYN bit being set, test for the SYN bit not being set or having the ACK bit set as well.

    ```
    noSYN(config)#access-list 110 permit tcp any host 172.16.50.65
      ➥established
    noSYN(config)#
    ```

3.  Any messages that matched the previous statement have exited the access list. So, now that you have a line that matches TCP traffic without just the SYN bit set, all other TCP segments, by definition, have only the SYN bit set. These are the potential instruments of attack to which special attention should be paid. Nevertheless, it is not necessary at this juncture to block these data structures but rather simply to compare their numbers to those from the previous line of the access list.

    ```
    noSYN(config)#access-list 110 permit tcp any host 172.16.50.65
    noSYN(config)#
    ```

4.  Because it is not the intent to block any traffic yet, the last line of the access list ensures that all other traffic based on IP is allowed to pass normally, which includes all other TCP traffic.

    ```
    noSYN(config)#access-list 110 permit ip any any
    noSYN(config)#
    ```

5.  Apply the access list to inbound traffic on the external interface of the noSYN router.

    ```
    noSYN(config)#interface f0/0
    noSYN(config-if)#ip access-group 110 in
    ```

6.  After an arbitrary period of time, look at the number of hits to the different lines in the access list. An inordinate number of initial segments to this server might indicate that it is the victim of a SYN flood attack. The following output shows a normal distribution of TCP traffic.

```
noSYN(config-if)#end
noSYN#show access-lists 110
Extended IP access list 110
    10 permit tcp any any established (60 matches)
    20 permit tcp any any (6 matches)
    30 permit ip any any (14 matches)
noSYN#
```

If the established line in the access list has very few matches, this means the local server has not generated repeat traffic from the supposed source of the TCP connection requests, possibly because the source IP addresses of these requests were bogus. If this is the case, and if the other TCP line in the list has relatively many matches, meaning a flood of SYN segments has appeared on the interface, use the configuration in the next section to minimize the connections opened by external sources.

### Controlling SYN Flooding

This section guides you through the process of turning your test into a shield in order to block some of the traffic you started out only counting.

1.  Enter Global Configuration mode.

    ```
    noSYN#config t
    noSYN(config)#
    ```

2.  As when testing for a flood of SYN messages, the first step is to permit those non-initial TCP messages that are part of an established connection or negotiation.

    ```
    noSYN(config)#access-list 110 permit tcp any host 172.16.50.65
       ➥established
    noSYN(config)#
    ```

3.  Because this access list is to be applied to the public interface of the noSYN router, allowing all VPN traffic to pass regardless of its nature, it is safe to deny all other TCP traffic, meaning that initial SYN-only messages are not allowed.

    ```
    noSYN(config)#access-list 110 deny tcp any host 172.16.50.65
    noSYN(config)#
    ```

When you are unable to block all initial TCP segments, due to the public nature of the server or other host, it is possible to use the same access list presented in the previous section. However, to extract the necessary information to lead you to the perpetrator of the attack, add the keyword log-input to the end of step 3 in the previous section. Similar ACLs along the reverse path are required to trace completely back to the source.

4. Because it is not the intent to block any other traffic, the last line of the access list ensures that all other traffic based on IP, including all other TCP messages, is allowed to pass normally.

```
noSYN(config)#access-list 110 permit ip any any
noSYN(config)#
```

5. Apply the access list to inbound traffic on the external interface of the noSYN router.

```
noSYN(config)#interface f0/0
noSYN(config-if)#ip access-group 110 in
```

6. Exit configuration.

```
noSYN(config-if)#end
noSYN#
```

## Criteria for Completion

You have completed this task when you have configured your router as noted and optionally tested access restrictions using equipment and connections similar to those outlined in Figure 3.3. You may substitute two computers, one for the entire public connection and one for the RAS server, in order to test your configuration more easily. Keep in mind that crossover Ethernet cables are required when connecting computers to routers.

# Task 3.9: Implementing File-Level Encryption

Today's operating systems have an Encrypting File System (EFS) that allows the currently logged-on user to encrypt files and folders on-the-fly so that no one else, when logged on under their own credentials, can read the encrypted objects. Even temporary files that are created while editing an encrypted file are encrypted. When you copy or move a file into an encrypted folder, the new file inherits encryption from the folder regardless of the source file's encryption status. By contrast, copying or moving a file into an unencrypted folder causes the file to retain its original encryption status.

If you have a computer that multiple users are likely to log on to, you have information that needs to be restricted to a single individual, and the added complexity of administering user and group rights to such information is not warranted, then EFS is an ideal tool. Be aware, however, that this feature works only while the data remains on the encrypting volume or once it arrives on another. While in transit, the data is not encrypted by EFS, so other precautions must be taken to encrypt data on the network. Furthermore, whenever you open an encrypted file, it is decrypted for use and then re-encrypted for storage. Very little danger lies within this process. It is the transmission over unencrypted links that you must watch out for, depending on the confidentiality of the data.

# Scenario

As the administrator of a publicly used computer, you have important files and folders that must not be altered. You would rather not get into file permissions to block others from accessing the files but instead wish simply to encrypt the specific files and folders while you are logged in, making sure that visiting users cannot gain access to these files and compromise them.

# Scope of Task

## Duration

This task should take about 45 minutes.

## Setup

For this task, you need access to a single computer's Windows graphical user interface (GUI).

## Caveat

Although it is true that no one else can view the encrypted information when not logged on as the user who encrypted the data, when they gain access to the system under the credentials of the user that performed the encryption, there is nothing to stop them from viewing the encrypted information. This means unauthorized users should not be allowed to use the credentials of others for any reason and that systems should be locked or powered down when unattended. It also means that passwords should be difficult to guess.

For Windows, EFSs only work on the NTFS filesystem, but you cannot use it to encrypt system objects or compressed objects. Even though a file is encrypted, that does not mean it cannot be destroyed. An administrator, for instance, can delete an encrypted file even though they cannot read it. Deletion rights are based on permissions, not encryption. Encryption does not follow an object to a different filesystem, such as onto CD-ROMs, but encryption is retained on backups of the original object.

# Procedure

In this task, you create a folder and various files in order to observe the effects of the Encrypting File System.

## Equipment Used

For this task, you need one computer with an EFS-compatible operating system, such as Windows XP Professional.

## Details

In the following procedure, you create a couple of folders and a couple of files, manipulating their encryption and observing the effect of copying and moving encrypted and decrypted files into encrypted and decrypted folders.

## Encrypting Files and Folders

This section details how to configure encryption for files and folders as well as what to expect when copying or moving objects with encryption in mind.

1. On your Desktop, double-click My Computer to bring up a list of the drives in your computer, as seen next.

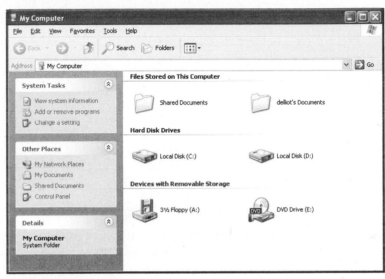

2. Double-click the icon of your primary hard drive and then right-click anywhere in the unaffiliated portion of the space in the rightmost pane and select New ➤ Folder.

3. Name the new folder Encryption and create a text document by right-clicking in the unaffiliated space in the right pane and clicking New ➤ Text Document, shown in the following image.

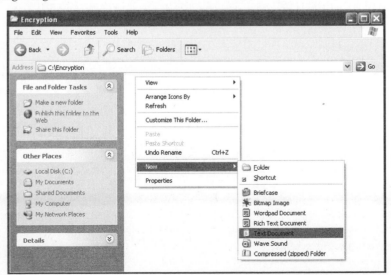

4.  Name the document Encrypted. Then create another text document and name it Decrypted.

5.  Right-click the file Encrypted and choose Properties to produce the General tab of the file's Properties dialog.

6. Click the Advanced button to bring up the Advanced Attributes dialog and then check the box labeled Encrypt Contents To Secure Data, as you see in the following image.

7. If the following Encryption Warning dialog pops up, fill in the radio button beside Encrypt The File Only and click the OK button.

8. If the fonts for the names of the Encrypted and Decrypted files are the same color, in the Windows Explorer window, click Tools ➢ Folder Options and select the View tab. Make sure there is a check mark in the box beside Show Encrypted Or Compressed NTFS Files In Color.

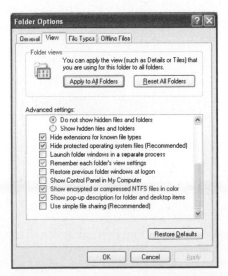

9. After clicking the OK button or if the preceding step was not necessary, notice whether the font of the name of the Encrypted file is different from that of the Decrypted file.

10. Create another folder in the Encryption folder and name it Copy or Move.

11. Encrypt the folder you just created in the same way that you encrypted the file earlier. The font of its name matches that of the encrypted file.

| Name ▲ | Size | Type | Date Modified | Attributes |
|---|---|---|---|---|
| Copy or Move | | File Folder | 5/2/2006 1:08 AM | AE |
| Decrypted | 0 KB | Text Document | 5/2/2006 1:07 AM | A |
| Encrypted | 0 KB | Text Document | 5/2/2006 1:08 AM | AE |

Another way to display whether objects are encrypted is to use the Details view in your folders and turn on the Attributes column. One attribute is the Encrypted attribute.

12. Copy or move the Encrypted and Decrypted files into the new folder. Open the folder and note the fact that because the folder has been set to encrypt its contents, by default, even the file named Decrypted has become encrypted.

13. Now, copy or move the files back to the Encryption folder and note that even though the Encryption folder is not set to encrypt its contents, objects placed in this decrypted folder retain their original encryption status.

14. Re-decrypt the file named Decrypted, reversing the procedure used earlier to encrypt an object.

## Determining Who Encrypted an Object

Occasionally, it becomes necessary to identify who encrypted an object so they can be contacted about decrypting it. If the user is no longer part of the organization, you have the option of reactivating their account and changing the password before logging on as them and decrypting the object. When all else fails, there is always the EFS recovery agent, which can decrypt objects without the user account that encrypted them.

1. Open a command prompt window and enter the command **efsinfo**. The following output shows what you can expect if you have not installed the executable from the Resource Kit.

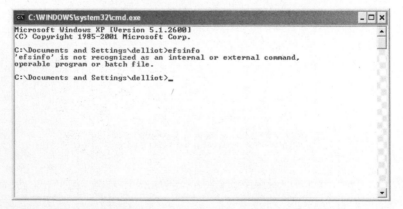

```
C:\WINDOWS\system32\cmd.exe                                              _ □ x
Microsoft Windows XP [Version 5.1.2600]
(C) Copyright 1985-2001 Microsoft Corp.

C:\Documents and Settings\delliot>efsinfo
'efsinfo' is not recognized as an internal or external command,
operable program or batch file.

C:\Documents and Settings\delliot>_
```

If, instead, the command executed without error, skip steps 2 through 11, which walk you through downloading the executable from Microsoft.

2. To install the executable that allows you to enter this command with success, first point your web browser to `www.microsoft.com/downloads`.

3. On the resulting web page, keep the default of All Downloads and, in the search field, enter **efsinfo** and either press the Enter key or click the Go button on the page.

4. This should result in something similar to the following. Don't concern yourself with the fact that you have a different operating system from the one displayed. Click the link in the result.

5. Go through the validation process, if required, installing the Windows Genuine Advantage software, if asked.

6. Once you are validated and taken to the download page, click the Download button near the top of the page. This produces the security warning shown next. If you wish to archive the file that installs the utility, click the Save button and navigate to where you want the file stored. Otherwise, simply click the Run button to start the installation process.

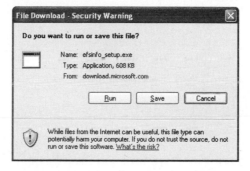

Note that you need to find the file you saved and run it to get to the same point as clicking the Run button without saving the file.

7. If you clicked the Run button earlier, you might see the following security warning pop-up, which simply asks you to confirm the fact that you wish to run this file. Click the Run button.

8. You see the following welcome screen, on which you click the Next button to continue to the EULA dialog.

9. Agree with the EULA, and click the Next button to bring up the Destination Directory dialog.

10. The default destination folder is \Program Files\Resource Kit on your primary hard drive volume, as shown for drive C in the following screen shot. Note the default and click the Install Now button to begin the installation.

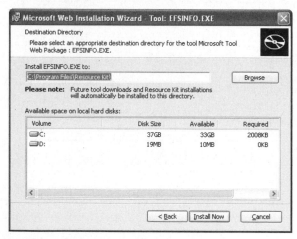

11. After the status bar runs across, you are taken to the final dialog for the installation. Click the Finish button to close the wizard.

12. The final steps refer to Figure 3.4. Start by going back to your command prompt window.

**FIGURE 3.4**    Command prompt results

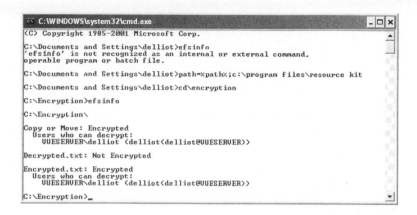

13.  At the command prompt, enter **path=%path%;c:\program files\resource kit**. Note that there are two mandatory spaces in the preceding string and C: is assumed, but substitute your drive letter. This command allows you to run the efsinfo utility from any folder. Refer back to Figure 3.4.

14.  Change your logged directory back to the Encryption folder with the command **cd\encryption**.

15.  At the new prompt, enter the command **efsinfo** to produce output similar to that in Figure 3.4. Note that David Elliot encrypted the objects and he is shown as the user that can decrypt them. Note also that the Decrypted file shows up as not being encrypted

### Right-Clicking to Encrypt (Optional)

Most users are not inconvenienced by the procedure to encrypt an object because they do not encrypt items that often. However you might have frequent need to encrypt objects, making an easier procedure worth the dangers of hacking your system's Registry.

**WARNING**    As with surgery, any time you edit your system's Registry, there are inherent risks. One inadvertent slip and you can render your system useless, requiring reinstallation of the operating system, likely producing data loss. While editing the Registry, only perform the steps in this task as written.

1.   Open the Registry Editor by clicking Start ➢ Run and entering **regedit**.

2.  Expand down to HKLM\SOFTWARE\Microsoft\Windows\CurrentVersion\
    Explorer\Advanced.

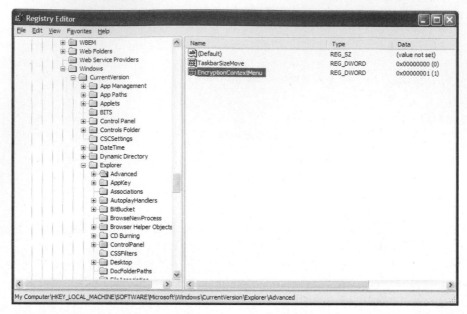

3.  Right-click in the unaffiliated space in the right pane and click New ➢ DWORD Value.

4.  Name the value EncryptionContextMenu.

5.  Double-click the EncryptionContextMenu name to bring up the Edit DWORD Value dia-
    log, change its value from 0 to 1, and click the OK button.

6.  No system reboot is required. Simply exit Registry Editor and right-click a file or folder
    to confirm the presence of the Encrypt selection. Be sure not to right-click a file that is not
    able to be encrypted and recall that encrypting a compressed file removes its compression.

## Criteria for Completion

You have completed this task when you create the files and folders noted in this task and
observe the encryption peculiarities mentioned herein.

# Task 3.10: Establishing Data Encryption between Routers

So far, you have seen how to encrypt routing advertisements between routers, but what if you
need to encrypt the user data that passes between two or more devices on opposite sides of a
vulnerable link? For that, you must establish some form of data encryption, which gets highly

complex very fast. There are various methods available to accomplish this task and sometimes varieties among these methods.

This task seeks to introduce you to one of the more basic yet effective methods, a simple IPSec encryption with pre-shared key authentication for anti-replay protection. Other methods are the fodder for complete volumes and beyond the scope of this one. Suffice it to say that unless you care to deal with certificate authorities (CAs) or entering RSA public keys, using pre-shared keys is a simple, effective method of providing fuel for the authentication machine.

## Scenario

You suspect that someone is eavesdropping on traffic between a remote client and a local server. Any other traffic to this local server does not concern you, but there are known trade secrets sent into the local network by this particular remote user. You decide to implement data encryption for this particular flow of information based on a static IP address that the remote client has.

## Scope of Task

### Duration

This task should take about 1 hour.

### Setup

For this task, you need space to set up two Cisco routers and the computer to configure them, as well as any optional equipment to create the scenario presented here.

### Caveat

Data encryption is not for the faint of heart. Entire advanced certifications are devoted to security alone. The procedure presented here unravels rather quickly with only slight deviation. If you do not understand certain steps in this task, independent research is highly recommended.

Be aware that not all Cisco IOS feature sets offer you the ability to perform this task. The 2611XM routers used to model this environment were running IOS image c2600-adventerprisek9-mz.123-14.T2.bin. A compatible image on a Cisco 3725 router is c3725-js-mz.122-15.T14.bin. These are specific images that include the firewall feature set. Many other images include this feature set. Consult Cisco's website or a Cisco sales representative for more information on other images that offer the commands used in this task.

A seemingly innocent event can prevent the entire security association (SA) from setting up, blocking all traffic that should be encrypted. Consider the innocuous example of configuring a host-to-host encryption on one router and a subnet-to-host encryption on the other, using Figure 3.5 as a reference. Assume router B encrypts any IP traffic it sees going from host B to host A. Further assume that router A encrypts any IP traffic it sees going from subnet A to host B. Configuring encryption this way could result in a successful SA if host B initiates contact but a failed SA if any subnet A member other than host A initiates contact. This is because inbound traffic is held to the converse of the outbound relationships you establish. As a result, router B does not expect any remote device other than host A to send encrypted information across the link.

**FIGURE 3.5**    Encryption example

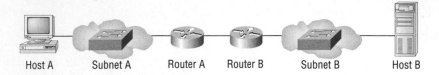

Host A        Subnet A      Router A      Router B      Subnet B      Host B

# Procedure

In this task, you will configure two Cisco routers with mirror-image pairings and then encrypt all IP traffic from both directions.

## Equipment Used

For this task, you need two Cisco routers with at least two network interfaces each. Optionally, any pairing of interface types can be made to work, in theory, with additional considerations if serial interfaces are used. Testing the task's results is assumed in the following procedure. Therefore, two computers, as well as hubs, switches, or crossover cables, are necessary.

## Details

The following steps walk you through targeting traffic for encryption and implementing encryption on the link between routers. Figure 3.6 shows a sample portion of an internetwork that will be referenced throughout this task.

**FIGURE 3.6**    Task sample network

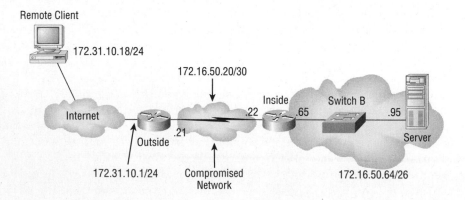

## IP Configuration

Each device's IP address is crucial. Not configuring the devices correctly leads to unrecognized addresses and the router's refusal to encrypt or even transmit data between hosts.

1.  Execute the following on router Inside.

```
Inside#config t
Inside(config)#int s0/0
Inside(config-if)#ip address 172.16.50.22 255.255.255.252
Inside(config-if)#int f0/0
Inside(config-if)#ip address 172.16.50.65 255.255.255.192
Inside(config-if)#
```

2.  Execute the following on router Outside.

```
Outside#config t
Outside(config)#int s0/0
Outside(config-if)#ip address 172.16.50.21 255.255.255.252
Outside(config-if)#int f0/0
Outside(config-if)#ip address 172.31.10.1 255.255.255.0
Outside(config-if)#
```

3.  Set up two computers, one on each end of the network. Configure each one with the appropriate address, mask, and default gateway, according to Figure 3.6.

4.  To avoid configuring dynamic routing, which is a preference in a lab setting but not a requirement, configure the following static routes on the corresponding device.

```
Inside(config-if)#exit
Inside(config)#ip route 172.31.10.0 255.255.255.0 172.16.50.21
Inside(config)#
```

```
Outside(config-if)#exit
Outside(config)#ip route 172.16.50.64 255.255.255.192 172.16.50.22
Outside(config)#
```

5.  Pinging from the computers is now possible. The following output is from the server in Figure 3.6.

```
C:\>ping 172.31.10.18

Pinging 172.31.10.18 with 32 bytes of data:

Reply from 172.31.10.18: bytes=32 time<1ms TTL=128
Reply from 172.31.10.18: bytes=32 time<1ms TTL=128
Reply from 172.31.10.18: bytes=32 time<1ms TTL=128
Reply from 172.31.10.18: bytes=32 time<1ms TTL=128
```

```
Ping statistics for 172.31.10.18:
    Packets: Sent = 4, Received = 4, Lost = 0 (0% loss),
Approximate round trip times in milli-seconds:
    Minimum = 0ms, Maximum = 0ms, Average = 0ms


C:\>
```

## Defining Traffic to Encrypt

Access lists are used to define what traffic you wish to encrypt over the link as well as what traffic you do not wish to encrypt. A `permit` parameter means encrypt the traffic on this line. A deny parameter means do not. A crypto access list is not a filter for transmission. Denied traffic is not encrypted, but it is still eligible for transmission.

Following are the corresponding access lists for each router. Note that the implicit deny stops all other traffic from being encrypted. You define the source (first address) as the device or network on the same side of the encrypted link as the router being configured and the destination as the device or network on the opposite side. Always avoid using any keyword in crypto access lists.

```
Inside(config)#access-list 120 permit ip host 172.16.50.95 host
➥172.31.10.18
Inside(config)#


Outside(config)#access-list 120 permit ip host 172.31.10.18 host
➥172.16.50.95
Outside(config)#
```

## Defining How to Encrypt and Authenticate

*Transform set* is the term used for a combination of security protocols and algorithms. Both encryption and authentication protocols are specified in a transform set that you conceive. Your transform set will be based on encryption by the encapsulating security payload (ESP) use of the Data Encryption Standard (DES) algorithm.

Specify the ESP-compatible SHA HMAC authentication algorithm (SHA stands for secure hash algorithm and HMAC stands for hash message authentication code), which will use the pre-shared key you specify later on each router to verify the source of the encrypted data as the opposite router. Name your transform set ENCRYPT.

```
Inside(config)#crypto ipsec transform-set ENCRYPT esp-des esp-sha-hmac
Inside(cfg-crypto-trans)#exit
Inside(config)#


Outside(config)#crypto ipsec transform-set ENCRYPT esp-des esp-sha-hmac
Outside(cfg-crypto-trans)#exit
Outside(config)#
```

## Mapping the Traffic to the Encryption

Cisco uses a crypto map to tie the access list representing the traffic to be encrypted to the protocols and algorithms that perform the encryption and authentication. Use the following commands to create crypto maps based on the traffic you chose to encrypt and the transform set created earlier as well as to identify the other end of the encrypted link.

1. Name the crypto map STATIC, realizing that you could have implemented dynamic crypto maps had the peers been less deterministic. You receive a warning to let you know that you still have work to do to complete the map.

```
Inside(config)#crypto map STATIC 1 ipsec-isakmp
% NOTE: This new crypto map will remain disabled until a peer
        and a valid access list have been configured.
Inside(config-crypto-map)#

Outside(config)#crypto map STATIC 1 ipsec-isakmp
% NOTE: This new crypto map will remain disabled until a peer
        and a valid access list have been configured.
Outside(config-crypto-map)#
```

2. Within the new configuration context, define the other router's serial interface's IP address as the peer identity for the encryption SA.

```
Inside(config-crypto-map)#set peer 172.16.50.21
Inside(config-crypto-map)#

Outside(config crypto map)#set peer 172.16.50.22
Outside(config-crypto-map)#
```

3. Relate the crypto map back to the transform set called ENCRYPT that you created earlier.

```
Inside(config-crypto-map)#set transform-set ENCRYPT
Inside(config-crypto-map)#

Outside(config-crypto-map)#set transform-set ENCRYPT
Outside(config-crypto-map)#
```

4. Finally, specify the access list from which to obtain the addresses of the source and destination flows to be encrypted.

```
Inside(config-crypto-map)#match address 120
Inside(config-crypto-map)#exit
Inside(config)#

Outside(config-crypto-map)#match address 120
Outside(config-crypto-map)#exit
Outside(config)#
```

## Get the Interface Involved

No encryption or authentication occurs just by virtue of the foregoing steps. An interface must be affiliated with the crypto map, which in turn references the traffic to be encrypted and how to encrypt it.

1.  Enter Interface Configuration mode and apply the crypto map, STATIC.

```
Inside(config)#int s0/0
Inside(config-if)#crypto map STATIC
%CRYPTO-6-ISAKMP_ON_OFF: ISAKMP is ON
Inside(config-if)#end
Inside#


Outside(config)#int s0/0
Outside(config-if)#crypto map STATIC
%CRYPTO-6-ISAKMP_ON_OFF: ISAKMP is ON
Outside(config-if)#end
Outside#
```

2.  It seems perfectly logical that a simple ping from one computer to the other will result in an SA being formed between the routers. No outward sign is given without turning on debugging.

```
Inside#debug crypto ipsec
Crypto IPSEC debugging is on
Inside#debug crypto isakmp
Crypto ISAKMP debugging is on
Inside#


Outside#debug crypto ipsec
Crypto IPSEC debugging is on
Outside#debug crypto isakmp
Crypto ISAKMP debugging is on
Outside#
```

3.  Ping one of the computers from the other and notice that what was once successful now fails.

```
C:\>ping 172.31.10.18

Pinging 172.31.10.18 with 32 bytes of data:
```

```
Request timed out.
Request timed out.
Request timed out.
Request timed out.

Ping statistics for 172.31.10.18:
    Packets: Sent = 4, Received = 0, Lost = 4 (100% loss),


C:\>
```

4. Observe the local router's debug output. What follows are the lines of output pertinent to the discussion. Note that the first block is output by the IPSec debug while the rest is due to the Internet Security Association Key Management Protocol (ISAKMP) debugging.

```
*IPSEC(sa_request): ,
  (key eng. msg.) OUTBOUND local= 172.16.50.22, remote=
172.16.50.21,
    local_proxy= 172.16.50.95/255.255.255.255/0/0 (type=1),
    remote_proxy= 172.31.10.18/255.255.255.255/0/0 (type=1),
    protocol= ESP, transform= esp-des esp-sha-hmac  (Tunnel),
    lifedur= 3600s and 4608000kb,
    spi= 0x5828C451(1479066705), conn_id= 0, keysize= 0, flags=
0x400A
*ISAKMP: Created a peer struct for 172.16.50.21, peer port 500
*insert sa successfully sa = 8525B564
*ISAKMP:(0:0:N/A:0):Can not start Aggressive mode, trying Main
mode.
*ISAKMP:(0:0:N/A:0):No pre-shared key with 172.16.50.21!
*ISAKMP:(0:0:N/A:0): No Cert or pre-shared address key.
*ISAKMP:(0:0:N/A:0): construct_initial_message: Can not start
Main mode
*ISAKMP: Deleting peer node by peer_reap for 172.16.50.21:
8525BC50
*ISAKMP:(0:0:N/A:0):purging SA., sa=8525B564, delme=8525B564
*ISAKMP:(0:0:N/A:0):purging node 657521518
```

Everything appears to start out well, but eventually the SA that was created is purged. UDP port 500 springs into action only to be torn back down eventually. ISAKMP is doing what ISAKMP does. It's looking for a CA-provided or pre-shared key to use in the authentication with the neighbor. Planning to use the pre-shared method, but having established no pre-shared key yet, you get ISAKMP to raise a red flag.

### Creating the Pre-shared Key

Only the `crypto isakmp key` command is required to create a pre-shared key, but the key must be identical, like a password, on both ends, with each end pointing to the other.

1.  On each router issue the `crypto isakmp key` command, using the same case-sensitive alphanumeric key and the appropriate opposite-end address.

    ```
    Inside#config t
    Inside(config)#crypto isakmp key WILEY address 172.16.50.21
    Inside(config)#end
    Inside#

    Outside#config t
    Outside(config)#crypto isakmp key WILEY address 172.16.50.22
    Outside(config)#end
    Outside#
    ```

> Note that hostnames are recommended over addresses when routers have more than one address and more than one interface involved in SAs. In the case of the two routers in this procedure, only one encrypted path exists, making addresses acceptable.

2.  Try the ping again. It is unsuccessful again.

    ```
    C:\>ping 172.31.10.18

    Pinging 172.31.10.18 with 32 bytes of data:

    Request timed out.
    Request timed out.
    Request timed out.
    Request timed out.

    Ping statistics for 172.31.10.18:
        Packets: Sent = 4, Received = 0, Lost = 4 (100% loss),

    C:\>
    ```

3.  Note the output on the local router.

    ```
    *IPSEC(sa_request): ,
      (key eng. msg.) OUTBOUND local= 172.16.50.22, remote=
    172.16.50.21,
    ```

```
      local_proxy= 172.16.50.95/255.255.255.255/0/0 (type=1),
      remote_proxy= 172.31.10.18/255.255.255.255/0/0 (type=1),
      protocol= ESP, transform= esp-des esp-sha-hmac  (Tunnel),
      lifedur= 3600s and 4608000kb,
      spi= 0xB449223F(3024691775), conn_id= 0, keysize= 0, flags=
0x400A
*Created a peer struct for 172.16.50.21, peer port 500
*insert sa successfully sa = 8525B564
*ISAKMP:(0:0:N/A:0):Can not start Aggressive mode, trying Main
mode.
*ISAKMP:(0:0:N/A:0):Looking for a matching key for 172.16.50.21
in default
*ISAKMP:(0:0:N/A:0): : success
*ISAKMP:(0:0:N/A:0):found peer pre-shared key matching
172.16.50.21
*ISAKMP:(0:0:N/A:0):incorrect policy settings. Unable to
initiate.
*ISAKMP: Deleting peer node by peer_reap for 172.16.50.21:
857B8808
*ISAKMP:(0:0:N/A:0):purging SA., sa=8525B564, delme=8525B564
*ISAKMP:(0:0:N/A:0):purging node 614749934
```

You start out on very familiar ground. Then, everything seems to get better; the pre-shared keys seem to do the trick, only to uncover another issue lurking in the wings. Apparently, the default ISAKMP policy settings for Internet Key Exchange (IKE) negotiations are not compatible with your effort to use pre-shared keys. In fact, the default authentication method is RSA signatures.

4.  Create a prioritized ISAKMP policy on both routers to be used during initial and subsequent IKE key negotiations, which provides each router with the other router's private key for decrypting the data that it sends later. The priority number, 1 being the highest priority and 10000 being the lowest, does not have to match on both ends, but use a priority that allows for overriding current policy entries while continuing to use uncontested entries simply by creating an additional policy of higher priority.

```
Inside#config t
Inside(config)#crypto isakmp policy 10
Inside(config-isakmp)#authentication pre share
Inside(config-isakmp)#end
Inside#

Outside#config t
Outside(config)#crypto isakmp policy 10
```

```
Outside(config-isakmp)#authentication pre-share
Outside(config-isakmp)#end
Outside#
```

There is a default policy of the lowest priority, call it 10001, that supplies you with the other defaults. Authentication is the only parameter that conflicts with your plans to use pre-shared keys. Thus, authentication is the only parameter you need to specify. Other parameters that you accept from the default policy are as follow:

- 56-bit DES-CBC encryption
- SHA-1 hash algorithm
- Group 1 Diffie-Hellman (a key agreement protocol, in which group 1 uses 768-bit encryption to enable two peers to exchange a secret key over a public link without any prior secrets)
- A one-day lifetime.

5.  Subsequent pings meet with success.

```
C:\>ping 172.31.10.18

Pinging 172.31.10.18 with 32 bytes of data:

Reply from 172.31.10.18: bytes=32 time<1ms TTL=128
Reply from 172.31.10.18: bytes=32 time<1ms TTL=128
Reply from 172.31.10.18: bytes=32 time<1ms TTL=128
Reply from 172.31.10.18: bytes=32 time<1ms TTL=128

Ping statistics for 172.31.10.18:
    Packets: Sent = 4, Received = 4, Lost = 0 (0% loss),
Approximate round trip times in milli-seconds:
    Minimum = 0ms, Maximum = 0ms, Average = 0ms


C:\>
```

6.  Noting the debug output on the local router, the flood gates appear to have opened. In fact, the remote router now has recipient debug activity slightly different from the following output, where there was none before.

```
*IPSEC(sa_request): ,
  (key eng. msg.) OUTBOUND local= 172.16.50.22, remote=
172.16.50.21,
    local_proxy= 172.16.50.95/255.255.255.255/0/0 (type=1),
    remote_proxy= 172.31.10.18/255.255.255.255/0/0 (type=1),
    protocol= ESP, transform= esp-des esp-sha-hmac  (Tunnel),
    lifedur= 3600s and 4608000kb,
    spi= 0x50E86232(1357406770), conn_id= 0, keysize= 0, flags=
```

```
0x400A
*Created a peer struct for 172.16.50.21, peer port 500
*insert sa successfully sa = 8525B564
*ISAKMP:(0:0:N/A:0):Can not start Aggressive mode, trying Main
mode.
*ISAKMP:(0:0:N/A:0):Looking for a matching key for 172.16.50.21
in default
*ISAKMP:(0:0:N/A:0): : success
*ISAKMP:(0:0:N/A:0):found peer pre-shared key matching
172.16.50.21
*ISAKMP:(0:0:N/A:0): beginning Main Mode exchange
*ISAKMP:(0:0:N/A:0): sending packet to 172.16.50.21 my_port 500
peer_port 500 (I) MM_NO_STATE
*ISAKMP (0:0): received packet from 172.16.50.21 dport 500 sport
500 Global (I) MM_NO_STATE
*ISAKMP:(0:0:N/A:0): processing SA payload. message ID = 0
*ISAKMP:(0:0:N/A:0):Checking ISAKMP transform 1 against priority
10 policy
*ISAKMP:          encryption DES-CBC
*ISAKMP:          hash SHA
*ISAKMP:          default group 1
*ISAKMP:          auth pre-share
*ISAKMP:          life type in seconds
*ISAKMP:          life duration (VPI) of  0x0 0x1 0x51 0x80
*ISAKMP:(0:1:SW:1): sending packet to 172.16.50.21 my_port 500
peer_port 500 (I) MM_SA_SETUP
*ISAKMP (0:134217729): received packet from 172.16.50.21 dport
500 sport 500 Global (I) MM_SA_SETUP
*ISAKMP:(0:1:SW:1): processing KE payload. message ID = 0
*ISAKMP:(0:1:SW:1): processing NONCE payload. message ID = 0
*ISAKMP:(0:1:SW:1): processing vendor id payload
*ISAKMP:(0:1:SW:1): speaking to another IOS box!
*ISAKMP:(0:1:SW:1):Send initial contact
*ISAKMP:(0:1:SW:1):SA is doing pre-shared key authentication
using id type ID_IPV4_ADDR
*ISAKMP (0:134217729): ID payload
        next-payload : 8
        type         : 1
        address      : 172.16.50.22
        protocol     : 17
        port         : 500
        length       : 12
```

```
*ISAKMP:(0:1:SW:1):Total payload length: 12
*ISAKMP:(0:1:SW:1): sending packet to 172.16.50.21 my_port 500
peer_port 500 (I) MM_KEY_EXCH
*ISAKMP (0:134217729): received packet from 172.16.50.21 dport
500 sport 500 Global (I) MM_KEY_EXCH
*ISAKMP:(0:1:SW:1): processing ID payload. message ID = 0
*ISAKMP (0:134217729): ID payload
        next-payload : 8
        type         : 1
        address      : 172.16.50.21
        protocol     : 17
        port         : 500
        length       : 12
*ISAKMP:(0:1:SW:1):: peer matches *none* of the profiles
*ISAKMP:(0:1:SW:1): processing HASH payload. message ID = 0
*ISAKMP:(0:1:SW:1):SA authentication status:
        authenticated
*ISAKMP:(0:1:SW:1):SA has been authenticated with 172.16.50.21
*ISAKMP: Trying to insert a peer 172.16.50.22/172.16.50.21/500/, and inserted
successfully 857B8808.
```

You can see that the IPSec information has never changed. Now, however, you see success in ISAKMP where there was none before. Negotiations succeed and expected addresses, port and protocol numbers, and policy and priority numbers appear with no critical errors.

7. (Optional) Subsequent pings produce nothing from the debugs running. If you would like to re-create the original flurry of success, execute the following on either router. Prepare for a litany of debug messages, as the security associations are broken.

```
Inside#clear crypto sa
Inside#
```

Now, the first ping from either computer results in debug output similar to the first successful debugs you witnessed.

8. Turn debugging off when you are done.

```
Inside#undebug all
Port Statistics for unclassified packets is not turned on.

All possible debugging has been turned off
Inside#
```

```
Outside#undebug all
Port Statistics for unclassified packets is not turned on.

All possible debugging has been turned off
Outside#
```

## Criteria for Completion

You have completed this task when you have completed the configuration of all four devices and verified that keys are being exchanged and IPSec is being triggered for the appropriate traffic.

# Task 3.11: Creating Data Backups

Backing up your computer regularly limits your loss of information to the period since your last backup. All machines fail. Not performing backups is tantamount to a guarantee that you will one day lose your data. The only question is when, not if. In the early days of personal computing, backup devices and media were somewhat prohibitive in cost for the individual user. With time, this cost came down to a more manageable level, but never has the industry offered a more affordable solution as is found in today's inexpensive hard drives and other forms of mass storage.

Today, it is feasible to purchase the hard drive you need in terms of size and another one twice as large for multiple levels of backup or to back up multiple systems. External drive chassis allow you to take advantage of painless USB and FireWire attachment without the need for and reduced convenience of permanent installation.

Regular full backups can be time consuming, a disincentive that can quickly burn you out, especially if you have not been hit yet by data loss. Different levels of backup exist that allow you the confidence of full coverage and the convenience of quick processing the majority of the time. At the heart of the backup process is the archive bit, one of the many attribute bits that the file system sets or resets for each object. Whenever a file is opened and then saved, the archive bit is set to a value of one. Following are the different backup levels offered by today's Windows operating systems, what they accomplish, and their effect on the archive bit:

**Normal**   Backs up the files you select regardless of archive-bit value. Normal changes the archive bits of the files to zero, so future incremental and differential backups skip them. Normal is the backup level used in full backups.

**Copy**   Backs up the files you select regardless of archive-bit value. Copy does not change the archive bit, so future incremental and differential backups might not skip them, depending on their original archive-bit values.

**Incremental** Backs up the files you select only if they were created or changed since the last normal or incremental backup. Incremental resets the archive bit of the files, so future incremental and differential backups skip them.

**Differential** Backs up the files you select only if they were created or changed since the last normal or incremental backup. Differential does not reset the archive bit of the files, so future incremental and differential backups do not skip them.

**Daily** Backs up the files you select only if they were created or modified today. Daily does not reset the archive bit of the files, so future incremental and differential backups do not skip them.

From the foregoing list, various strategies develop. For example, a single normal backup can be augmented by alternating differential backups, for redundancy, until the differentials become so large that another normal backup is indicated. You would restore the normal backup and then the latest differential backup. Alternatively, cumulative incremental backups augment the normal backup. You restore the normal backup and then all incremental backups in order. A single differential backup is the same size as the full collection of incremental backups, assuming the backups were made over the same period.

## Scenario

Regular network backups are being made, but there is a server that is not part of the enterprise domain. This server is not included in the regular backups that take place. You have purchased an external USB-attached hard drive for the purpose of making a backup of the local `Documents and Settings` folders of all users who have ever logged on to the server and thus had profiles created for them.

## Scope of Task

### Duration

This task should take about 1 hour.

### Setup

For this task, you need enough space to set up a single computer with, at most, an external hard drive.

### Caveat

Resist the temptation to use the same physical drive as your backup destination. A primary reason you perform backups to begin with is to avoid expensive data recovery if your hard drive fails. If your common physical device fails, both your original data and your backup of that data are lost. This is not to say that accidental deletion and corruption are not common causes for recovery, just that when possible, backup sets should be kept separate from the protected data.

Be sure to restore data in the proper order. Restoring newer incremental backup sets before earlier ones and restoring incremental or differential backup sets before the normal set overwrites newer information with older versions when overlapping files exist.

Depending on the value of the data, it is usually wise to store backups off site. In the case of fire, flood, theft, or other disasters that compromise the original data physically, the backup sets can be endangered as well.

## Procedure

In this task, you create a normal backup set made up of the Documents and Settings folders on your computer for each profile automatically.

### Equipment Used

For this task, you need a single computer with additional available storage equal to or exceeding the used portion of the boot partition (Microsoft's term for the partition with the operating system files, including Documents and Settings folders, by default). Figure 3.7 shows a typical external hard drive with AC power and USB connections.

### Details

In the following procedure, you use your operating system's built-in backup utility to back up the Documents and Settings folder for each account that has logged on to the computer. In this example, Windows XP Professional is used.

**FIGURE 3.7**    An external hard drive

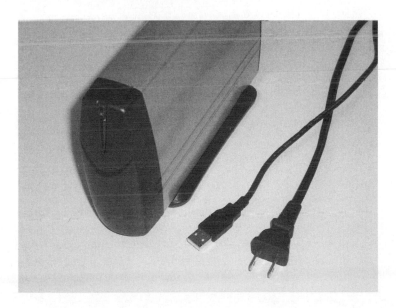

## Backing Up Your Data

Backing up data presents a variety of options, including what to back up, where to store the backup set, and what type of backup to perform.

1.  Open the Backup Or Restore Wizard by clicking Start ➤ All Programs ➤ Accessories ➤ System Tools ➤ Backup.

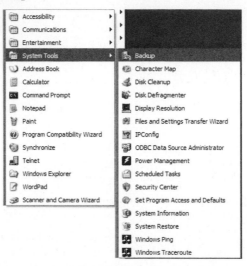

2.  On the Backup Or Restore Wizard Welcome screen, click the Next button. Alternatively, you can use the full version of the utility by clicking the Advanced Mode link, producing the utility interface in the next image.

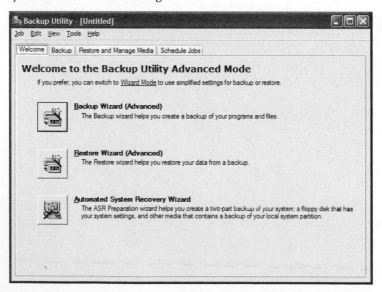

To return to Wizard mode once in the middle of Advanced mode, choose Tools ➤ Switch To Wizard Mode. Wizard mode is advised for anyone who does not require the added control of Advanced mode. You will know if Wizard mode does not provide the control you require, at which point you need only close the utility and start it again.

3.  In the Backup Or Restore screen, you must decide which function you wish to perform. For this example, choose Back Up Files And Settings, the default, and click the Next button.

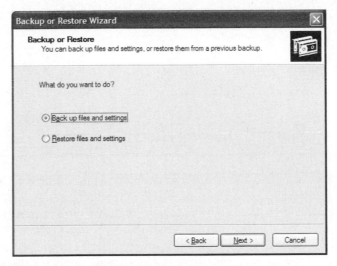

4.  In the What To Back Up screen, you have four choices:

    ▪  My Documents And Settings backs up only the Documents and Settings folder for the currently logged-on user. This folder includes such common areas as My Documents, the Start menu, and the Desktop itself.

    ▪  Everyone's Documents And Settings backs up the same information as the previous choice but for every known user of the computer. If there is only one primary user, this selection does not add much beyond the previous choice. With many regular users, this selection can produce a relatively large backup set.

    ▪  All Information On This Computer backs up literally everything on the computer and creates a system recovery disk that can be used, after a fresh copy of the operating system is installed, to restore the system to its state at the time of the backup. Obviously, this selection requires the most backup space.

    ▪  Let Me Choose What To Back Up begins a more advanced wizard, allowing you to pick and choose the files and folders to be backed up.

Fill in the radio button beside Everyone's Documents And Settings and click the Next button to move on to the Backup Type, Destination, and Name dialog.

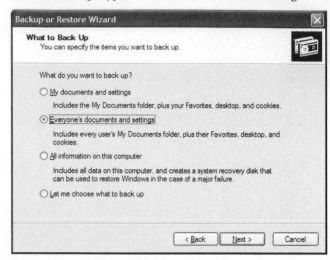

5. Click the Browse button and navigate to a drive and folder where you wish to place the backup file, preferably not on the same drive with the information being backed up. Give the backup set a name, such as WileyBackup, and click the Save button to return to the screen, which looks similar to the following. Then click the Next button to advance to the next wizard screen.

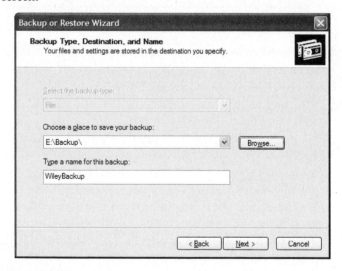

**6.** In the Completing The Backup Or Restore Wizard screen, click the Advanced button to explore the options for the level of backup you wish to perform.

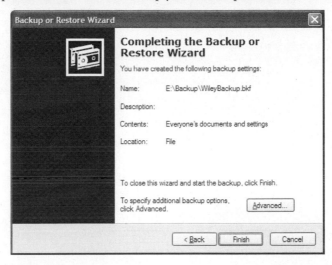

**7.** In the Type Of Backup screen, the default backup type is normal, which backs up every file you choose regardless of how its archive bit is set. To keep your backup manageable during this task, choose Differential from the drop-down, shown next. Click the Next button.

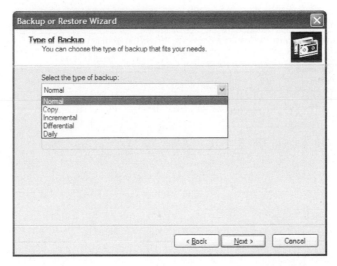

8.  Clear all check boxes in the How To Back Up dialog. Doing so speeds the backup along, avoiding verification. Verification is not a bad idea in production, especially with critical information on the line. Additionally, you make sure that all files, even those in use, get backed up. Click the Next button.

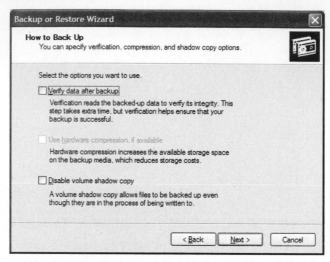

9.  In the Backup Options screen, choose Replace The Existing Backups. Doing so reduces confusion later in this example if you perform the backup more than once or use an existing file for the backup set. In production, placing related backups, such as a normal backup and all subsequent incremental backups, in the same backup set is not a bad idea. You just have to remember there are multiple backups in the same backup file. Click the Next button.

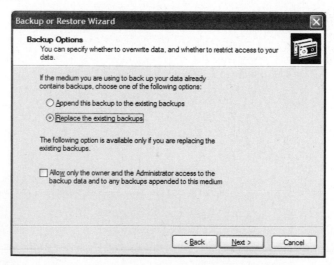

**10.** The When To Back Up screen allows you to schedule the backup for when the computer is least busy. For this example, leave the default, Now, selected. Click the Next button.

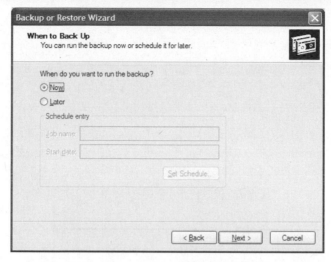

**11.** You are once again taken to the Completing The Backup Or Restore Wizard screen. This time, it has no Advanced button. Making modifications now involves clicking the Back button to return to previous screens until you arrive at the one with the information you wish to alter. Click the Finish button to start the backup process.

The Backup Progress pop-up appears briefly. Very soon another pop-up, similar to the following, displays the progress in estimating the number of files and bytes to be backed up.

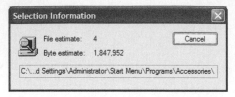

The Backup Progress pop-up returns to the foreground as it ticks off the advancement of the backup process with a green bar. Eventually, the Backup Progress pop-up looks similar to the following, indicating the backup is complete.

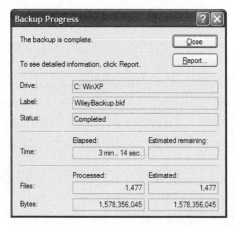

Clicking the Report button generates a Notepad text file with slightly more in-depth information compared to what the Backup Progress pop-up displays. Click the Close button to end the wizard completely and conclude the backup.

## Restoring Files from a Backup

Restoring backed-up files provides another opportunity to make choices about how you wish to proceed. Different options work best in certain situations.

1.  Find the backup set you just created and double-click it. This brings up the same Backup or Restore Wizard from which you started your backup.

2.  Click Next to go to the Backup Or Restore screen, where you select restore files and settings this time. Click the Next button to proceed to the What To Restore screen.

3.  The What To Restore screen is a simple tree that includes the most recent backup (notice the WileyBackup file in the following screen shot), as well as any past backup sets that you have not deleted. Click the plus sign to the left of the backup set you just

created to expand it, and put a check mark in the box beside the entry you wish to restore. Click the Next button.

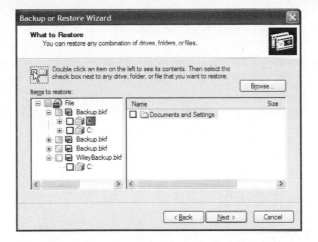

Note in the preceding image that the other expanded backup set called backup.bkf shows two entries. This is what happens when a backup is appended to an existing backup set. Be sure to pay attention to the dates on these two backups, if they are related, so you restore them in the proper order, with the oldest one being restored first and so on.

4. In the Completing The Backup Or Restore Wizard screen, click the Advanced button to bring up the Where To Restore screen.

5. In the Where To Restore screen, you can choose to restore all files to the exact location from which they came or some other location, including a single folder that you can sort out later.

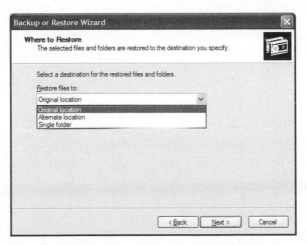

If you wish to perform the restore, select Original Location and click the Next button, progressing to the How To Restore screen. Otherwise, click the Cancel button to end the wizard completely and skip all remaining steps.

6. In the How To Restore screen, choose the default, recommended option (as shown in the following image), which makes sure the restore you are about to perform does not alter your data, which has not been compromised as in the case of actual data loss. Click the Next button.

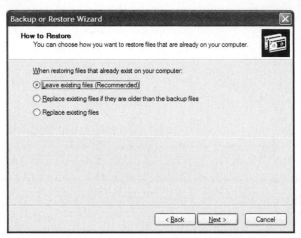

7. The Advanced Restore Options screen in the following image is best kept at its default settings unless you have good cause to change anything. Click the Next button.

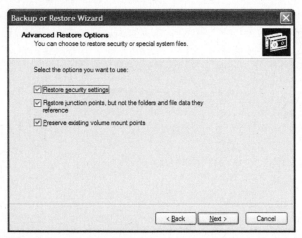

8. You return to the Completing The Backup Or Restore Wizard screen, now with the Advanced button missing. Click the Finish button to begin the restore process and click the Close button when the restore is complete.

## Criteria for Completion

You have completed this task when you have created a backup file in a location of your choosing and optionally restored its contents to their original location.

# Task 3.12: Running an Antivirus Scan

Computer viruses need no introduction. They have plagued the industry for decades now. Whenever one virus gets neutralized, another one—or more—is waiting to take its place. Methods for combating these plagues vary from single-system programs to enterprise-wide distributed applications. Just a few antivirus software publishers lead the market, although a throng of them exists. Just as viruses change regularly, so do the definitions for the software that fights them. The Internet, the very medium that most commonly propagates viruses, is invaluable for keeping these software packages up-to-date, and even for delivering the software to begin with.

Norton AntiVirus, by Symantec, is used in this task, but similar procedures work with VirusScan, by McAfee, Inc., and AVG, by Grisoft, as well as with the majority of other antivirus applications. With regular scans and updates for new virus definitions, the destructive nature of viruses, which can bring computers to their knees and lead to complete operating system reinstallations, can be kept at bay.

## Scenario

One of your servers is acting questionably. You have performed some basic troubleshooting to no avail. You are suspicious that you might be dealing with a virus and realize that somehow, this server slipped through the cracks with no antivirus coverage, as it is not under the domain umbrella. As such, you intend to download and use a popular antivirus package to see if the symptoms improve.

## Scope of Task

### Duration

This task should take about 1 hour, depending on the level of virus scan performed.

### Setup

For this task, you need enough space to set up a single computer.

### Caveat

Occasionally, a virus can become so entangled in one or more files that in order to remove the virus, the files must be sacrificed. There is a trade-off between spending longer hunting the source of your infliction and cutting your losses by reinstalling the operating system. During your attempt to search and destroy, other systems can become inadvertently infected. It's always wise, when a system is attacked by a virus, to remove the device from the network and then, using an uninfected system, download any tools required and conduct your raid with the infected unit offline.

## Procedure

In this task, you use an antivirus utility to scan for viruses on your computer. Symantec's Norton AntiVirus is used as an example. Other packages have different user interfaces, but the broad concepts shown here can be applied to any antivirus software. You just might need to investigate the features of your software to discover the similarities.

### Equipment Used

For this task, you need a single computer with an installed antivirus utility.

### Details

In the following procedure, you follow the use of Norton AntiVirus (NAV) to scan for and remove viruses, porting general concepts to your own antivirus package.

1. With NAV installed and working properly, you see a yellow, circular system tray icon similar to the following.

2. Double-clicking the system tray icon produces the NAV control applet.

3. Click the Full System Scan link to display information on this type of scan, as well as a button that you can click to perform a scan immediately.

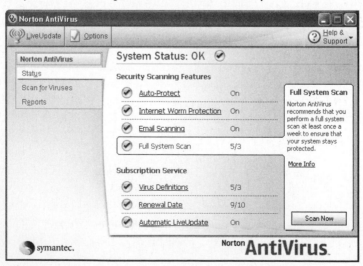

Alternatively, you can click the Scan For Viruses link on the left for more granular control over your system scan. Note from the following screen shot that a schedule has been set for the Scan My Computer entry.

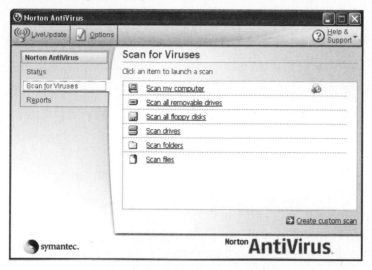

In this view, clicking the Scan Drives link brings up the Scan Drives dialog, which allows you to select only the drives you wish to scan, as shown in the following image. The Scan button begins the scan, and the Cancel button returns you to the Scan For Viruses page.

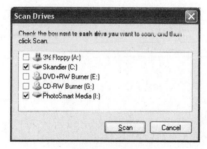

4.  From the Scan For Viruses page, clicking the Scan Folders link brings up a dialog similar to the following. From here, you place a check mark in the box beside each folder you want scanned. The Scan and Cancel buttons perform as previously mentioned.

From the Scan For Viruses page, clicking the Scan Files link generates a dialog that enables you to choose only the specific files you desire for the scan. The next screen shot depicts an example of this interface. Multiple files can be selected within a single folder. Clicking the Open button begins the scan, which includes about 150 other nonselected files by default. The Cancel button returns you to the Scan For Viruses page.

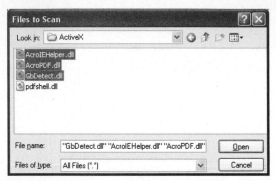

Select a scan to perform using one of the methods in this step. The following illustration shows a virus scan in progress.

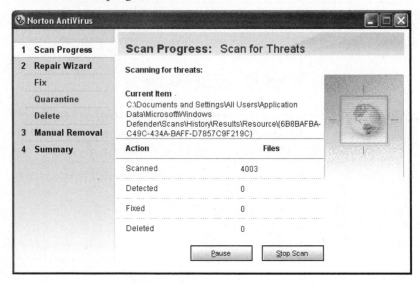

**5.**  When the scan is complete, a report similar to the following is displayed. Click the Finished button to return to the NAV control applet.

**6.**  On the control applet, click Options in the upper-left portion to display the following dialog.

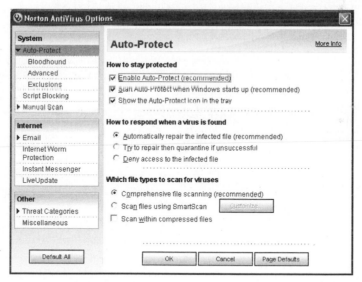

This is a set of three categories totaling nine pages, each selectable from the list on the left, that allows you to customize how the program works and handles scans and viruses that are detected. Many of the pages offer you the option of NAV silently taking care of issues it finds or warning you before taking any such action so you can be comfortable that NAV is not going overboard. Eventually, once your confidence in NAV is in place, you can adjust these settings to allow NAV to work completely in the background without your input.

In the Internet category, the Instant Messenger page, shown next, offers an intelligent way to monitor which users utilize which of the popular instant messenger offerings and how.

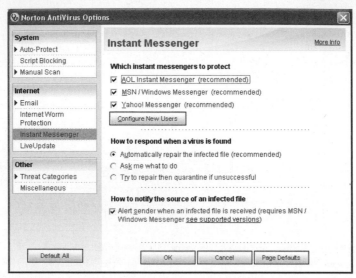

In the Other category, Threat Categories, seen in the following image, allows you to dial in the level of protection that you feel you require. Perhaps you use this to ignore classes of threats that you are not concerned about.

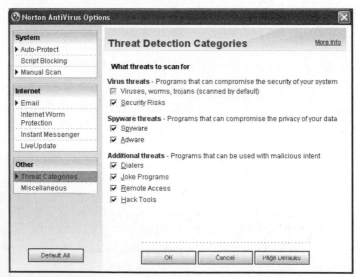

**7.** Beside Options on the control applet is LiveUpdate, Symantec's real-time update utility that runs regularly, by default, and that you can run on demand using the following procedure. Clicking here brings up the LiveUpdate Wizard, which begins by displaying what NAV components are installed already.

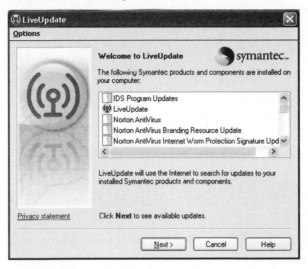

**8.** Click the Next button to begin a search for updates to the application and virus definitions. The following illustration shows a connection established to `liveupdate.symanteciveupdate.com` as well as the progress indicator for the search.

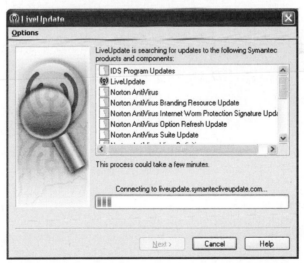

If the search results in updates, they are displayed and checked by default, shown next, for example.

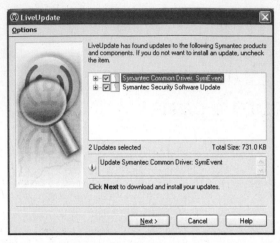

**9.** Click the Next button to download and install all checked items. This brings up another progress indicator.

**10.** Eventually, the following screen is displayed, confirming successful updating of the NAV software. Click the Finish button to exit the LiveUpdate Wizard.

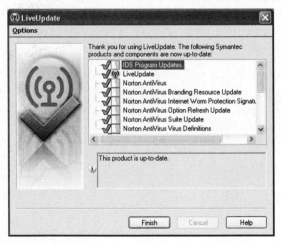

**11.** If you are met with the Restart Required warning, make sure to save your work in all your open programs and then click the OK button to reboot. The warning can be dragged out of the way by its title bar until you are ready to reboot.

## Criteria for Completion

You have completed this task when you have conducted a scan for viruses with your own anti-virus application.

# Task 3.13: Running an Anti-spyware Scan

Although not quite as malicious in intent as viruses and similar to spam in email vernacular, spyware, which was created more as a marketing tool, is an increasingly prevalent class of often unwanted Internet fare. Spyware is the toilet paper on the shoe of the casual Internet browser. Without defenses in place, which can lead to issues during browsing, spyware is free to install itself and eventually clog the main arteries of the operating system. In some cases, spyware inhibits the successful execution of legitimate programs, making it more like an unintentional virus.

The market is replete with anti-spyware utilities of varying caliber. Counterintuitively, some of the best ones are free. Others are free until you become so impressed that you spring for a donation. Regardless, a system that has been online for more than a few weeks but has never had an anti-spyware scan performed on it tends to begin operating more efficiently and correctly immediately after its first scan. One popular freeware utility that accepts voluntary donations is Spybot - Search & Destroy. In this task, Spybot - Search & Destroy is used to illustrate the relative ease of performing an anti-spyware scan.

## Scenario

The server you recently scanned for viruses still is acting questionably. You are suspicious that the symptoms you have been observing might be the result of spyware more than viruses, as previously suspected. You decide to download and use Spybot - Search & Destroy to perform a scan for spyware.

## Scope of Task

### Duration

This task should take about 1 hour.

### Setup

For this task, you need enough space to set up a single computer with Spybot - Search & Destroy installed or an Internet connection over which to download it.

## Caveat

Some items targeted as spyware are welcome utilities that you intentionally installed on your computer, such as your Yahoo toolbar or your coupon software. It is always a good idea to visually confirm that all the suspicious processes found by the scan are indeed spyware. Usually, simply removing the check mark beside an item in the list prevents it from being destroyed. Generally, an anti-spyware utility allows the user to specify exceptions that they want to ignore during future scans.

Be aware that there are many anti-spyware products on the market. Spybot - Search & Destroy is a decent representative of how they all work. The use of this package in this task is only as an example. Compare the steps here to your own anti-spyware application.

# Procedure

This task guides you through downloading the latest version of Spybot - Search & Destroy and conducting a scan for spyware on your computer.

## Equipment Used

For this task, you need a single computer with Spybot - Search & Destroy or an Internet connection.

## Details

In the following procedure, you install and execute Spybot - Search & Destroy on a computer in the attempt to discover and eradicate spyware.

### Downloading and Installing

1.  Point your web browser to www.download.com and enter **spybot** in the Search field. Click the Go button.

2.  If not the first, one of the first results is Spybot - Search & Destroy, shown next. Click the Download label to the right, which brings up a Security Warning dialog.

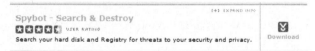

3.  In the Security Warning dialog, click the Run button. If you prefer to save the installation file and run it separately, the Save button accomplishes this.

4.  After clicking the Run button, or after executing the downloaded file, and after the progress indicator makes it all the way across, you'll get another security warning. Simply click the Run button to confirm that the program's execution is intentional.

5.  Choose the language in which you wish to install. Click the OK button to bring up the welcome dialog.

6. On the welcome dialog, click the Next button to advance to the License Agreement dialog.

7. Accept the license agreement and click the Next button to go to the Select Destination Location dialog.

8. Generally, the default installation destination, as shown in the following image, is recommended. If you have a reason to change this location, click the Browse button to navigate to a new location. Installing to the same location as an older version over-writes the older version for efficiency. Click the Next button to produce the Select Components dialog.

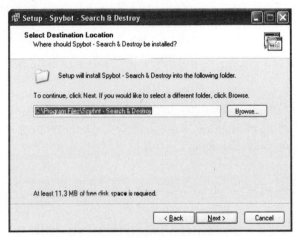

9. As shown next, there are not many options in the Select Components dialog, but one that you might consider is Download Updates Immediately.

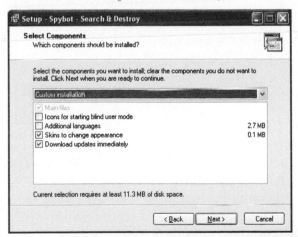

Checking this selection causes Setup to look for updates during the installation process, which requires an Internet connection. Clearing this box allows you to install from a downloaded file without a connection. Updates can be downloaded at any time later. Click the Next button, which takes you to the Select Start Menu Folder dialog.

10. The Select Start Menu Folder dialog is where you allow the installation process to create a folder on your Start menu or choose to use an existing folder. Click the Browse button to select your own folder on the Start menu or enter a new name to create a new folder with a different name from the default. Click the Next button to continue to the Select Additional Tasks dialog.

11. In the Select Additional Tasks dialog, choose the icons you want created as well as the real-time protection methods you desire. Remember, you can find the executable in the Start menu folder you chose. If you chose not to use a Start menu folder, you still can find the application in the destination location you picked out earlier. Click the Next button to advance to the Ready To Install dialog.

12. Confirm your settings and click the Back button to return to previous dialogs or click the Install button to begin downloading any additional files for the installation.

13. If you chose to update during installation and updates were found, the following screen appears. You want to use the default, which is the path where the program was just installed.

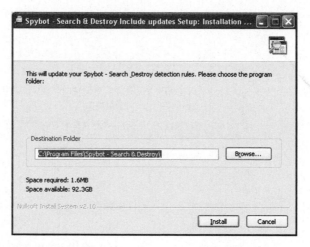

14. When the Include Updates Setup is done, click the Close button to be brought to the wizard completion dialog, where the only choice is to run Spybot - Search & Destroy now or not. Either way, click the Finish button to leave the wizard.

## Running the Application

1. If you did not choose to run the application after installation or you already had Spybot - Search & Destroy installed, double-click the icon to start the program. The first time you run the application, you are presented with a series of steps to finalize your installation.

The first major step among these is to back up your system's Registry. If a software package includes this feature, there's probably a very good reason. Click the Create Registry Backup button in the middle of the pop-up. When the Next arrow returns, click it to move along.

2.  The next major milestone is to search for and install updates, as shown in the following screen shot. If you chose to do this during installation and you just completed that part of the installation, there will not be anything to download and the associated button remains ghosted. Otherwise, click the Search For Updates button; if any are found, the Download All Available Updates button becomes active. Click the Download All Available Updates button to do so. Click the Next arrow to continue.

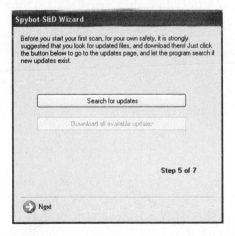

3.  Once all updates are downloaded, it is a good idea to immunize your system, which applies any downloaded definitions to the application. Click the Immunize This System button to complete the update process. Click the Next arrow to finalize the installation of the application.

4.  In the final step of the installation, click the button that reads Start Using The Program. If you prefer to peruse the tutorial or help file, there are buttons for those as well.

5.  Once the full application executes, click the Update icon in the left frame of the application to bring up the manual update search and download window.

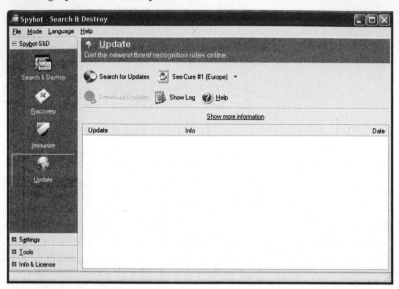

6.  Click the Immunize icon on the left to bring up a window similar to the following. This process is best completed each time you download updates. If someone else downloads updates, including the computer during automated updates, immunization may not occur regularly, obviating some of the updates.

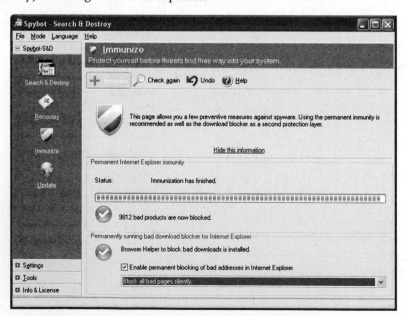

7. The Recovery icon is the key to displaying previous spyware fixes so that you can run through the list and place a check mark in any box. Checked items can then have a common policy applied to them. They are either recovered or purged completely from the system. Note, in the following illustration, that there are two levels of check boxes, one to accept the entire group and then one for each of the entries within a group. You can check these boxes in any combination; a check mark placed or cleared in a group box affects all entries within that group.

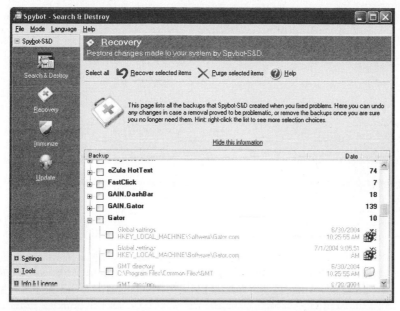

8. The Search & Destroy icon on the left takes you to the meat of the application, the point from which scans are begun, shown next. Click the Check For Problems icon to begin the actual scan.

9.  You hope to find no problems, in general, returning results that appear similar to the following. However, if you do find problems, run down the list and make sure check marks are in the boxes you want them in. Then, click the Fix Selected Problems icon to rid the system of the detected items that you designate.

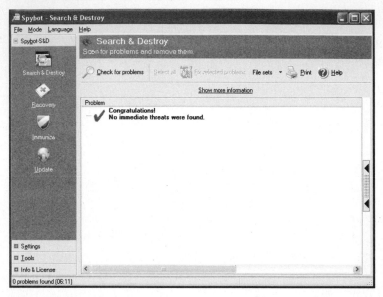

10. Spybot - Search & Destroy has a direct link to the Windows Scheduled Tasks utility. Windows makes this available through Start ➤ All Programs ➤ Accessories ➤ System Tools ➤ Scheduled Tasks. Spybot - Search & Destroy places its interface under the Settings bar and the Scheduler icon, shown next. The two check boxes in this window are convenient for scheduled, unattended scans. In fact, you would never know the scan took place if the log did not confirm as much.

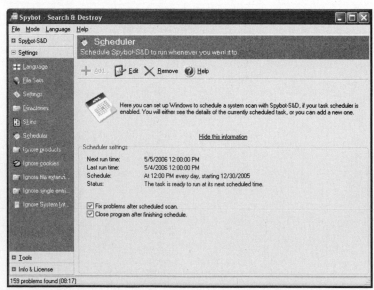

**11.** If you do not have any tasks scheduled for Spybot - Search & Destroy, click the Add icon to bring up the following Scheduled Task pages. If you do have one set already, click the Edit icon to bring up the same view. The Task page shown has one crucial item, the Run As field, that does not default properly and must be set for the task to perform as scheduled.

**12.** Enter the account name, preceded by the authenticating device—usually the local system— or domain and then click the Set Password button to enter the current password for the username entered. Note that whenever the password for the username changes, further scheduled tasks will not execute until a matching password is entered here.

**13.** The Schedule page is where you actually enter the time and frequency of the scans to be performed. See the following illustration for an example.

14. The Advanced button brings up more detailed settings, including when to start the back-ups, which can be set for a future date. For example, you might use this feature if you currently handle the scans manually but intend to be away from the computer starting on a certain date and yet the computer will be used by someone else for which the program is unavailable. The Advanced Schedule Options dialog is shown next.

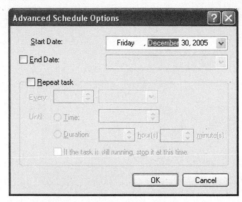

15. The Windows interface for all tasks scheduled looks similar to the following. Note that the same values from Spybot - Search & Destroy are shown for the program in this window.

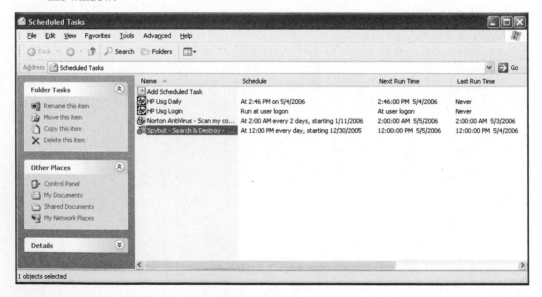

16. In the Spybot - Search & Destroy application, the Settings bar on the left also has a Settings entry. Clicking the entry brings up a long list of very specific items, shown next, that you can tweak to make the application run to your exact specifications.

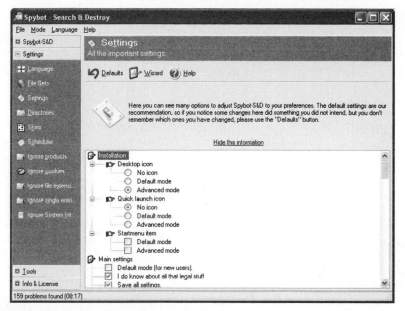

17. The Tools bar on the left displays a number of check boxes for various items. The ones you check appear on the left under the Tools bar so that you can access their specific settings, which are not available without a check mark in the correct box on the right.

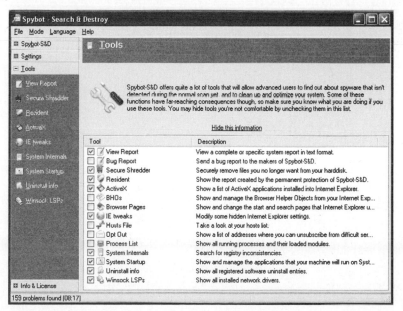

**18.** Finally, the Info & License bar on the left is where you can go to make a donation for the publisher of the free software. You can also see the legal information and credits here. The following screen shot shows the Info & License bar.

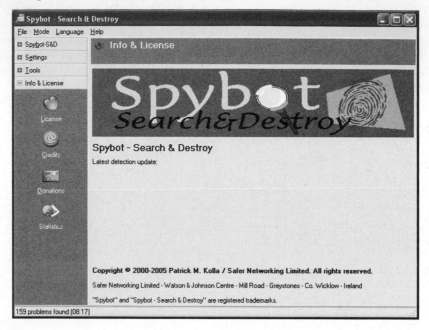

## Criteria for Completion

You have completed this task when you have conducted a scan for spyware with Spybot - Search & Destroy and fixed any problems found.

# Task 3.14: Searching for Operating System Updates

Different operating systems offer updates to their code in various ways. Some provide patches for download or on CD-ROMs or DVD-ROMs. Microsoft implements a web-based update service called Windows Update for genuine installations of its operating systems. Windows Update can be fairly automated, or you can take more control over the process if you choose. Today's Windows operating systems are capable of automatically updating themselves on a regular basis without user intervention as long as an Internet connection is present. Nevertheless, noncritical updates do not update automatically. Occasionally, manually updating your operating system to take care of these discrepancies is necessary.

## Scenario

You have a server that is not part of the enterprise domain. As a result, it does not obtain regular updates from the update server. You use the Automatic Updates icon in Control Panel, shown in Figure 3.8, to verify that the server is set to retrieve and install operating system updates. You have automatic updates turned on, as shown in Figure 3.9, but you are concerned that some nonessential updates have not been pushed to the system. You decide to go to Microsoft's website to find out if there are any updates available and, if so, download and install them.

## Scope of Task

### Duration

This task should take about 30 minutes.

### Setup

For this task, you need a single computer with an Internet connection.

**FIGURE 3.8**    Applet's icon in Control Panel

Administrative    Automatic    Bluetooth
   Tools         Updates     Configuration

**FIGURE 3.9**    Automatic Updates applet

## Caveat

Microsoft offers a server-based update service. When coupled with Group Policy objects (GPOs) limiting user access to the individual updates, the result of trying to update your operating system is a message similar to the following.

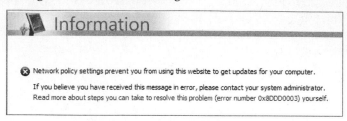

Some updates require you to reboot your system. Make sure you do not update your system manually while in the middle of other critical processes.

# Procedure

This task points you to Microsoft's Windows Update site and directs you through a search for updates for your operating system.

## Equipment Used

For this task, you need a single computer with an Internet connection.

## Details

In the following procedure, you check the Windows Update site for updates to your operating system.

### Express for High-Priority Updates

1.   Check to see if there is a Windows Update entry in your Start menu, probably visible right on the All Programs menu, as shown next. Click this icon if it exists.

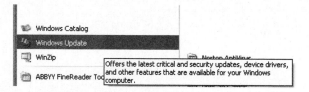

Otherwise, point your web browser to `http://windowsupdate.microsoft.com`. The website checks for a client-side component to the Windows Update application.

2.  On the Welcome To Windows Update page, there are two buttons, Express and Custom. Click the Express button to see what high-priority updates the software discovers.

3.  After a progress indicator makes its way across the scale, a page similar to the following displays if high-priority updates are discovered. Click the Install Updates button to continue.

4.  Accept the End User License Agreement (EULA) if presented with one.

5.  A progress indicator will list progress for both downloading and installation of updates. If a dialog similar to the one shown next appears, click the Close button. Normally, it is fine to click the Restart Now button as long as you have all work saved and an immediate reboot would not be destructive.

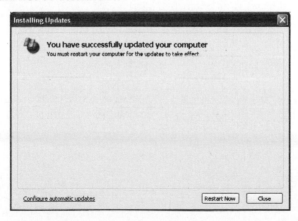

Clicking the Close button takes you back to the results page from the Windows Update website, which looks similar to the following.

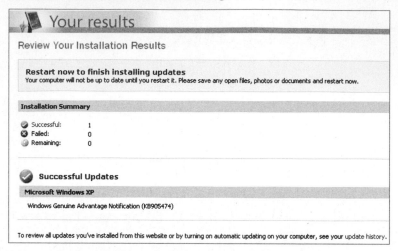

 Note that the need to restart for this particular update is reiterated here. Also, there is a link to display your system's past updates.

## Custom for Optional Updates

1. After rebooting, if necessary—additional updates do not install until mandatory restarts take place—run the Windows Update service again, but click the Custom button.

2. After a brief search for all types of updates, output similar to the following appears. It is no surprise to see no high-priority updates this time, but be on the lookout for lower-priority optional updates that you wish to download and install.

**3.** Click the Software Or Hardware link in the left frame. If updates were found for the category you choose, a display that looks very much like the next screen appears.

**4.** Placing a check mark in each update you wish to install adds it to the list to be downloaded and installed. Click the Review And Install Updates link, shown next, to continue to the page titled the same.

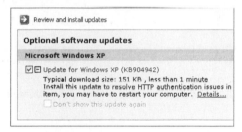

**5.** Click the Install Updates button, shown in the next screen, to start the process.

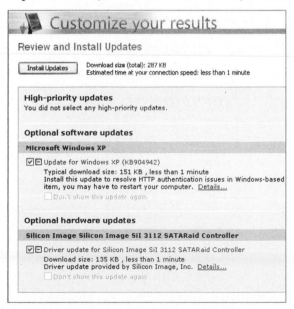

## Microsoft Update

At the time this book was written, Microsoft was introducing a new service, called Microsoft Update, to update non–operating system Microsoft components, such as Microsoft Office, much like Windows Update works for the operating system. In fact, the interface looks remarkably similar. These updates have been available online for some time, just not all in one convenient service. The following steps take you through the process of checking for and, if necessary, installing the client-side portion of the Microsoft Update service.

1. Check to see if you already have the Microsoft Update icon in your Start menu. If so, click it. If you do not have the icon, point your web browser to `http://update.microsoft.com` and click the Start Now button to begin installation.

2. If you have to install the client side of the service on you computer, the following page eventually displays. Click the Check For Updates button to begin a search for non–operating system updates.

3. A page similar to the following screen shot appears, showing you the updates that were found and the products for which the updates apply.

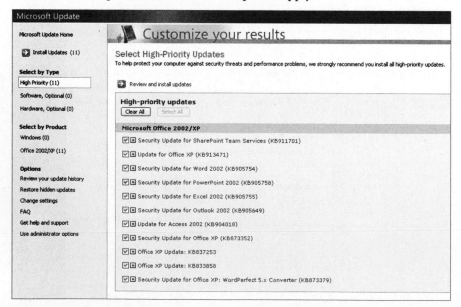

4.  If updates were found, review them and check or clear the boxes next to them as you wish.

5.  Click the Review And Install Updates link.

6.  Accept the EULA.

7.  Once the updates are installed, click the Close button on the confirmation dialog.

8.  A page similar to the following (and similar to the corresponding page displayed by Windows Update) tells you that the process is complete and allows you to view your update history.

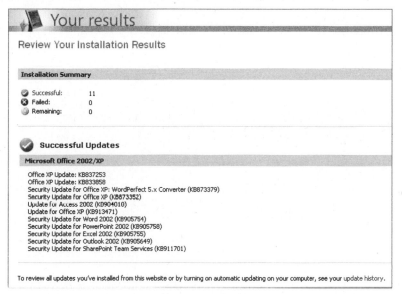

## Criteria for Completion

You have completed this task when you have accessed Microsoft's Windows Update site and searched for, downloaded, and installed any high-priority updates found. Optionally, you might have chosen to enhance your experience with this procedure by installing, if necessary, and accessing Microsoft Update as well.

# Phase
# 4

# Troubleshooting the Network

In this phase, many of the tools available to a network administrator during troubleshooting are presented. The utilities and protocols you will use in phase 4 as you enhance your troubleshooting skills are ARP, `netstat`, FTP, ping, `ipconfig`, trace route, Telnet, and `nslookup`.

Additionally, you get to practice with a protocol analyzer for a much closer look at the traffic on your network. Finally, you will take a look into the event logs of your computer to find out how to monitor those events that matter most during day-to-day operation.

**NOTE** The tasks in this phase map to domains 2 and 4 in the objectives for the CompTIA Network+ exam.

# Task 4.1: Using ARP Utilities

IP devices keep a table known as an ARP cache. A cache is a temporary table, the contents of which age and disappear from the table from lack of use, based on a configurable timer. Each time the entry is used, its individual timer is reset, lengthening its stay in the cache. An ARP cache stores IP-address-to-MAC-address resolutions for other IP devices on the local subnet. Recall that IP hosts build their ARP cache through link-local broadcasts that remain on the immediate subnet only. An ARP broadcast goes out when the routing process, on either a source or intermediate system, determines the next-hop device, even if it's the final destination, which lies in its local subnet by definition.

The Layer 2 frame's header encapsulates the IP header, and receiving hardware passes the bits of the inbound frame to the Layer 2 entity, say Ethernet, for processing. As a result, the MAC address for the next device in the path to the destination is the only functional address in the frame. Until a routing decision has to be made or until the final destination is reached, the IP address is simply raw data to the Layer 2 processes along the way.

Sometimes, it becomes necessary to look into the mind of the local device to see what it knows about its local network. For example, does a computer know the MAC address of its default gateway? Most ARP utilities give the user or administrator a way to statically configure entries for devices that the local machine accesses on a semiregular basis. There is no need to make static entries for often-accessed devices because the MAC addresses of these devices never age out of the cache. There is no value in making static entries for rarely accessed devices because the broadcasts that go out for these hosts are negligible. The devices that are accessed only frequently enough to barely miss the cut-off and just barely fall off the list when they are ARPed for again are the ones that the local system benefits from having entered statically in its cache.

## Scenario

One of your servers is inaccessible from the rest of the internetwork. You plan to use its ARP utility to make sure it knows the MAC address of its default gateway. In fact, you plan to go ahead and statically configure this association, just to reduce the broadcast traffic on the network.

## Scope of Task

### Duration

This task should take about 30 minutes.

### Setup

For this task, you need to set up a single computer with connectivity to another IP device.

### Caveat

Be careful not to forget about static cache entries that you set. All it takes is for a NIC to be replaced or the general IP addressing scheme to change and entries based on the old information are null and void. In fact, they might interfere with the proper functioning of the system. If you create them statically, you must remove them manually as well. You will have to keep an eye on your static entries or they could become troubleshooting tasks in and of themselves. You do not want to make a static entry for a device whose IP address was learned by DHCP. The association between IP and MAC addresses becomes invalid as soon as the device obtains a different IP address from the DHCP server.

## Procedure

In this task, you use the ARP utility to discover and set IP-to-MAC associations, using a Microsoft operating system and a Cisco router. Figure 4.1 illustrates the sample network connectivity between a computer and a router.

**FIGURE 4.1**   Sample network layout

## Equipment Used

For this task, you need a computer with a Windows operating system and a Cisco router. Connect the computer's Ethernet interface to the router's Ethernet interface. Also connect the computer to the console port of the router for configuration access.

## Details

This task walks you through configuring a computer and a router for IP access to one another and then confirming Layer 2 connectivity through each device's ARP utility.

1. Use an Ethernet crossover cable to connect the computer to the router or use a switch or hub with two straight cables.

2. Configure the computer and router to be on the same IP subnet, as in Figure 4.1.

### ARP on the Computer

1. Ping the router from the computer.

```
C:\>ping 172.16.50.65

Pinging 172.16.50.65 with 32 bytes of data:

Reply from 172.16.50.65: bytes=32 time=1ms TTL=64
Reply from 172.16.50.65: bytes=32 time=1ms TTL=64
Reply from 172.16.50.65: bytes=32 time=1ms TTL=64
Reply from 172.16.50.65: bytes=32 time=1ms TTL=64

Ping statistics for 172.16.50.65:
    Packets: Sent = 4, Received = 4, Lost = 0 (0% loss),
Approximate round trip times in milli-seconds:
    Minimum = 1ms, Maximum = 20ms, Average = 5ms


C:\>
```

2. On the computer, open a command prompt.

3. Enter the command **arp -a** at the computer's command prompt. You should see the IP-to-MAC association for the router. In the Type column of the output, **dynamic** means that the resolution was automatic when the two devices were forced to communicate during the ping, or before, perhaps. For a list of Unix-style switches for the **arp** command, enter **arp /?** Or simply enter **arp** with no arguments.

```
C:\>arp -a

Interface: 172.16.50.66
  Internet Address        Physical Address        Type
  172.16.50.65            00-0c-85-c4-d3-20        dynamic


C:\>
```

4. Enter the command **arp -s** *IP_address MAC_address*, where *IP_address* and *MAC_address* are the addresses for the router in the previous ARP output.

```
C:\>arp -s 172.16.50.65 00-0c-85-c4-d3-20

C:\>
```

5. Now, when you enter the **arp -a** command, the dynamic entry has become static.

```
C:\>arp -a

Interface: 172.16.50.66
  Internet Address      Physical Address      Type
  172.16.50.65          00-0c-85-c4-d3-20     static

C:\>
```

6. Use the **arp -d** *IP_address* command to remove the static entry and let the association be learned dynamically the next time it is needed.

```
C:\>arp -d 172.16.50.65

C:\>
```

## ARP on the Router

1. On the router, show the ARP cache with the EXEC command **show arp**.

```
ARProuter#show arp
Protocol  Address       Age (min) Hardware Addr   Type   Interface
Internet  172.16.50.66       -     000f.1fbd.76a5  ARPA   Fa0/0
ARProuter#
```

2. In order to enter the same association statically, do the following.

```
ARProuter#config t
ARProuter(config)#arp 172.16.50.66 000f.1fbd.76a5 arpa
ARProuter(config)#end
ARProuter#
```

There is no clear-cut way to know that the entry is static, except for the absence of the interface value in the last column.

```
ARProuter#show arp
Protocol  Address       Age (min) Hardware Addr   Type   Interface
Internet  172.16.50.66       -     000f.1fbd.76a5  ARPA
ARProuter#
```

3.  Negate the command that created the static entry, leaving off the MAC address, to go back to dynamic, as shown in the following code. Displaying the cache again eventually shows that the interface value returned. Ping the computer to hurry things along, if necessary.

```
ARProuter#config t
ARProuter(config)#no arp 172.16.50.66
ARProuter(config)#end
ARProuter#
```

## Criteria for Completion

You have completed this task when you have displayed and configured static ARP entries on the computer and on the router.

# Task 4.2: Using the NETSTAT Utility

The Internet, and every other IP-based network for that matter, fosters communication between devices using a data structure known as a socket. Specifically, a TCP/IP socket is a 48-bit numerical value consisting of an IP address and a TCP or UDP port number. Although they're numerically identical, you can distinguish between TCP and UDP sockets by tracking the Layer 4 protocol. In essence, a socket describes a specific application running anywhere in the internetwork. The IP address leads to the device executing the application (HTTP, for example), and the Layer 4 protocol and port number uniquely lead to the specific application in question.

   Microsoft operating systems and those based on Unix use a utility known as NETSTAT, which is short for network statistics, to report on the state of sockets that exist on the device executing the command. With this utility, a network administrator can investigate the TCP/IP activity going on to or from a specific device at any given moment.

## Scenario

One of your servers has been enduring quite a bit of traffic lately. Concerned about its source and purpose, you set out to discover the nature of this increase in load. Using the NETSTAT utility on the server, you shed some light on this discrepancy.

## Scope of Task

### Duration

This task should take about 20 minutes.

## Setup

For this task, you need to set up a single computer with connectivity to the Internet or an intranet.

## Caveat

Unless you know the history of a connection, it is sometimes difficult to determine whether the local device is the initiator of the connection. Further investigation might be required to ascertain the purpose of a suspicious connection. Be careful not to jump to the conclusion that an unfamiliar connection is an attack on the local system.

# Procedure

In this task, you use the NETSTAT utility to view the current connections to a network-attached system.

## Equipment Used

For this task, you need a computer with a connection to a TCP/IP network with one or more types of server.

## Details

This task details the common uses of the `netstat` command in a Windows operating system.

1. Test your system for Internet or intranet connectivity by using HTTP, Telnet, or some other network service to a remote device.
2. Open a command prompt window.
3. Enter the command **netstat**. If you are not issuing the command on a server, you might see a cyclical connection to your own device, similar to the following. Call this the set of default connections.

```
C:\>netstat

Active Connections

  Proto  Local Address      Foreign Address      State
  TCP    filesrv:1068       localhost:6139       ESTABLISHED
  TCP    filesrv:6139       localhost:1068       ESTABLISHED

C:\>
```

See page 20 of RFC 793 for an explanation of TCP connection states.

4.  To display the corresponding IP address instead of the NETBIOS or DNS name for each entry, issue the command **netstat -n**.

```
C:\>netstat -n

Active Connections

    Proto  Local Address          Foreign Address        State
    TCP    127.0.0.1:1068         127.0.0.1:6139         ESTABLISHED
    TCP    127.0.0.1:6139         127.0.0.1:1068         ESTABLISHED

C:\>
```

5.  In your Command Prompt window, issue the command **netstat 3**. Quickly point your web browser to http://www.wiley.com. Go back and watch the progress in your Command Prompt window. The number 3 causes the command to repeat every three seconds. You see a developing set of connections similar to the following.

```
C:\>netstat 3

Active Connections

    Proto  Local Address          Foreign Address        State
    TCP    filesrv:1659           www.wiley.com:http     ESTABLISHED

Active Connections

    Proto  Local Address          Foreign Address        State
    TCP    filesrv:1663           208.215.179.180:http   ESTABLISHED
    TCP    filesrv:1664           208.215.179.180:http   ESTABLISHED
    TCP    filesrv:1665           www.wiley.com:http     LAST_ACK

Active Connections

    Proto  Local Address          Foreign Address        State
    TCP    filesrv:1664           208.215.179.180:http   ESTABLISHED
    TCP    filesrv:1666           www.wiley.com:http     TIME_WAIT
    TCP    filesrv:1669           208.215.179.180:http   ESTABLISHED
^C
C:\>
```

6. Press Ctrl+C to stop the command from running.

7. Issue the command **netstat 3** again in your command prompt window. Return to your web browser and enter the address **ftp://ftp.microsoft.com**. Note the connection display, similar to the following.

```
C:\>netstat 3

Active Connections

    Proto  Local Address        Foreign Address        State
    TCP    filesrv:1068         localhost:6139         ESTABLISHED
    TCP    filesrv:6139         localhost:1068         ESTABLISHED

Active Connections

    Proto  Local Address        Foreign Address        State
    TCP    filesrv:1068         localhost:6139         ESTABLISHED
    TCP    filesrv:6139         localhost:1068         ESTABLISHED
    TCP    filesrv:1891         ftp.microsoft.com:ftp  ESTABLISHED
^C
C:\>
```

8. (Optional) Try to think of other ways to generate traffic that results in your computer establishing connections that you can verify using different forms of the netstat command, which you can investigate by issuing the command **netstat /?**.

## Criteria for Completion

You have completed this task when you have displayed your computer's sockets using the NETSTAT utility while establishing connections using various protocols.

# Task 4.3: Using the FTP Utility

The File Transfer Protocol (FTP), part of the TCP/IP suite and detailed in RFC 959, is an integral component of many user interfaces. Many believe that the front ends (FTP utilities) are themselves FTP. In fact, FTP is only the Application layer protocol that these utilities employ to do their job. That job is to facilitate the transfer of files and folders from one host on an internetwork to another. From the simplest forms, such as a command-line interface, to more complex forms, such as a Windows Explorer view and, the most complex, full-featured applications, FTP utilities abound. They all have one thing in common: they use the FTP protocol.

## Scenario

One of your servers has never been used as a client workstation, but you would like to be able to view Word files without the danger of altering them. Your plan is to go to the Microsoft FTP site to download an executable that will install a Word viewer. Your secondary goal, while you are able to get away from the masses for a few minutes, is to evaluate two FTP client products that you have heard about, WebDrive and BulletProof.

## Scope of Task

### Duration

This task should take about 45 minutes.

### Setup

For this task, you need to set up a single computer with connectivity to the Internet.

### Caveat

Don't confuse FTP with Server Message Block (SMB), which is the protocol used to transfer files from one device to another in a Windows resource sharing environment. Whenever you share a folder on one computer and transfer files to and from that folder using another computer, it is SMB that packages the information up and transfers it, not FTP.

Using the command-line FTP utility can try the patience of the most stoic of administrators. If this is your only option, be sure to look for, download, and peruse index files that explain large directories with files that have names that are too cryptic to be able to decipher efficiently.

## Procedure

In this task, you use the Microsoft command-line FTP utility, as well as the Microsoft Explorer FTP utility. Optionally, you can follow along with the use of two popular try-before-you-buy FTP clients.

### Equipment Used

For this task, you need a computer with an Internet connection.

### Details

#### Microsoft Command Line

This section details the steps to attach to and navigate the Microsoft FTP server and then download the Word Viewer installation file from the Softlib/MSLFILES directory.

1. Test your system for Internet connectivity by pinging or using HTTP to browse to a remote device.

2.  Open a command prompt window.

3.  Enter the command **ftp ftp.microsoft.com**. Alternatively, you can start the FTP utility by entering **ftp**. Then, at the ftp> prompt, enter **open ftp.microsoft.com**. Microsoft's FTP server prompts you for a user name.

```
C:\>ftp ftp.microsoft.com
Connected to ftp.microsoft.com.
220 Microsoft FTP Service
User (ftp.microsoft.com:(none)):
```

4.  Unless someone at Microsoft gives you a temporary username and password to access a restricted area of the server, use **anonymous** as the username and your email address as the password. You still get access with the wrong email address, but there is no reason not to enter a legitimate one. Many front ends use an arbitrary value with the username anonymous when you choose to log on as a guest.

```
User (ftp.microsoft.com:(none)): anonymous
331 Anonymous access allowed, send identity (e-mail name) as password.
Password:
230-Welcome to FTP.MICROSOFT.COM. Also visit
http://www.microsoft.com/downloads.

230 Anonymous user logged in.
ftp>
```

> At the ftp> prompt, enter a question mark (?) to obtain a list of legal commands.

5.  Following is the output of the ls command, which is a Unix command, similar to the dir /b command in Microsoft networks, that lists only folder and filenames, no details. In fact, if you did not know, you would be hard-pressed to differentiate between the two.

```
ftp> ls
200 PORT command successful.
150 Opening ASCII mode data connection for file list.
bussys
deskapps
developr
KBHelp
MISC
MISC1
peropsys
Products
```

```
PSS
ResKit
Services
Softlib
226 Transfer complete.
ftp: 101 bytes received in 0.00Seconds 101000.00Kbytes/sec.
ftp>
```

6. Change directories to the Softlib directory, which is the next step in getting to the file you need to download. Use the cd command with the directory name. Obtain a directory listing for the Softlib directory.

```
ftp> cd softlib
250 CWD command successful.
ftp> ls
200 PORT command successful.
150 Opening ASCII mode data connection for file list.
index.txt
MSLFILES
README.TXT
226 Transfer complete.
ftp: 33 bytes received in 0.00Seconds 33000.00Kbytes/sec.
ftp>
```

7. Although you have been informed that the file you are looking for, the Word Viewer installation file, is in the MSLFILES directory, meaning that you must change directories one more time, enter the **dir** command to confirm that MSLFILES is a directory and not just a file. A dash (-) in the first column indicates a file, while a d indicates the entry is a directory, confirming the status of MSLFILES.

```
ftp> dir
200 PORT command successful.
150 Opening ASCII mode data connection for /bin/ls.
-r-xr-xr-x   1 owner     group       205710 May 10  2000 index.txt
dr-xr-xr-x   1 owner     group            0 Feb  1 22:43 MSLFILES
-r-xr-xr-x   1 owner     group         2401 Sep  3  1999 README.TXT
226 Transfer complete.
ftp: 210 bytes received in 0.00Seconds 210000.00Kbytes/sec.
ftp>
```

8. Change to the MSLFILES directory.

```
ftp> cd mslfiles
250 CWD command successful.
ftp>
```

**9.** Say you want to download the file to the Desktop of the Administrator user account. This location has a path of `C:\Documents and Settings\Administrator\Desktop`. There are at least two ways to make sure this is the destination for the file. One way is to change the local directory to the desired path. Another way is to specify the path in the download step. Use the `lcd` command, as follows, to go with the first method and change the local directory. With no arguments, the `lcd` command displays the current directory.

```
ftp> lcd
Local directory now C:\.
ftp>
```

**10.** Unfortunately, the FTP shell does not support spaces in filenames, as evidenced by the following output, indicating the currently logged directory is still the same.

```
ftp> lcd documents and settings
lcd local directory.
ftp> lcd
Local directory now C:\.
ftp>
```

**11.** The solution is to use Microsoft's convention for converting long names to the original 8.3 format, an eight-character filename and a three-character extension. For filenames longer than eight characters, or for those with spaces in them, use the first six characters followed by a tilde (~) and then a sequential number assigned by the operating system to eliminate conflicts. If there is only one filename with those first six characters, the number used is 1. Assume that is the case for `Documents and Settings`. Remember, case does not matter.

```
ftp> lcd docume~1
Local directory now C:\Documents and Settings.
ftp>
```

**12.** Continue navigating down the directory tree. While filenames with spaces are not allowed, those that violate the original 8.3 format are allowed. That fact notwithstanding, optionally, you can specify the Administrator directory name as **admini~1**. You can also combine multiple steps, as in the case of **lcd administrator\desktop**.

```
ftp> lcd administrator
Local directory now C:\Documents and Settings\Administrator.
ftp> lcd desktop
Local directory now C:\Documents and Settings\Administrator\Desktop.
ftp>
```

**13.** The get command is used to download a single file. Contrast the get command with the put command to upload, provided you have write access to the server. An additional version of each command, mget and mput, allows for multiple files to be transferred at once. You can specify the entire transaction in a single command, as you can with the copy command at the Microsoft command prompt, or just issue the get command and let the interface walk you through the other parameters. You need to download the `index.txt` file shown in that previous directory listing because the `MSLFILES` directory has a very large number of files in it.

```
ftp> get
Remote file index.txt
Local file index.txt
200 PORT command successful.
150 Opening ASCII mode data connection for index.txt(205710 bytes).
226 Transfer complete.
ftp: 205710 bytes received in 1.81Seconds 113.84Kbytes/sec.
ftp>
```

**14.** Look for the Index file on the Desktop of the Administrator, as shown next.

**15.** Now, open the `index.txt` file and search for "word viewer," which is all you have to go on. The following image gives an example of what you might find.

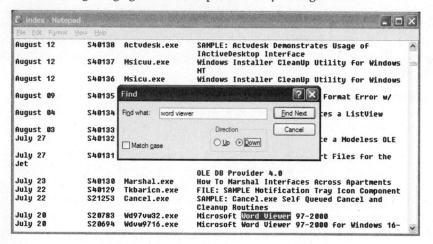

**16.** Unfortunately, your local directory change is fickle. It is only good for one use. Issuing the `lcd` command with no arguments shows you are back to the default directory after your last file transfer, which would make finding your downloaded files a bit challenging if you were not aware of this peculiarity.

```
ftp> lcd
Local directory now C:\.
ftp>
```

17. Now that you know the file you require is named WD97VW32.EXE, for the version of the viewer for 32-bit operating systems, download it to the Administrator's Desktop. Use the method that does not involve changing the local directory.

```
ftp> get
Remote file wd97vw32.exe
Local file c:\docume~1\admini~1\desktop\wd97vw32.exe
200 PORT command successful.
150 Opening ASCII mode data connection for wd97vw32.exe(3952016 bytes).
226 Transfer complete.
ftp: 3952016 bytes received in 252.88Seconds 15.63Kbytes/sec.
ftp>
```

18. You can see the file exists on the Desktop of the Administrator account.

19. You have at least three choices for exiting your FTP session. The least elegant method is simply to close the Command Prompt window with no further effort. Another way is to issue the bye command, which closes the FTP session and the FTP utility, ejecting you back out to a standard command prompt. The third way is to issue the close command, which ends the FTP session but leaves you in the FTP interface in case you want to open a new connection next. The quit command leaves the FTP utility from here. The following output shows this last method.

```
ftp> close
221 Thank you for using Microsoft products.
ftp> quit

C:\>
```

## Windows Explorer

A much simpler way to accomplish the foregoing task, but a method that is not always available, depending on the operating system or the group policy in place, is the use of the Explorer interface to gain access to an FTP server.

1. Open either a Windows Explorer or Internet Explorer window and navigate to ftp:// ftp.microsoft.com.

It is acceptable to leave off the `ftp://` prefix when the server name is ftp, just as it is not problematic to leave off `http://` when the server name is www.

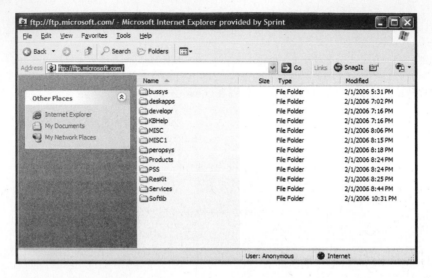

**2.** When you double-click the `Softlib` object in the window, the following listing is displayed, from which it is not difficult to spot that `index.txt` is a file and `MSLFILES` is a directory, unlike the ambiguity when using the `ls` command in the FTP command-line utility. All you need to do to read the `index.txt` file is to double-click it.

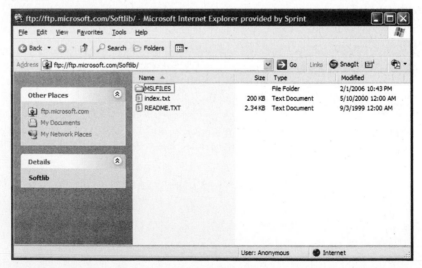

**3.** Double-click the MSLFILES folder object and look for WD97VW32.EXE, as illustrated next.

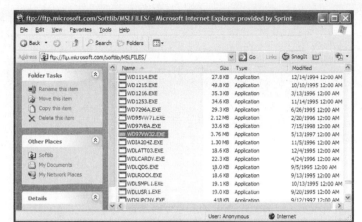

**4.** Making sure the Explorer window with the FTP content is not maximized, and that you can see part of the Desktop, simply drag the file to the Desktop and drop it. A copy of the file is placed on the Desktop. Other methods that work between Explorer windows work in this case as well—for example, right-clicking and choosing Copy from the shortcut menu and then pasting it to the destination any one of a variety of ways.

## BulletProof

By browsing to http://www.download.com and performing a search on "ftp client," you can find the latest version of an application called BulletProof FTP Client. Keep your eye on Web-Drive, as well, which comes up in the same search.

**1.** After downloading and installing BulletProof, you find a full-featured FTP client with quite a few more bells and whistles than the Explorer method of FTP access offers.

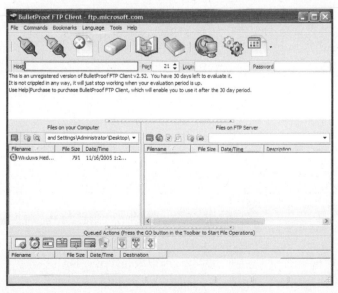

2.   Traverse the local tree in the Files On Your Computer pane to the same directory you used earlier—for example, `C:\Documents and Settings\Administrator\Desktop`.

3.   Type **ftp.microsoft.com** in the Host field and click the first large icon at the top to connect to the server and you are presented with a notification of the success of the connection, as in the next illustration. Note that anonymous access is the default.

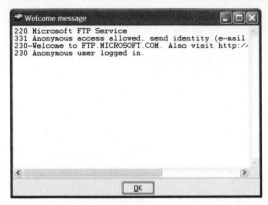

4.   In the following image, in the Files On FTP Server pane, notice the same directories that you saw earlier in the output from the `ls` command.

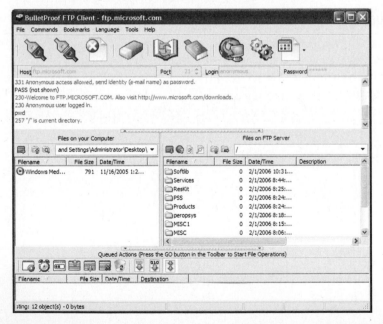

5.   In order to view the `index.txt` file, you must first download it, much as you did with the command-line method earlier. There is a drag-and-drop feature, but it is only from one pane to another within the application, not out to the Desktop or an Explorer window. After you double-click the file `index.txt`, it appears queued up in the bottom pane of the

application, as you can see at the bottom of the following screen shot. In fact, you can click the first icon at the bottom to start the transfer now or wait a configurable amount of time, no more than 30 seconds or so by default, and the application transfers it automatically. Then, you must find the file and open it, as with the command-line method.

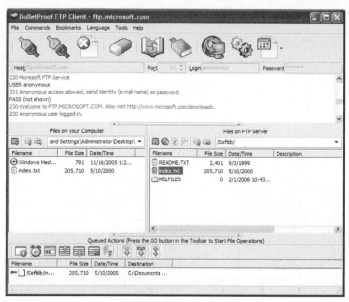

6. Traverse the directory tree on the server to where you found the Word Viewer file before and start the transfer. Notice the progress indicator at the very bottom of the application, as shown next.

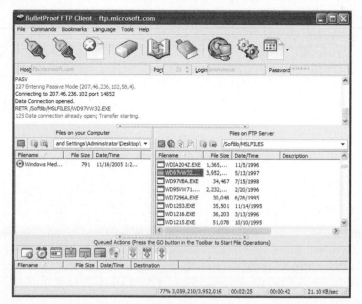

When the transfer is complete, the file appears in the Files On Your Computer pane on the left.

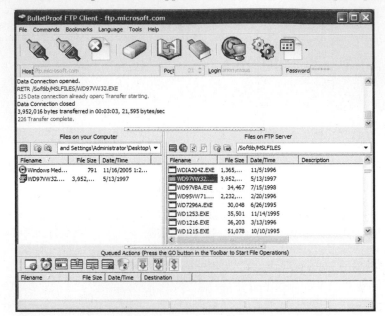

## WebDrive

Of the methods presented here, WebDrive arguably offers the best mix of features and convenience. You are able to choose the protocol you wish to use between client and server; you're not limited to just FTP. You can choose something more secure if you like. You also are able to map the server to a drive letter, making the drag-and-drop feature possible again. The following image depicts the initial state of WebDrive after installation.

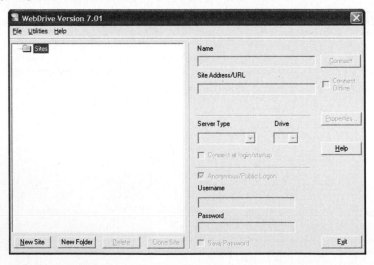

1.  Click the New Site button to bring up the following New Site Wizard screen. Enter a friendly name for the configuration, and then click the Next button to move on to the Server type selection.

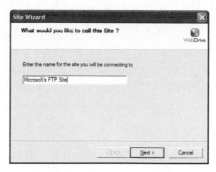

2.  By dropping the menu down, you can see the variety of protocols with which this client front end is compatible, as shown next. Click on your server choice and then click the Next button.

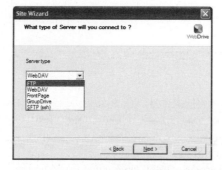

3.  In the dialogs that ensue, enter `ftp.microsoft.com` as the URL for the server; choose any available drive letter form the drop-down for the drive to map to the server; leave the Username and Password fields blank—or specify **anonymous** and your email address, respectively, if you wish.

4.  Click the Finish button, to leave the wizard and try out your new connection.

5. Note, from the following screen shot, that your friendly site name appears under the Sites folder and all your optional settings are to the right and editable, as long as your site is selected. Click the Connect button to produce an Explorer window for the drive you specified.

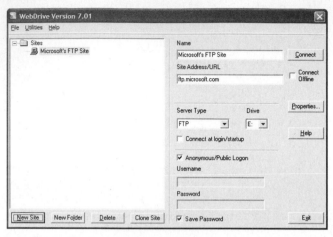

6. Traverse the directory structure of the server until you arrive at the MSLFILES directory and then find the WD97VW32 object (which is the WD97VW32.EXE file), as shown in the following screen shot. You can drag this file to the location of your choosing. You might have to make sure the Explorer window is not maximized.

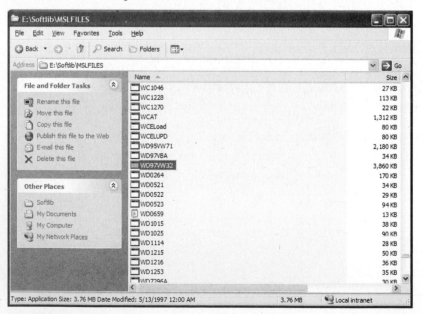

## Criteria for Completion

You have completed this task when you have performed a file transfer using the command-line and Explorer methods. Optionally, downloading and installing the trial versions of Bullet-Proof FTP Client and WebDrive offers experience with additional FTP utilities.

# Task 4.4: Using Ping Utilities

Nearly every class of IP-compatible device has built in to it a way to test connectivity to the rest of the network with a single command. The vast preponderance of these devices uses the ping utility. The term is often capitalized like an acronym and expanded as Packet INternet Groper, but ping's author has dismissed this urban legend. Perhaps the industry has a bit more pent-up creativity than it knows what to do with. Its name is derived from the fact that it works in a similar fashion to a sonar ping in that it sends a packet out and expects one back. The variable delay tends to be proportionate to the distance and the number of devices in between.

## Scenario

One of your established servers has stopped responding to client requests. You plan to use the ping utility, among others if necessary, to ascertain the full nature of the connectivity issues plaguing this server and the network in general.

## Scope of Task

### Duration

This task should take about 30 minutes.

### Setup

For this task, you need to connect a computer and a router.

### Caveat

There is no substitute for knowing how your network is laid out. Simply knowing what to expect by running connectivity verification utilities tends to keep you from going off on a wild-goose chase. Assuming that problems are with the source or destination of a ping exchange only leaves out any intermediate devices that might have connectivity issues of their own, leading to wasted efforts to fix a problem that might not exist. Also knowing how the ping process works is beneficial as well.

## Procedure

In this task, you use the ping utility on a computer running Windows and on a Cisco router to test connectivity from one to the other. Figure 4.2 illustrates the sample network connectivity between a computer and a router.

**FIGURE 4.2** Sample network layout

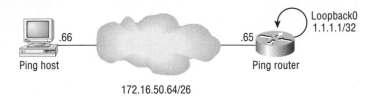

## Equipment Used

For this task, you need a computer with a Windows operating system and a Cisco router. Connect the computer's Ethernet interface to the router's Ethernet interface. Also connect the computer to the console port of the router for configuration access.

## Details

In this task, you use the ping utility on an interconnected computer and router to investigate the differences in their interfaces as well as the nature of IP routing.

1.  Use an Ethernet crossover cable to connect the computer to the router or use a switch or hub with two straight cables.

2.  Configure the computer and router according to Figure 4.2.

3.  At a Command Prompt on the computer, ping the router's nearest interface. This works because when a device pings another, it sources the ICMP echo request on the exit interface. This IP address is the destination address that the device you ping uses to send an echo reply. Because both addresses are on the same IP subnet, they know to use their common interface to send traffic to each other.

```
C:\>ping 172.16.50.65

Pinging 172.16.50.65 with 32 bytes of data:

Reply from 172.16.50.65: bytes=32 time=1ms TTL=64
Reply from 172.16.50.65: bytes=32 time=1ms TTL=64
Reply from 172.16.50.65: bytes=32 time=1ms TTL=64
Reply from 172.16.50.65: bytes=32 time=1ms TTL=64
```

```
Ping statistics for 172.16.50.65:
    Packets: Sent = 4, Received = 4, Lost = 0 (0% loss),
Approximate round trip times in milli-seconds:
    Minimum = 1ms, Maximum = 20ms, Average = 5ms

C:\>
```

4. On the router, reverse the source and destination for the ping just to show that neither end has a problem generating the echo request.

```
PingRouter#ping 172.16.50.66

Type escape sequence to abort.
Sending 5, 100-byte ICMP Echos to 172.16.50.66, timeout is 2 seconds:
!!!!!
Success rate is 100 percent (5/5), round-trip min/avg/max = 1/1/4 ms
PingRouter#
```

5. Now, attempt to ping the router's loopback interface from the computer. If the computer's default gateway is other than the router's local interface, the computer thinks it has a path everywhere in the world. When the default gateway device does not know how to handle a destination network, it forwards it on to its default gateway. By the time the unreachable messages begin to flow back to the source of the pings, the source has timed out waiting for a response.

```
C:\>ping 1.1.1.1

Pinging 1.1.1.1 with 32 bytes of data:

Request timed out.
Request timed out.
Request timed out.
Request timed out.

Ping statistics for 1.1.1.1:
    Packets: Sent = 4, Received = 0, Lost = 4 (100% loss),

C:\>
```

6. On the router, execute an extended ping by entering only the command **ping**. The rest of the settings appear as follows. Again, the source and destination are reversed from the previous step.

```
PingRouter#ping
Protocol [ip]:
Target IP address: 172.16.50.66
```

```
Repeat count [5]:
Datagram size [100]:
Timeout in seconds [2]:
Extended commands [n]: y
Source address or interface: 1.1.1.1
Type of service [0]:
Set DF bit in IP header? [no]:
Validate reply data? [no]:
Data pattern [0xABCD]:
Loose, Strict, Record, Timestamp, Verbose[none]:
Sweep range of sizes [n]:
Type escape sequence to abort.
Sending 5, 100-byte ICMP Echos to 172.16.50.66, timeout is 2 seconds:
Packet sent with a source address of 1.1.1.1
.....
Success rate is 0 percent (0/5)
PingRouter#
```

NOTE
> Note that the ping was unsuccessful. This is because you sourced the ping
> from the loopback interface, which has an IP address to which the computer
> is unable to return traffic, as evidenced in step 5. This is a way to test connec-
> tivity of a remote device to a local address without the need to conduct the
> ping from the remote device.

7. Teach the computer how to find the address of the router's Loopback interface.

   C:\>**route add 1.1.1.1 mask 255.255.255.255 172.16.50.65**

   C:\>

8. Now, try the ping from both directions. The router has no problem responding to the computer's source address, which is on a local subnet with the router. After the alteration to the computer's routing table, the computer has no trouble getting to the Loopback interface of the router even though it is not a local address.

   C:\>**ping 1.1.1.1**

   ```
   Pinging 1.1.1.1 with 32 bytes of data:

   Reply from 1.1.1.1: bytes=32 time=495ms TTL=120
   Reply from 1.1.1.1: bytes=32 time=428ms TTL=120
   ```

```
Reply from 1.1.1.1: bytes=32 time=428ms TTL=120
Reply from 1.1.1.1: bytes=32 time=465ms TTL=120

Ping statistics for 1.1.1.1:
    Packets: Sent = 4, Received = 4, Lost = 0 (0% loss),
Approximate round trip times in milli-seconds:
    Minimum = 428ms, Maximum = 495ms, Average = 454ms

C:\>


PingRouter#ping
Protocol [ip]:
Target IP address: 172.16.50.66
Repeat count [5]:
Datagram size [100]:
Timeout in seconds [2]:
Extended commands [n]: y
Source address or interface: 1.1.1.1
Type of service [0]:
Set DF bit in IP header? [no]:
Validate reply data? [no]:
Data pattern [0xABCD]:
Loose, Strict, Record, Timestamp, Verbose[none]:
Sweep range of sizes [n]:
Type escape sequence to abort.
Sending 5, 100-byte ICMP Echos to 172.16.50.66, timeout is 2 seconds:
Packet sent with a source address of 1.1.1.1
!!!!!
Success rate is 100 percent (5/5), round-trip min/avg/max = 1/2/4 ms
PingRouter#
```

## Criteria for Completion

You have completed this task when you have configured the devices according to the task procedure and observed the success and failure of the ping utility. Because this feature is so prevalent and crucial to daily troubleshooting, it is highly recommended that you devise your own scenarios and conduct similar attempts to verify connectivity.

# Task 4.5: Using the IPCONFIG Utility

One of the most informative yet simple utilities an IP-compatible operating system offers is the one that allows you to see the current IP address, mask, default gateway, name servers, and other components that go into a well-rounded IP installation. For Microsoft's latest operating systems, this command-line utility is known as IPCONFIG. In Unix and MacOS, you can use the IFCONFIG utility for similar results.

## Scenario

One of your established servers has stopped responding to client requests. You plan to use the ping utility, among others, if necessary, to ascertain the full nature of the connectivity issues plaguing this server and the network, in general.

## Scope of Task

### Duration

This task should take about 30 minutes, 20 to 30 minutes longer if you need to configure your own DHCP server.

### Setup

For this task, you need a computer that has access to a network with a DHCP server. You can optionally make your own LAN with a cable directly to a wireless router (or a similar device) that provides DHCP information. Editing the DHCP server portion of such a device allows you to witness the effects of server changes, because among other things, the IPCONFIG utility reports local DHCP-learned settings and even allows you to release and renew such settings.

### Caveat

Utilities, such as IPCONFIG and IFCONFIG, allow the display of IP information on the local device. They do not go beyond the local network interfaces of the computer on which the command is issued. Furthermore, these utilities are not used to change this information, only to display it. Each operating system offers other utilities, both command-line and graphical, for changing such information.

Be sure you know which interface you are reading the information for when using these utilities. When multiple interfaces exist on a device, the display can scroll beyond a single screen. Scroll the display back to ensure that you are not studying the information for the wrong interface.

# Procedure

In this task, you use the IPCONFIG utility of the Microsoft operating system to display information as you alter it in other areas of the operating system and over the network.

## Equipment Used

For this task, you need a computer with a Windows operating system and a source of DHCP services connected to the network interface of the computer.

## Details

This task guides you through using the IPCONFIG utility to confirm changes you make to the IP addressing of a workstation and to display other IP-based details.

### General Use

1.  Connect the computer to the source of the DHCP information, whether through the network or directly to the device running the DHCP services.

2.  At a Command Prompt on the computer, issue the command `ipconfig`.

    ```
    C:\>ipconfig

    Windows IP Configuration


    Ethernet adapter Broadcom 570x Gigabit Integrated Controller:

            Media State . . . . . . . . . . . : Media disconnected

    Ethernet adapter Intel(R) PRO Wireless 2200BG Network Connection:

            Connection-specific DNS Suffix  . :
            IP Address. . . . . . . . . . . . : 172.16.10.103
            Subnet Mask . . . . . . . . . . . : 255.255.255.192
            Default Gateway . . . . . . . . . : 172.16.10.65

    C:\>
    ```

    From the sample display, you can see that there are two network interfaces, one wired and one wireless. The wired interface is not connected to a network. The wireless interface currently is connected.

3.  The `ipconfig` command offers minimal information without being enhanced through the use of software switches, which might be all you are looking for in a particular situation.

Sometimes, however, more is required. Issuing the command ipconfig /? displays a list of switches you can use. The following is an excerpt from the help switch's output.

```
USAGE:
    ipconfig [/? | /all | /renew [adapter] | /release [adapter] |
             /flushdns | /displaydns | /registerdns |
             /showclassid adapter |
             /setclassid adapter [classid] ]


    Options:
       /?           Display this help message
       /all         Display full configuration information.
       /release     Release the IP address for the specified adapter.
       /renew       Renew the IP address for the specified adapter.
       /flushdns    Purges the DNS Resolver cache.
       /registerdns Refreshes all DHCP leases and re-registers DNS names
       /displaydns  Display the contents of the DNS Resolver Cache.
       /showclassid Displays all the dhcp class IDs allowed for
       /adapter.
       /setclassid  Modifies the dhcp class id.
```

```
The default is to display only the IP address, subnet mask and
default gateway for each adapter bound to TCP/IP.

For Release and Renew, if no adapter name is specified, then the IP address
leases for all adapters bound to TCP/IP will be released or renewed.
```

## Local DNS Resolution Cache

1.  Clearly, the ipconfig command can be used for purposes beyond simple local-address display. What if you wanted to see the current set of DNS resolutions sitting in your local cache, that is, the set of resolutions for which you do not need to query a DNS server? For this, you use the /displaydns switch. Clear your current cache with the /flushdns switch and then take a look at it. Except for the IP loopback entries and some possible entries for your proxy server, there should be nothing, if you have no Internet clients running in the background.

```
C:\>ipconfig /flushdns


Windows IP Configuration


Successfully flushed the DNS Resolver Cache.


C:\>ipconfig /displaydns
```

```
Windows IP Configuration

       1.0.0.127.in-addr.arpa
       ----------------------------------------
       Record Name . . . . . : 1.0.0.127.in-addr.arpa.
       Record Type . . . . . : 12
       Time To Live  . . . . : 593525
       Data Length . . . . . : 4
       Section . . . . . . . : Answer
       PTR Record  . . . . . : localhost


       localhost
       ----------------------------------------
       Record Name . . . . . : localhost
       Record Type . . . . . : 1
       Time To Live  . . . . : 593525
       Data Length . . . . . : 4
       Section . . . . . . . : Answer
       A (Host) Record . . . : 127.0.0.1



C:\>
```

2. Now, ping a few hosts by name, whether on the Internet or on your enterprise intranet. The following output is truncated for pertinence.

```
C:\>ping www.wiley.com

Pinging www.wiley.com [208.215.179.146] with 32 bytes of data:

C:\>ping www.yahoo.com

Pinging www.yahoo.akadns.net [68.142.226.43] with 32 bytes of data:

C:\>ping www.embarq.com

Pinging embarq.com [144.226.116.35] with 32 bytes of data:

C:\>
```

**3.** Display the new entries associated with your recent lookups. The loopbacks and proxies remain but are omitted in the following output.

```
C:\>ipconfig /displaydns

Windows IP Configuration

        www.embarq.com
        ----------------------------------------
        Record Name . . . . . : www.embarq.com
        Record Type . . . . . : 5
        Time To Live  . . . . : 14378
        Data Length . . . . . : 4
        Section . . . . . . . : Answer
        CNAME Record  . . . . : embarq.com


        www.yahoo.com
        ----------------------------------------
        Record Name . . . . . : www.yahoo.com
        Record Type . . . . . : 5
        Time To Live  . . . . : 9
        Data Length . . . . . : 4
        Section . . . . . . . : Answer
        CNAME Record  . . . . : www.yahoo.akadns.net


        www.wiley.com
        ----------------------------------------
        Record Name . . . . . : www.wiley.com
        Record Type . . . . . : 1
        Time To Live  . . . . : 607
        Data Length . . . . . : 4
        Section . . . . . . . : Answer
        A (Host) Record . . . : 208.215.179.146


C:\>
```

## Detailed IP Configuration Display

1.  Use the /all switch to display more detailed information than the ipconfig command alone displays.

    C:\>**ipconfig /all**

    Windows IP Configuration

            Host Name . . . . . . . . . . . . : mycomp
            Primary Dns Suffix  . . . . . . . : ad.domain.com
            Node Type . . . . . . . . . . . : Hybrid
            IP Routing Enabled. . . . . . . . : No
            WINS Proxy Enabled. . . . . . . . : No
            DNS Suffix Search List. . . . . . : ad.domain.com
                                                domain.com


    Ethernet adapter Broadcom 570x Gigabit Integrated Controller:

            Media State . . . . . . . . . . . : Media disconnected
            Description . . . . . . . . . . . : Broadcom 570x Gigabit Integrated
    Controller
            Physical Address. . . . . . . . . : 00-0F-1F-BD-76-A5


    Ethernet adapter Intel(R) PRO Wireless 2200BG Network Connection:


            Connection-specific DNS Suffix  . :

            Description . . . . . . . . . . . : Intel(R) PRO/Wireless 2200BG
    Network Connection
            Physical Address. . . . . . . . . : 00-0E-35-4E-F2-15
            Dhcp Enabled. . . . . . . . . . . : Yes
            Autoconfiguration Enabled . . . . : Yes
            IP Address. . . . . . . . . . . . : 172.16.10.103
            Subnet Mask . . . . . . . . . . . : 255.255.255.192
            Default Gateway . . . . . . . . . : 172.16.10.65
            DHCP Server . . . . . . . . . . . : 172.16.10.65
            DNS Servers . . . . . . . . . . . : 205.152.37.23
                                                205.152.132.23

```
Lease Obtained. . . . . . . . . : May 10 4:34:12 PM
Lease Expires . . . . . . . . . : May 11 4:34:12 PM
```

`C:\>`

Note the added information, not only for the interfaces, which now show the DHCP lease information as well as the DNS servers they use, but for the system in general. NetBIOS node information and DNS domain search suffixes are presented before any interface details. Recall that with DHCP, the client first attempts to renew the lease when 50 percent of the lease has expired. Therefore, for the 24-hour lease shown here, in 12 hours the date and time information will change to the following, assuming the DHCP server is active.

```
Lease Obtained. . . . . . . . . : May 11 4:34:12 AM
Lease Expires . . . . . . . . . : May 12 4:34:12 AM
```

1. If you look closely, you see that the *PM*s changed to *AM*s and the new lease was obtained the next morning, 12 hours before the old lease was to expire. The new expiration is 24 hours (the lease duration) after the new lease was obtained.

2. Release your DHCP lease and then re-obtain it, using the `/release` and `/renew` switches. It is always wise to release before renewing because renewing alone does not always flush the DHCP information properly.

`C:\>`**`ipconfig /release`**

```
Windows IP Configuration


No operation can be performed on Broadcom 570x Gigabit Integrated Controller
while it has its media disconnected.


Ethernet adapter Broadcom 570x Gigabit Integrated Controller:

        Media State . . . . . . . . . . . : Media disconnected


Ethernet adapter Intel(R) PRO Wireless 2200BG Network Connection:

        Connection-specific DNS Suffix  . :
        IP Address. . . . . . . . . . . . : 0.0.0.0
        Subnet Mask . . . . . . . . . . . : 0.0.0.0
        Default Gateway . . . . . . . . . :
```

`C:\>`**`ipconfig /renew`**

```
Windows IP Configuration
```

No operation can be performed on Broadcom 570x Gigabit Integrated Controller while it has its media disconnected.

Ethernet adapter Broadcom 570x Gigabit Integrated Controller:

      Media State . . . . . . . . . . . : Media disconnected

Ethernet adapter Intel(R) PRO Wireless 2200BG Network Connection:

      Connection-specific DNS Suffix  . :
      IP Address. . . . . . . . . . . . : 172.16.10.103
      Subnet Mask . . . . . . . . . . . : 255.255.255.192
      Default Gateway . . . . . . . . . : 172.16.10.65

C:\>

3. Now, display the lease information for the active interfaces. Note that the 24-hour window has been restarted from the current time. Impertinent information is omitted in the following output.

      Lease Obtained. . . . . . . . . . : May 10 5:08:46 PM
      Lease Expires . . . . . . . . . . : May 11 5:08:46 PM

4. (Optional) If you have access to the DHCP server configuration, explore the effects of changing the lease duration (as well as the address pool and other options) on what the ipconfig command displays with various switches.

### Criteria for Completion

You have completed this task when you have explored each of the switches for the IPCONFIG command-line utility. Optionally, manipulating the DHCP server and observing the results on the client using the ipconfig command and various switches can be attempted.

# Task 4.6: Using Traceroute Utilities

The ping utility is ideal in situations in which the intermediate network infrastructure is known or trusted. When a ping fails, however, the broken link can be caused by the source, destination, or any device in between. The ping utility has no way of pinpointing the break in the path from a single execution. If the echo from source to destination fails, you must choose another device along the path to ping in order to begin determining where the problem lies.

With the traceroute utility, it is possible to conduct a trace from a single device in one step. The source of the traceroute does not send out ICMP packets, as in the case of the ping utility, but the destination and intermediate devices send ICMP error messages back to the source, which lets the source know the traceroute is working. Think of the traceroute process as a series of intentional errors.

As you may know, traceroute sends nonsensical messages—after all, the payload is not functional—to the destination in the form of UDP datagrams to port 33434 by default, the first port in a range reserved for traceroute. However, the destination of the traceroute is not the primary target of the trace, unless there are no intermediate devices in the path. By manipulating the time to live (TTL) field in the IP header, with the first datagram's TTL set to 1, the traceroute source sequentially discovers each device in the path to the destination.

When the first intermediate device receives the packet with the UDP datagram, the routing process requires that the device first decrement the TTL by one before considering any further processing of the IP packet. It is the new TTL of 0 that dictates that the intermediate device must cease processing of the packet, discard it, and send an executioner's message—an "ICMP time exceeded in transit" message—back to the IP source of the packet. Of course, this is exactly what the source device has in mind. With the time-exceeded message comes the IP address of the executioner.

By incrementing the TTL of a new IP packet each time it receives a time-exceeded message, the source discovers each successive intermediate device in order, because it becomes the job of the next device in the path to zero out the TTL and reveal itself. Finally, when the destination receives the datagram destined for a UDP port that no IP host is allowed to have active, an "ICMP destination port unreachable" message is returned to the source. Such a message from the traceroute destination is the trigger that ends the trace.

## Scenario

Having tried to ping a remote device in the internetwork to no avail, your next step is to run a traceroute to the same device to see how far your traffic can get.

## Scope of Task

### Duration

This task should take about 30 minutes.

### Setup

For this task, you need to connect a computer and a router through at least one other router. Additionally, the computer needs Internet access, either by another path or through the two routers.

## Caveat

It is important to realize that a traceroute is not a specialized echo request (ping). An ICMP echo reply is never returned during a traceroute. Blocking ICMP echoes does not stop the traceroute utility. Any security involving the denial of ping packets needs to deny datagrams to the destination UDP port range 33434 as well. You must keep in mind the following caveat about this practice: As shown in the procedure of this task, you can choose any unassigned UDP port number and end up with the same results. So blocking of all traceroute traffic takes a bit of strategy and knowledge of your internetwork. You cannot stop all ICMP messages or your IP internetwork comes to a grinding halt.

Baseline traceroutes are advised prior to using the utility in a troubleshooting setting. This means as you implement the network, run a traceroute between strategic end devices to paint a picture of the path normal traffic takes. Barring this, you must have an impeccable grasp, through being able to reference blueprints or from firsthand design knowledge, of the interconnections in your network. Without one of these three prerequisites, there is little chance of your troubleshooting the problem without assistance or traveling to the last known device to see where it normally connects.

Be careful not to put too much stock in any one utility. Even traceroute, which seems to be foolproof in determining the last working device in the path to a destination, has its shortcomings, depending on the situation. For example, if the path that the executioner takes to send the source a time-exceeded message is not the reverse path of the traceroute message, any failure in the reverse path makes the executioner look like the device with the problem. Look at subsequent TTLs to see if the trace begins working again. If so, there might be other reachability problems in the network that traceroute has uncovered. Think of all scenarios while interpreting traceroute results.

## Procedure

In this task, you use the traceroute utility on a computer running a Microsoft operating system and on a Cisco router to test connectivity from one to the other. Figure 4.3 illustrates the sample network connectivity between the computer and router.

**FIGURE 4.3**    Sample network layout

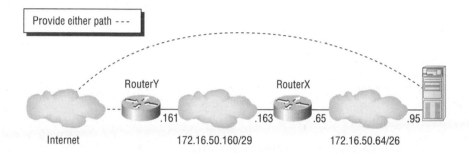

## Equipment Used

For this task, you need a computer with Internet access, as well as connectivity to one router, which in turn is connected to another router, as in Figure 4.3. You need hubs, switches, and cabling to reproduce the network shown in the same diagram.

## Details

In this task, you use the traceroute utility to discover the path to remote endpoints.

1.  Use an Ethernet crossover cable to connect the computer to the router or use a switch or hub with two straight cables.

2.  Connect the two routers together.

3.  Configure the computer and routers according to Figure 4.3.

4.  Add the following configuration to RouterY.

```
RouterY#config t
RouterY(config)#ip route 172.16.50.64 255.255.255.192
➥172.16.50.163
RouterY(config)#end
RouterY#
```

5.  Add the following configuration to the computer.

```
C:\>route add 172.16.50.160 mask 255.255.255.248 172.16.50.65

C:\>
```

6.  On RouterY, conduct a traceroute to the computer at 172.16.50.95.

```
RouterY#traceroute 172.16.50.95

Type escape sequence to abort.
Tracing the route to 172.16.50.95

  1 172.16.50.163 4 msec 4 msec 4 msec
  2 172.16.50.95 4 msec 4 msec *
RouterY#
```

The escape sequence referenced in the output of the command is Ctrl+Shift+6. Hold down the Ctrl and Shift keys while tapping the 6 key above the keyboard—not on the numeric keypad—until you return to a prompt. The traceroute command continues until a TTL of 30 is reached or the destination returns the "destination port unreachable" message. A failed traceroute can continue through 30 slow, pointless iterations without the escape sequence.

**7.** On the computer, issue the tracert command with no arguments or switches.

```
C:\>tracert

Usage: tracert [-d] [-h maximum_hops] [-j host-list] [-w timeout] target_name

Options:
    -d                 Do not resolve addresses to hostnames.
    -h maximum_hops    Maximum number of hops to search for target.
    -j host-list       Loose source route along host-list.
    -w timeout         Wait timeout milliseconds for each reply.


C:\>
```

While there are very few switches, one or two of them tend to make life much easier. For example, if you know there are only so many intermediate devices (routers) between source and destination devices, limit the number of hops with the -h switch so that the traceroute does not seem to go on forever on a failure. If the name of each device along the way is not beneficial, there is a way to stop those from displaying as well, the -d switch.

**1.** On the computer, pick an Internet (or corporate intranet) location and traceroute to it by name or address.

```
C:\>tracert www.yahoo.com

Tracing route to www.yahoo.akadns.net [216.109.118.70]
over a maximum of 30 hops:

  1     62 ms     92 ms    105 ms   172.16.10.65
  2     14 ms     91 ms     93 ms   68.216.218.66
  3     15 ms     68 ms     88 ms   68.216.218.49
  4     42 ms     50 ms     53 ms   205.152.181.25
  5     44 ms     89 ms     81 ms   65.83.237.36
  6     32 ms     83 ms     74 ms   65.83.236.9
  7     30 ms     89 ms     79 ms   65.83.236.116
  8     42 ms     85 ms     56 ms   65.83.236.66
  9     52 ms     60 ms     60 ms   65.83.237.228
 10     44 ms    100 ms     64 ms   ge-0-0-0-p100.msr1.dcn.yahoo.com
        [216.115.108.1]
```

```
11    46 ms    78 ms    68 ms  ge3-1.bas1-m.dcn.yahoo.com
      [216.109.120.149]
12    43 ms    46 ms    58 ms  p7.www.dcn.yahoo.com [216.109.118.70]
```

Trace complete.


C:\>

Note that the utility seeks to run a reverse DNS lookup on all results. For those that come back with a corresponding DNS name, the IP address is listed in square brackets after the name. Use the -d switch to stop names from displaying.

2. Going back to the router and performing an extended traceroute by issuing the traceroute command with no arguments gives you the opportunity to experiment with alternate port numbers. This can be used to test security designed to prohibit traceroute activity. The extended traceroute also gives you the opportunity to test the remote device's ability to send traffic to an interface on the router that does not source pings and traceroute messages to the destination by default. Consider a Loopback0 interface on RouterY with an address of 1.1.1.1/32. The following traceroute sources from the Loopback0 interface, limits the number of TTL iterations to 5, and sends messages to UDP port number 33500. Notice in the list at http://www.iana.org/assignments/port-numbers that this port number is unassigned and has a good chance of working for traceroute.

```
RouterY#traceroute
Protocol [ip]:
Target IP address: 172.16.50.95
Source address: 1.1.1.1
Numeric display [n]:
Timeout in seconds [3]:
Probe count [3]:
Minimum Time to Live [1]:
Maximum Time to Live [30]: 5
Port Number [33434]: 33500
Loose, Strict, Record, Timestamp, Verbose[none]:
Type escape sequence to abort.
Tracing the route to 172.16.50.95

  1 172.16.50.163 4 msec 4 msec 4 msec
  2 172.16.50.95 4 msec 4 msec *
RouterY#
```

3. You can also use this method to test the existence of a working UDP port on the destination device. Say the computer is a DNS server listening on UDP port 53 for client resolution queries. Specifying that port will not result in "destination port unreachable" messages returning to the router, indicating that port is active on that host.

```
RouterY#traceroute
Protocol [ip]:
Target IP address: 172.16.50.95
Source address:
Numeric display [n]:
Timeout in seconds [3]:
Probe count [3]:
Minimum Time to Live [1]:
Maximum Time to Live [30]: 5
Port Number [33434]: 53
Loose, Strict, Record, Timestamp, Verbose[none]:
Type escape sequence to abort.
Tracing the route to 172.16.50.95

  1 172.16.50.163 4 msec 4 msec 4 msec
  2 *   *   *
  3 *   *   *
  4 *   *   *
  5 *   *   *
RouterY#
```

## Criteria for Completion

You have completed this task when you have configured the devices according to the task procedure and observed the success and failure of the traceroute utility.

# Task 4.7: Using Telnet

Telnet is a very popular protocol for remote login service between a client and the server that allows such access. Telnet is detailed in RFC 854 and is used by equipment manufacturers to simulate a local command-line interface across an IP network, using TCP port 23. Cisco routers, for example, allow Telnet access across any network interface, producing a command-line interface (CLI) that exactly resembles the one you receive during a console-port session.

## Scenario

Traveling to a nearby city to configure one of your routers is not convenient. Your plan is to enable Telnet access to this router across the network so you can be more productive.

## Scope of Task

### Duration

This task should take about 30 minutes.

### Setup

For this task, you need to connect a computer and a router through at least one other router.

### Caveat

While this task seeks to familiarize you with Telnet, it does not intend to imply that this protocol is recommended over all other similar protocols. For example, the Secure Shell version 2 (SSH-2) protocol, which uses TCP port 22 and is detailed in RFC 4251, is secure, whereas Telnet is not. In fact, Telnet sends all information in cleartext, allowing an eavesdropper to acquire passwords and other confidential information that is not otherwise encrypted. However, Telnet is more prolific, and for this reason, it continues to enjoy mainstream acceptance. Running Telnet through a VPN is one way to keep this information from the public, but internal corporate eavesdroppers still must be considered. Be sure a device allows Telnet access—meaning it runs a Telnet server service—before counting on such access in a mission-critical scenario. Most equipment allows such access only after it has been configured to do so.

## Procedure

This task explains how to enable the Telnet server on a Cisco router and subsequently telnet to the router for remote configuration across the network. Figure 4.4 illustrates the sample network connectivity between the computer and router.

**FIGURE 4.4**    Sample network layout

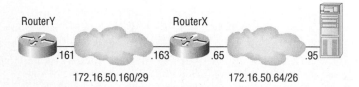

## Equipment Used

For this task, you need a computer connected to one router, which in turn is connected to another router, as in Figure 4.4. You need hubs, switches, and cabling to reproduce the network shown in this figure.

## Details

In this task, you configure the Telnet server on a Cisco router and then gain access to its CLI from a computer and another Cisco router.

### General Setup

1. Use an Ethernet crossover cable to connect the computer to the router or use a switch or hub with two straight cables.

2. Connect the two routers.

3. Configure the computer and routers according to Figure 4.4.

4. Add the following configuration to RouterY.

```
RouterY#config t
RouterY(config)#ip route 172.16.50.64 255.255.255.192
➥172.16.50.163
RouterY(config)#end
RouterY#
```

5. Add the following configuration to the computer.

```
C:\>route add 172.16.50.160 mask 255.255.255.248 172.16.50.65

C:\>
```

6. On RouterY, create a username for authentication and a password to go with it. Use **delliot** as the username and **wiley** as the password.

```
RouterY#config t
RouterY(config)#username delliot password wiley
RouterY(config)#
```

7. On RouterY, configure the default Telnet ports for access using the local user database.

```
RouterY(config)#line vty 0 4
RouterY(config-line)#login local
RouterY(config-line)#end
RouterY#
```

## Using Telnet from Router to Router

1.  On RouterX, Telnet to RouterY, using the credentials created for David Elliot. Try to enter Privileged EXEC mode. If your router has an enable secret configured, enter that when prompted; if it has only an enable password, enter that. However, if you have configured neither, you are not allowed into Privileged mode over a Telnet connection, as shown in the following output.

```
RouterX#172.16.50.161
Trying 172.16.50.161 ... Open

User Access Verification

Username: delliot
Password:
RouterY>enable
% No password set
RouterY>
```

2.  Configure an enable secret on RouterY, if necessary.

```
RouterY#config t
RouterY(config)#enable secret wiley
RouterY(config)#end
RouterY#
```

3.  Try to enter Privileged mode again in the Telnet session to RouterY from RouterX. Enter the enable secret you just configured. This time, it works.

```
RouterY>enable
Password:
RouterY#
```

4.  Begin the process to exit the Telnet session by executing the key sequence Ctrl+Shift+6, x. To do this, hold the Ctrl and Shift keys down and then tap the 6 key once. Release the Ctrl and Shift keys and tap the letter x key once. This brings you back to the host router you used to telnet into RouterY.

```
RouterY#
RouterX#
```

5.  Issue the show sessions command to confirm that the Telnet session is just suspended, not disconnected.

```
RouterX#show sessions
Conn Host                Address           Byte  Idle Conn Name
*  1 172.16.50.161       172.16.50.161      0     0 172.16.50.161

RouterX#
```

6. Issue the `disconnect` command with the connection number of the Telnet session to RouterY and confirm that you wish to disconnect your session. Showing the suspended sessions again confirms you have completely exited your session with RouterY.

```
RouterX#disconnect 1
Closing connection to 172.16.50.161 [confirm]
RouterX#sh sessions
% No connections open
RouterX#
```

## Using Telnet from Computer to Router

1. On the computer, open HyperTerminal; one way to open it is by choosing Start ➤ All Programs ➤ Accessories ➤ Communications ➤ HyperTerminal (the application, not the folder, if one exists). This produces the opening dialog for HyperTerminal. Name the session and click the OK button.

2. In the Connect To dialog, choose TCP/IP (Winsock) from the Connect drop-down. Doing so takes away the modem information that might have displayed by default. Instead, you now have a location to enter a hostname or address and accept or change the default port number. Port 23 is correct for Telnet. Enter the IP address for RouterY. Click the OK button to continue to the HyperTerminal session.

3. In the HyperTerminal session, you are prompted for the username and password just as you were when connecting from router to router. Enter the appropriate information, similar to the following.

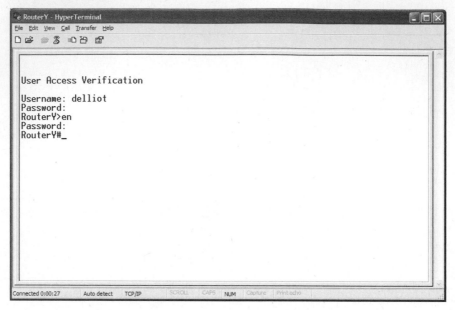

## Criteria for Completion

You have completed this task when you have configured the devices according to the task procedure and successfully used Telnet to gain access to a Cisco router from another Cisco router and from a computer.

# Task 4.8: Using the NSLOOKUP Utility

An unfortunately underutilized utility for a poorly understood global naming system is NSLOOKUP (the NS stands for Name Server or Name Service). It refers to the ability to make DNS lookups more controllable so that you can troubleshoot problems or suspected problems with DNS name-to-IP-address resolution. Most technicians and engineers can spot a DNS problem when they see one. Pinging by name fails, but pinging by address works. Browsing to a known valid web page results in an error page. Of course, that is caused by DNS issues and so much more, but you know you have that gut "uh-oh, it's DNS" feeling when that error page pops up in the place of http://www.wiley.com.

The NSLOOKUP utility takes almost all of the guesswork out of the equation, even allowing you to test name resolution with servers that are not part of the standard DHCP scope you feel you are restricted to. When you ping or trace to a destination, you get to see one of the possibly many IP addresses the hostname you specify resolves to. With the NSLOOKUP utility, you are able to see *all* addresses and aliases associated with a name. More options might make future troubleshooting less of a struggle.

## Scenario

Your DNS server is not returning IP addresses for Internet sites. You take it upon yourself to test its resolution capacity manually, as well as compare it to the capacity of other known DNS servers in the Internet.

## Scope of Task

### Duration

This task should take about 30 minutes.

### Setup

For this task, you need a computer with Internet access. Alternatively, a corporate intranet connection is sufficient if you know the name or address of DNS servers that are not your primary and secondary servers.

### Caveat

The NSLOOKUP utility, as its name implies, is for the display of information only. Permanently changing such information for full-time use on a device must be done through other avenues. Be certain the name server you attempt to use is a known server. This utility will return negative results that can lead you to the wrong conclusion if you happen to use the wrong DNS server name or address. At the very least, ping the DNS server's name or address before attempting to use it with the NSLOOKUP utility.

## Procedure

In this task, you use the NSLOOKUP utility of the Microsoft operating system to display information provided by DNS servers regarding name resolution.

### Equipment Used

For this task, you need a computer with an Internet connection or an intranet connection that leads to multiple DNS servers. All associated devices and cabling to provide this access is assumed.

## Details

The following steps lead you through the more common uses of the NSLOOKUP command-line utility in a Microsoft operating system. Stemming from a Unix environment, this utility is present in other operating systems, both under the same name and others, such as dig.

1. Connect the computer to a network that offers multiple DNS servers. This procedure uses the Internet.

2. At a Command Prompt on the computer, issue the command `ipconfig/all`. Pay special attention in the output to the IP addresses of the DNS servers.

   ```
   DNS Servers . . . . . . . . . . . : 205.152.37.23
                                       205.152.132.23
   ```

3. At a Command Prompt on the computer, issue the command `nslookup`.

   ```
   C:\>nslookup
   Default Server:  dns.asm.bellsouth.net
   Address:  205.152.37.23

   >
   ```

   As you can see, you are thrust into another command shell, call it the nslookup prompt. You are no longer sitting at a DOS command prompt. The address of one of your DNS servers appears with a name that has been resolved in reverse by that very server. Your prompt is now a simple greater-than symbol (>). This is known as the interactive mode of the NSLOOKUP utility.

4. Enter a question mark (**?**) and study the help display. The command `help` accomplishes the same result. The output is too extensive to present here, because the entire display is worthwhile.

5. At the nslookup prompt, you can simply specify a name for which you want to see the resolution.

   ```
   > www.wiley.com
   Server:  dns.asm.bellsouth.net
   Address:  205.152.37.23

   Non-authoritative answer:
   Name:   www.wiley.com
   Address:  208.215.179.146

   >
   ```

   The same result can be obtained from the command prompt by placing the name you want resolved directly after the `nslookup` keyword. This is the noninteractive mode of the

NSLOOKUP utility. Once your resolution is returned, you are placed back at the command prompt.

```
C:\>nslookup www.wiley.com
Server:  dns.asm.bellsouth.net
Address:  205.152.37.23

Non-authoritative answer:
Name:    www.wiley.com
Address:  208.215.179.146


C:\>
```

6. Say your regular DNS servers do not appear to be working. In interactive mode, issue the command server ns1.mindspring.com, which changes the default server while in this mode. Then look up the same name you looked up earlier.

```
> server ns1.mindspring.com
Default Server:  ns1.mindspring.com
Address:  207.69.188.185

> www.wiley.com
Server:  ns1.mindspring.com
Address:  207.69.188.185

Non-authoritative answer:
Name:    www.wiley.com
Address:  208.215.179.146

>
```

7. If you prefer to use another server only for this lookup, you can specify the name and server on the same line. Subsequent lookups consult the original default server. Note that you must change the default server back to its original value for the following procedure to work properly. You can use the exit command to leave interactive mode and then enter the nslookup command at the command prompt to reenter interactive mode, if you prefer. This returns your name server to its default setting.

```
> www.wiley.com ns1.mindspring.com
Server:  ns1.mindspring.com
Address:  207.69.188.185

Non-authoritative answer:
```

```
Name:     www.wiley.com
Address:  208.215.179.146

> www.sybex.com
Server:  dns.asm.bellsouth.net
Address:  205.152.37.23

Non-authoritative answer:
Name:     www.sybex.com
Address:  208.215.179.220

>
```

The equivalent noninteractive procedure places the server you wish to use at the end of the earlier noninteractive command, as follows.

```
C:\>nslookup www.wiley.com ns1.mindspring.com
Server:  ns1.mindspring.com
Address:  207.69.188.185

Non-authoritative answer:
Name:     www.wiley.com
Address:  208.215.179.146


C:\>
```

Perhaps you need to look up all common server addresses for a particular domain name, say yahoo.com. For example, you want to know if Yahoo!'s web server has a different IP address from its FTP server and its mail servers, as well as how many addresses are used to get you to the same server and if any aliases to the common names exist. From interactive mode, change the default domain name to yahoo.com so that you do not have to enter it repeatedly.

```
> set srchlist=yahoo.com
>
```

Now, until you exit interactive mode, any unqualified names you enter are appended by yahoo.com.

```
> www
Server:  dns.asm.bellsouth.net
Address:  205.152.37.23

Non-authoritative answer:
```

```
Name:     www.yahoo.akadns.net
Addresses:  216.109.118.73, 216.109.118.74, 216.109.118.75, 216.109.117.109
            216.109.117.110, 216.109.117.207, 216.109.118.66, 216.109.118.72
Aliases:  www.yahoo.com

> mail
Server:  dns.asm.bellsouth.net
Address:  205.152.37.23

Non-authoritative answer:
Name:     login.yahoo.akadns.net
Address:  209.73.177.115
Aliases:  mail.yahoo.com, login.yahoo.com

> smtp
Server:  dns.asm.bellsouth.net
Address:  205.152.37.23

Non-authoritative answer:
Name:     smarthost.yahoo.com
Addresses:  216.109.112.27, 216.109.112.28, 216.145.54.171, 216.145.54.172
            216.145.54.173
Aliases:  smtp.yahoo.com

> pop3
Server:  dns.asm.bellsouth.net
Address:  205.152.37.23

Non-authoritative answer:
Name:     pop3.yahoo.com
Address:  206.190.46.10

> dns
Server:  dns.asm.bellsouth.net
Address:  205.152.37.23

Non-authoritative answer:
Name:     dns.yahoo.com
Address:  63.250.206.138
```

```
> ns
Server:  dns.asm.bellsouth.net
Address:  205.152.37.23

Non-authoritative answer:
Name:    ns.yahoo.com
Address:  66.218.71.63

> mail1
Server:  dns.asm.bellsouth.net
Address:  205.152.37.23

Non-authoritative answer:
Name:     reactivate1.mail.vip.sc5.yahoo.com
Address:  216.136.224.155
Aliases:  mail1.yahoo.com

> www2
Server:  dns.asm.bellsouth.net
Address:  205.152.37.23

Non-authoritative answer:
Name:    rc.yahoo.akadns.net
Address:  216.109.112.135
Aliases:  www2.yahoo.com, rc.yahoo.com

>
```

Set the default server to dns.yahoo.com and look up the address for ns.yahoo.com again.

```
> server dns.yahoo.com
Default Server:  dns.yahoo.com
Address:  63.250.206.138

> ns
Server:  dns.yahoo.com
Address:  63.250.206.138

Name:    ns.yahoo.com
Address:  66.218.71.63

>
```

Notice that the answer is authoritative, unlike before, because the DNS server dns.yahoo.com is authoritative for all things ending in yahoo.com.

8.  To resolve names from the first domain that produces a match when the domain name is appended to the unqualified name, create an ordered list with the `set srchlist` command in interactive mode. An example follows.

```
> set srchlist=wiley.com/yahoo.com
> www
Server:    dns.asm.bellsouth.net
Address:   205.152.37.23

Non-authoritative answer:
Name:    www.wiley.com
Address:   208.215.179.146

> dns
Server:    dns.asm.bellsouth.net
Address:   205.152.37.23

Non-authoritative answer:
Name:    dns.yahoo.com
Address:   63.250.206.138

>
```

In this example, because wiley.com comes first in the list, which must be delimited by slashes, it is appended first to any unqualified names, such as www. When a match occurs, it is presented. In the case of the name dns, appending wiley.com does not produce a match, so yahoo.com, the second domain name in the list, is appended and produces a match.

While there certainly is much more that can be done with the NSLOOKUP utility, you are well on your way to mastering its capabilities. You also have the necessary navigation skills to be able to carry on your own experiment with the command structure.

## Criteria for Completion

You have completed this task when you have practiced the foregoing techniques for using the NSLOOKUP utility in both interactive and noninteractive modes. You can manipulate the name server to use in resolutions as well as the domain list that is to be appended to unqualified names.

# Task 4.9: Using a Protocol Analyzer

One of the power tools in the back pocket of administrators that understand the nuts and bolts of networking is the protocol analyzer. These gems come in many shapes and forms. There are simple software applications installed on one or more systems, some of which only monitor their own inbound and outbound traffic. And there are stand-alone devices that monitor literally every frame that passes by. Regardless of the form in which the analyzer comes, the basic effect is the same. These tools capture frames from the network and allow you to dissect them for pertinent information or trend analysis.

Microsoft's server operating systems offer a basic form of protocol analyzer called Network Monitor. The version that installs with each server allows frames to be captured only if they are sourced by or destined for the local device. Microsoft's Systems Management Server (SMS) includes a more liberal version that monitors all network traffic available to its network interface.

## Scenario

One of your servers seems to be under a higher level of utilization than expected. Your plan is to run Network Monitor on that server to analyze the activity, just to make sure it is all aboveboard.

## Scope of Task

### Duration

This task should take about 30 minutes.

### Setup

For this task, you need to set up a server connected across a network, even if fabricated with a crossover cable.

### Caveat

You must understand the encapsulation of messages in packets and packets in frames before any of this will make complete sense. You can still follow the logic presented here, but striking out on your own to use this tool in troubleshooting can have disastrous results stemming from misinterpretation of the captured information. Be sure to use other resources to educate yourself on the underlying technology, if necessary.

## Procedure

In this task, you use Microsoft's Network Monitor utility on a server product to capture frames from the network and inspect the contents of the frames and the packets they encapsulate.

## Equipment Used

For this task, you need a server with network access to at least one other device that can generate known traffic to the server for analysis.

## Details

This task walks you through accessing and executing the Microsoft Network Monitor on a contemporary Windows Server product.

### General Use

1. Open Network Monitor. You can do this by clicking Start ➤ All Programs ➤ Administrative Tools ➤ Network Monitor.

2. After the program starts, the F8 key allows you to create a filter for your capture. Alternatively, follow Capture ➤ Filter, along the menu bar at the top. Unless the server is an SMS server, this brings up the following informational message. Click the OK button to continue.

3. As you can see, in the Capture Filter dialog (shown next), you have the option to filter on types of frames, on addresses—both MAC and IP—and on any patterns in the data in which you are interested.

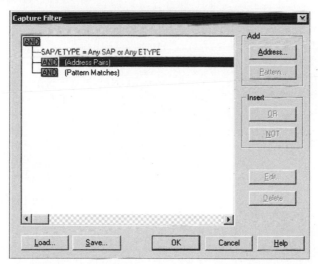

Double-click the SAP/ETYPE line. Doing so produces the Capture Filter SAPs And ETYPEs dialog.

**4.** In the Capture Filter SAPs And ETYPEs dialog, you can change the default action to capture all type of frames by double-clicking on any entry. Alternatively, you can click the entry and then click the Disable button. The following image shows a filter that does not capture Bridge Protocol Data Units (BPDUs)—not a bad idea if you have them and don't care about them. BPDUs come out every 2 seconds per switch or bridge interface by default. Click the OK button to return to the Capture Filter dialog.

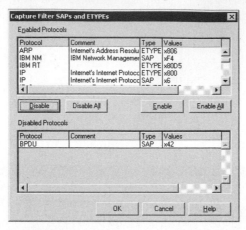

**5.** In the Capture Filter dialog, double-click the (Address Pairs) line. Alternatively, you can click the line once and then click the Address button. This launches the Address Expression dialog, shown in the following image.

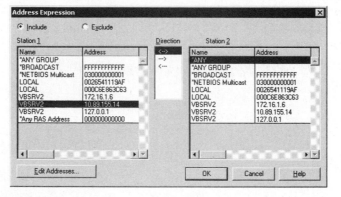

Each pass of the Address Expression dialog adds another address-based expression to the filter. How the expressions are grouped affects how the filter works—more on that later. In the Address Expression dialog, make sure the Include radio button is filled. The Exclude radio button creates a NOT function similar to that offered for pattern expressions, shown later in this procedure. For Station 1, click the server's name on the line with the IP address you wish to monitor. Others can be added by repeating this step. Leave Station 2 set to *ANY and Direction set to bidirectional (<-->). Click the OK button to return to the Capture Filter dialog.

## Filter Operators

The graphic below shows the results of the previous step in this procedure.

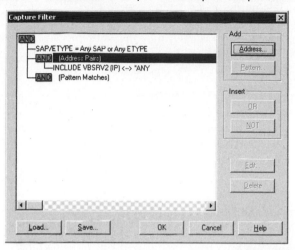

The AND farthest to the left dictates that SAP/ETYPE, address pairs, and pattern matches are all considered equally when matching traffic. A frame not matching all three of the criteria is not captured. If you do not specify Address Pairs or Pattern Matches, these criteria simply are not checked. Leaving all SAPs and ETYPEs enabled is tantamount to ignoring this criterion. Be careful what criteria you specify. It is very easy to leave yourself with a capture that yields no frames. The image below shows the same filter as before but with additional, more complex conditions

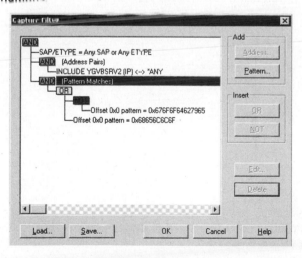

The patterns are the hexadecimal representations of the ASCII words *goodbye* and *hello*. Realize that these patterns do not appear at the 0x0 offset (very beginning) of any frames, but this is just an example to explain the operators. With pattern matches, you can use the OR and NOT operators. So the filter in Figure 4.6 reads as follows: If a frame comes along that was either sourced by or destined for the local server AND either the frame has the word *hello* right at the beginning OR it at least does NOT have the word *goodbye* right at the beginning, then capture the frame. Reproduce the logic in Figure 4.6, which is not as easy as it looks, and then use this logic to build your own meaningful filters later on.

Capture filters are not always where you want to put your effort. Sometimes it's best to go ahead and capture everything and then apply a display filter to the results. Be aware, though, that the hard drive space must be available to house the original capture on which to apply the display filter. Occasionally, this requirement makes capture filters a better choice. Display filters are presented later in this procedure.

6. On another computer that has access to the server, open a command prompt and prepare to ping the server.

7. Start the capture that you built the filter for simply by pressing the F10 key. If you prefer, you can follow Capture ➤ Start. You also can click the button that looks like the play button on your home electronics and that says Start Capture when you hover over it. Once you start the capture, go to the other computer and ping the server a few times. The following image shows a capture in progress on the server.

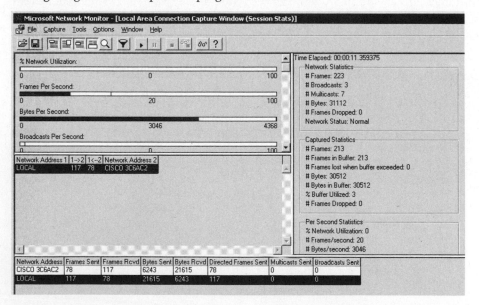

**8.** By clicking the Capture menu while a capture is in progress, you see that you have myriad options. For example, you can press the F11 key to stop the capture, or you can click the button with the "stop" square. If you hold the Shift key down while you press the F11 key, you not only stop the capture, you immediately bring up the screen to display the captured data. Alternately, you can stop first, then display. The buttons with the spectacles on them are equivalent to these key sequences. Using the method of your choice, stop the capture after the pings have completed and display the results. Note, by the following screen shot, there are still quite a few extraneous frames that have been captured, depending on what you are looking for, of course.

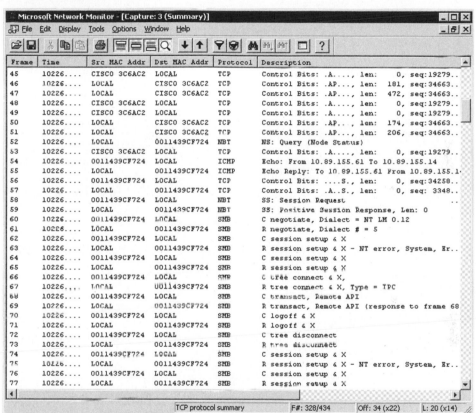

Nevertheless, you can scroll through them until you come to one of your ICMP packets, shown in greater detail in the following illustration.

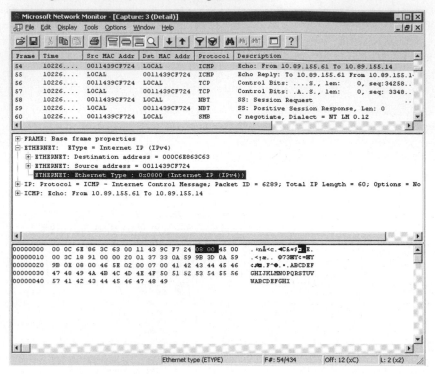

The preceding screen shot was produced by double-clicking the ICMP-based frame in what is called the summary pane. Doing so automatically produces the additional detail and hex panes, in that order, from top to bottom. By expanding the Ethernet section in the detail pane and clicking on the line that shows the Ethernet Type, for example, you see the corresponding value in the hex pane becomes highlighted. Note that 0x0800 appears in both panes.

9. Now, expand the IP section of the frame, as shown next.

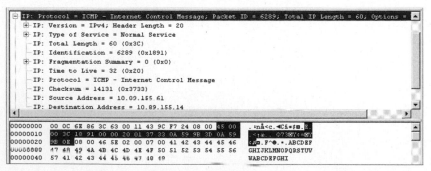

The highlighted portion in the hex pane is the entire IP header, 20 bytes. Note, in the detail pane, the protocol field points to ICMP. If you were to find that value in the hex pane, it would be the value 0x01 at byte number 24. Because numbering begins at an offset of 0x00, this is really byte 23, or offset 0x17 (23 in hex). Make a note of this for later. Also notice the repeating text in the hex pane. That's the standard dummy payload for a ping packet, a repeating uppercase *A* through *W*.

As an example of how close you can scrutinize this output, consider the following screen shot, which is a composite of a normal ping on top and a ping with the −f switch to set the do-not-fragment (DF) bit in the IP header, the only field with a 1 in either output. In practice, you might set this switch along with gradually increasing the payload size to see what the largest MTU along the path is. It would be the highest payload size that gets a successful response because packets with the DF bit set that are larger than the MTU of the immediate link are discarded.

```
⊟ IP: Fragmentation Summary = 0 (0x0)
    ├ IP: .0.............. = May fragment datagram if necessary
    ├ IP: ...0000000000000 = Fragment Offset 0 (0x0000)
    └ IP: ..0.............. = Last fragment in datagram
⊟ IP: Fragmentation Summary = 16384 (0x4000)
    ├ IP: .1.............. = Cannot fragment datagram
    ├ IP: ...0000000000000 = Fragment Offset 0 (0x0000)
    └ IP: ..0.............. = Last fragment in datagram
```

Also expand the ICMP section of the frame and note the telltale type 8, code 0 of an ICMP echo request or type 0, code 0 of an echo reply.

10. While in display mode, press the F8 key to open the Display Filter dialog. Alternatively, you can click the button with the picture of a funnel. Double-click the Protocol==Any line (or single-click and then click the Edit Expression button) to bring up the Expression dialog.

11. On the Protocol tab, click the Disable All button to start with a clean slate.

12. Scroll down in the Disabled Protocols pane and click on the entry with ICMP in the name column. Click the Enable button (not the Enable All button). You now see ICMP alone in the Enabled Protocols pane, as shown next. Click the OK button to return to the Display Filter dialog.

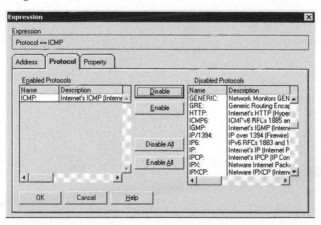

**13.** The Display Filter dialog now looks similar to the following, with ICMP in the place of ANY. Click the OK button.

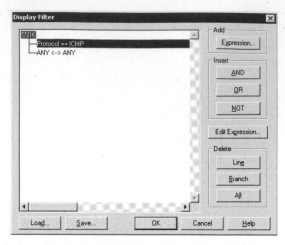

Now the display is pared down to include only ICMP packets, as shown in the following image.

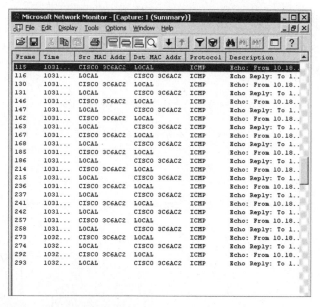

You can toggle the display filter on and off by clicking the button showing the funnel with the red circle and slash over it.

**14.** Close the capture display by choosing File ➤ Close, for example.

### Using a Capture Filter for ICMP and Telnet

1.  Press the F8 key to bring up the Capture Filter dialog again.

2.  Double-click Pattern Matches or single-click it and click the Pattern button. This opens the Pattern Match dialog. Now that you know where to find the signature of ICMP in a frame, enter the information you discovered earlier, as shown in the following illustration. Click the OK button.

This tells the capture engine to watch byte 23 (0x17) for the value 0x01, counting from the beginning of the frame, which is the 24th byte because the first one is byte 0. This is where the value for the protocol field of the IP header can be found. 0x01 means ICMP.

3.  Click once on your new Pattern Match entry. The OR and NOT buttons light up in the Insert section to the right. With the Offset 0x17 entry highlighted, click the OR button. This produces something in the dialog similar to the following. Note the OR flag under Pattern Matches.

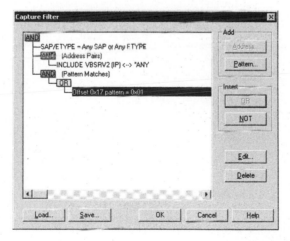

4.  To create another pattern match to be part of the OR expression, click on the OR label or the first pattern match you created for ICMP. Do not click on the preceding AND label beside Pattern Matches. Creating another pattern match that way puts it in series with the OR expression, not under it. Click the Pattern button.

5.  To include Telnet traffic from a Telnet server, fill in the information according to the following image.

This means that byte 34, the 35th byte, or 0x22, starts the pattern 0x0017. This is the location of the source port number in the TCP header, which is port 23 (0x17) for Telnet. You can discover this information by looking at unfiltered Telnet traffic. To monitor traffic destined for the Telnet server as well, make another OR pattern match for 0x0017 at byte 0x24.

6.  Now, as the next illustration shows, you have two pattern matches, either one of which causes a frame capture if all other requirements are met. Click the OK button.

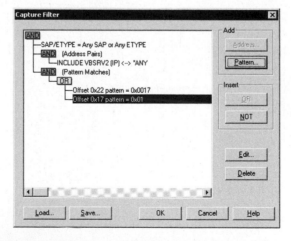

7.  Start a capture and then ping and try to Telnet to the server from the other computer. Even if there is no Telnet service active on that device, Telnet traffic is generated. The following graphic shows that when you stop and display the capture, except for the statistics frame,

there are only ICMP and TCP listed in the Protocol column, even without applying a display filter. However, all other frames are lost for good. There is nothing to toggle here.

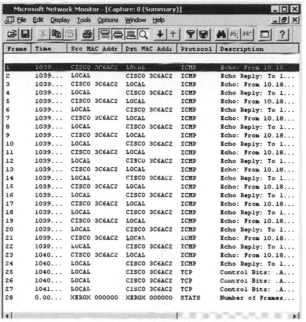

8. When you scrutinize one of the TCP-based frames, similar to the one shown next, note that it was sourced by a device acting as a Telnet server using port 23, if for no other reason than to tell the client that no Telnet service exists. Nevertheless, the destination port must be used as the source port or the client has no idea why it is receiving unsolicited information. At least this way the client understands that its intended target for Telnet was bogus and is able to report as much back to the user interface.

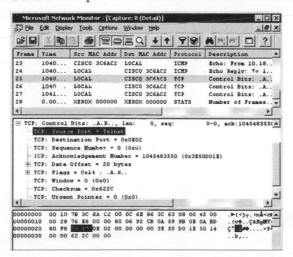

## Criteria for Completion

You have completed this task when you have conducted the captures using Network Monitor on a Microsoft Windows Server product.

# Task 4.10: Displaying Computer Event Logs

All modern operating systems have some method of allowing you to view logs of one type of event or another. Some operating systems have supplied such event viewers for a number of years. Some viewers are text based, just like a CLI, while others are graphical in nature. The graphical viewers generally don't offer any more information than the text-based utilities, just a more agreeable method of navigation through the events; there really are no "graphics" to speak of. Microsoft calls its utility the Event Viewer. There is an Event Viewer on every contemporary Windows offering for Intel-compatible processors.

## Scenario

You have been receiving error messages on startup for a few systems under your authority. You also are concerned about other issues that might be lurking on these computers. Your plan is to use the Event Viewer on these devices to look through the different classes of events that have been logged.

## Scope of Task

### Duration

This task should take about 30 minutes.

### Setup

For this task, you need a single computer running Microsoft Windows. The computer must have Administrative Tools available. See this task's procedure for how to display Administrative Tools on the Start menu.

### Caveat

The output of Event Viewer can be quite cryptic. For this reason, there has been some effort made to provide resources to decipher the messages generated. If you do not understand the meaning of an event, don't necessarily discount its pertinence to your problem. Consult one or more of the resources available to you, from public databases and even ID decoders to Microsoft technical support.

# Procedure

In this task, you use Microsoft's Event Viewer to observe the effect on audited events as you manipulate objects in a controlled environment. The Microsoft Event Viewer displays a security log, as well as the minimum of both an application and a system log. Other logs are optional and vary among installations.

## Equipment Used

For this task, you need a single computer with a modern Microsoft operating system installed.

## Details

This task guides you through the use of Event Viewer to monitor audited events on a Microsoft operating system.

### Displaying Administrative Tools

In a proper Windows installation, you can get to Event Viewer and other tools in more than one way. Sometimes, however, you must enable the precise method in which you are interested. This section shows you where to change the availability of Administrative Tools.

1. Confirm that you have Administrative Tools accessible on your system. At a minimum, you should have the following applet in Control Panel.

2. Alternatively, you might have access to these tools directly from the Start menu.

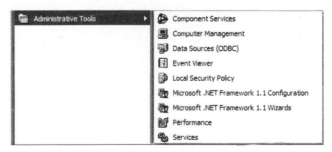

**3.** If you wish to have the tools on the Start menu but they are not there, use Figure 4.5 as a guide.

In this composite illustration, you see two locations where you can right-click and then click Properties to enter the Taskbar And Start Menu Properties dialog, either in an unaffiliated portion of the Start menu—on the left in the illustration—or on an unaffiliated portion of the Taskbar—on the right in the illustration.

**FIGURE 4.5**  Taskbar And Start Menu Properties

**4.** Choose one of these methods and enter the Taskbar And Start Menu Properties dialog.

**5.** Display the Start Menu page, shown next.

**6.** Click the Customize button.

7.  Display the Advanced page and scroll down to the bottom in the Start Menu Items portion of the page, shown next.

8.  Under the System Administrative Tools item in the list, fill in the first or second radio button but not the third, Don't Display This Item.

9.  Click the OK button to return to the Taskbar And Start Menu Properties dialog.

10. Click the OK button to close the Taskbar And Start Menu Properties dialog.

11. Now, confirm that Administrative Tools appears in the Start menu under All Programs.

## Running and Using Event Viewer

Now that you have your favorite method lined up for accessing the tools, it's time to investigate the use of one of them, Event Viewer.

1.  In Administrative Tools, find and double-click Event Viewer. This produces a window similar to the following, which is taken from a server running Microsoft Windows Server 2003.

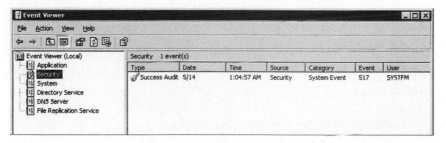

2. Spend a moment browsing the logs shown by clicking the items in the left pane of Event Viewer.

3. Right-click the item labeled Security in the left pane and click Clear All Events.

Feel free to perform step 3 whenever you want to see the effects of one of the following steps more clearly. The screen captures of the Event Viewer in this task are taken after performing this step.

4. Assuming you have an event 517 success audit, caused by clearing the log, double-click this entry in the right pane. This brings up the Event Properties dialog (shown in the following image), which adds detail to the abstract entry in the Event Viewer's right-hand pane. Note that the first line of the description states that the audit log was cleared.

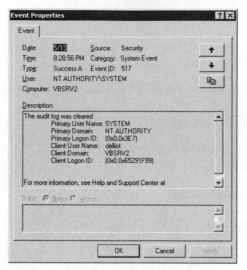

5. Leave Event Viewer open and minimize all open windows.

## Using Third-Party Tools

Various tools and utilities exist for organizing the logged information found in Event Viewer, which can grow quite unwieldy very quickly. One such tool is provided free by Microsoft's EventComb, part of its Security Operations Guide for Windows 2000 Server. You can find the installing application for EventComb by searching at www.microsoft.com/downloads for "sec-ops.exe," "Security Operations Guide for Windows 2000 Server," or "Security Guide Scripts Download."

A tool that provides ready detail for sometimes confusing event descriptions can be found at www.eventid.net. Subscribers can launch additional information sources directly from this site. The following screen shot illustrates the gist of looking up the 517 event ID on this website. Note that many sections are omitted from this output because an ID of 517 appears in more logs than just the security log, each with a different meaning.

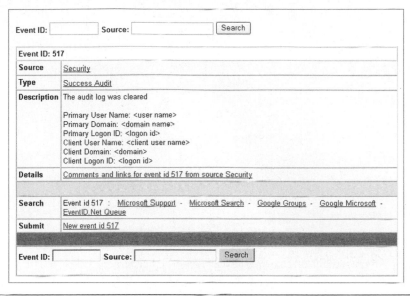

## Auditing Success

Now that Event Viewer is handy, this section guides you through a controlled environment for generating success entries in the log.

1.  Create a folder on the Desktop called Audit Me. Then right-click the folder and choose Properties from the shortcut menu to open the Properties tabs for your folder.

**2.** Click the Security tab to display the Security properties.

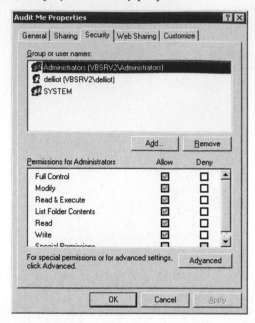

**3.** Click the Advanced button to bring up the Advanced Security Settings tabs for your folder and then click the Auditing tab for the folder.

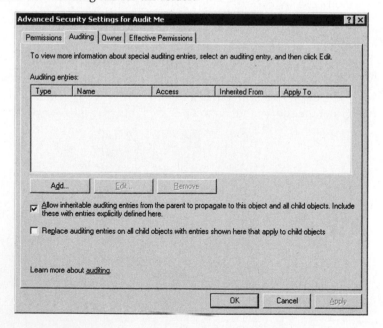

4.  Click the Add button to display the Select User Or Group dialog and type **Everyone**, for the group of the same name, in the text box. Click the OK button.

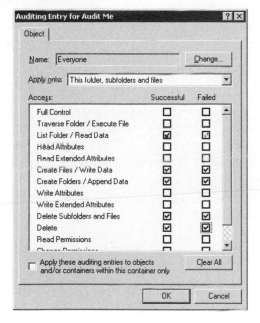

5.  In the Auditing Entry dialog for the Everyone group, check the boxes as shown in the following image to turn on auditing for success and failure in accessing and changing the Audit Me folder and its contents. Click the OK button to return to the Auditing page of the Advanced Security Settings dialogs.

6. Click the OK button on the Auditing page of the Advanced Security Settings tabs, which might bring up the a security warning, indicating that auditing has yet to be enabled on the system.

7. Open Local Security Settings in Administrative Tools. Expand Local Policies and click on Audit Policy to display a window similar to the following screen shot.

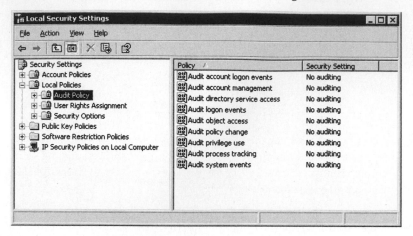

> An alternative way to get to the Security Settings branch of the Local Security Settings applet is through the Microsoft Management Console (MMC). Add the snap-in called Local Computer Policy and navigate to Local Computer Policy\ Computer Configuration\Windows Settings\Security Settings.

8. If possible, double-click each item in the right pane and remove the check marks from both check boxes.

9. Double-click the item in the right pane labeled Audit Object Access and check the boxes for both Success and Failure. Click the OK button to return to Local Security Settings.

10. Close Local Security Settings and return to where you created the Audit Me folder on the Desktop. Open the Audit Me folder.

11. Remember that you can clear the security event log if you want a clean start. Create a folder under Audit Me called Audit Junior.

12. Open Event Viewer and click on Application in the left pane and then back on Security. This is the best way to refresh the log if the security log view was left open. The refresh

function adds unnecessary entries to the log. You now see entries created by the audit you configured for the `Audit Me` folder, similar to the following.

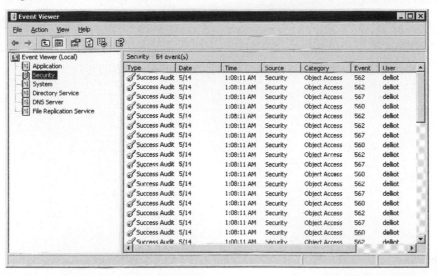

13. Assuming the items in your list are ordered by date and time, scroll down toward the bottom and the oldest entry. Double-click the oldest entry related to your folder creation and click the up arrow button on the Event Properties dialog until you find the event that shows New Folder in the Object Name field, as seen next.

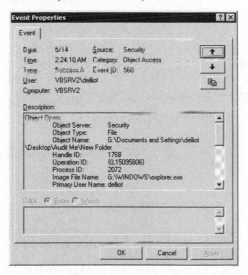

This entry was logged when you created the new folder and it was registered under the name `New Folder`, which happens as soon as the folder is created even though the name appears to be temporary because it is highlighted as editable.

**14.** Click the up arrow button on the Event Properties dialog until you find the next event that shows New Folder in the Object Name field, but notice when you scroll the description down, you eventually see DELETE in the Accesses field, similar to the following.

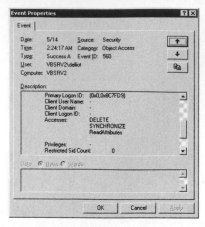

This entry was logged the split second before the folder's new name took effect. The old name, New Folder, has to be expunged before the new name can take its place, hence the deletion event for New Folder.

**15.** Click the up arrow button again until you find the event that shows Audit Junior in the Object Name field. This entry was logged after you entered the new name for the folder. This completes the major steps in the audit for creating a folder. Creating a file produces similar audits.

## Auditing Failure

This section shows you how to create a scenario that allows you to observe the Event Viewer entries made by attempted access to or control over an object without proper permissions.

**1.** Right-click the icon on your Desktop for the Audit Me folder and click Sharing And Security to bring up the Properties dialogs for Audit Me. The Sharing tab is selected by default.

**2.** Click the Security tab.

**3.** Click the Advanced button to bring up the Advanced Security Settings dialogs.

**4.** On the Permissions tab, clear the check mark from the box with the label that starts Inherit From Parent. This pops up a dialog that asks if you want to copy the current settings (the Copy button) or start from scratch (the Remove button).

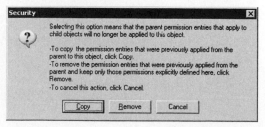

**5.** Click the Copy button so you can build from what your account already has.

**6.** As shown for David Elliot in the following screen shot, deny the permission to create folders and to delete anything. Click the OK button.

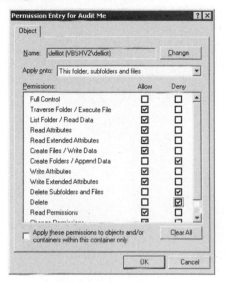

**7.** Click OK on the security warning drawing your attention to the possible unintentional lockout that denials of access might generate. You do not need to worry about that here.

**8.** Click the OK button on the Security tab of the Audit Me Properties dialog.

**9.** Attempt to create a folder in the Audit Me folder. You are met with the following error message. Click the OK button.

**10.** Go back to Event Viewer and click away from and back to the security section and notice the failure notifications caused by your attempt. The following screen shot illustrates how these events look in Event Viewer. Feel free to look at these more closely.

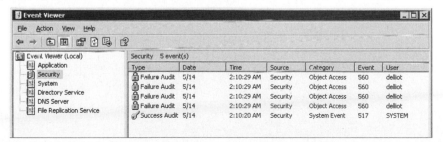

**11.** Note that the following dialog shows New Folder in the Object Name field, indicating the failure event was created after the default name was applied to the folder that you thought was never created.

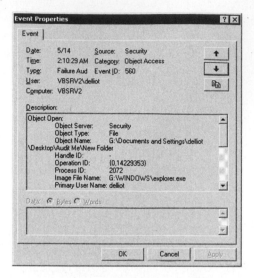

**12.** Now, try to delete the Audit Junior folder. You see the following error. Click the OK button.

**13.** In Event Viewer, find the failure entry that, when opened, specifies Audit Junior in the Object Name field and DELETE in the Accesses field.

## Criteria for Completion

You have completed this task when you have configured auditing globally and on an object, opened Event Viewer, and manipulated the object to generate controlled Event Viewer entries.

# Index

**Note to the Reader:** Throughout this index **boldfaced** page numbers indicate primary discussions of a topic. *Italicized* page numbers indicate illustrations.

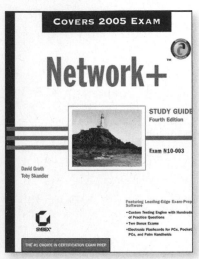